ARTS
MARKETING

Other publications by Keith Diggle

Marketing the Arts, an introduction and practical guide, published
in 1976 by The City University, London

"Only Connect", the arts provision system in the UK, published in
1980 by The Calouste Gulbenkian Foundation
(UK & Commonwealth Branch), London

Guide To Arts Marketing, published in 1984 by
Rhinegold Publishing Limited, London

KEITH DIGGLE

ARTS MARKETING

R·

RHINEGOLD PUBLISHING LIMITED
241 Shaftesbury Avenue, London WC2H 8EH
Tel: 0171 333 1721 Fax: 0171 333 1769

Arts Marketing
Keith Diggle

First published 1994 in Great Britain by
Rhinegold Publishing Limited, 241 Shaftesbury Avenue,
London WC2H 8EH, Great Britain.

British Library Cataloguing in Publication Data. A catalogue record
for this book is available from the British Library.

© Keith Diggle
ISBN 0 946890 58 7

Printed in Great Britain by Perfectaprint, Byfleet, Surrey

Book Design: Sarah Davies
Cover photograph: *'Same man, same shirt, new book'*: Tony Gamble.

PREFACE

In this, my third book on the subject of how best to approach the marketing of the arts – the performing arts in the main but the presenters of visual arts should find ideas of value herein – I offer what I believe to be the elements necessary for the understanding of a subject that many find difficult to grasp. The <u>objective</u> of marketing in what is not usually a profit-making area is defined so that it incorporates the social purpose of arts presentation: good financial management of both expenditure and income is the *sine qua non* of any form of marketing but with the arts there is also the 'people element' to be considered and this means not only audiences but artists as well – *arts* marketing must acknowledge the special position of the producers of what is to be marketed and not demand total subjugation to the box office demands of today. An <u>analysis</u> of the components of *arts* marketing is given which makes it clear that this is an holistic approach that takes into account the circumstances under which most arts are presented where all decisions are usually made and carried out by very few people operating under conditions of strict financial limitations. Apart from its holistic character this approach contains some important (and possibly new to some) ideas in terms of how the components are related one to another. Finally a precise <u>terminology</u> is offered which assists in understanding and remembering what the components do and how they work together. The art is then to make all the components work together and this, which can only come from experience, is echoed by the fairly obvious symbolism of the cover photograph.

Readers will, I hope, forgive me if, in spite of my efforts to suppress, there is a thread of regretfulness that emerges from time to time. Since the publication of my last book there have been opportunities to develop this work and thus improve audience levels and do more to compensate for the erosion of public financial support for the arts. In spite of my efforts (and they have on occasion been considerable) the opportunities have been lost. Now with a new Arts

Council of England and an Arts Marketing Association I permit myself cautious optimism and offer this book to those who have the power to take action.

I also offer this book to those whose job it is to make, select and present the arts: not only the beginners but also their bosses who may well find one or two useful thoughts here (a brown paper cover is recommended).

Finally, my thanks to the staff of Rhinegold Publishing Limited for their hard work and unfailing good spirits and, in particular, to Sarah Davies who has designed the book, and to Tony Gamble, my co-director, the MD of the company, who has not only tolerated my *idée-fixe* for years but even took the cover photograph without extracting the promise that this would positively be the end of the matter.

Keith Diggle
September 1994

CONTENTS

8

PART TWO

A CLOSER LOOK AT
PUBLIC RELATIONS AND ADVERTISING

Attenders and Intenders; A common language; Creating the message; Putting the message into a context that will persuade and sell; Stimulating the buying desire; Conveying the message; Delivering the message to the Attenders.

PART THREE

THE UNAVAILABLE AUDIENCE

CHAPTER TWELVE   PAGE 209

EDUCATIONAL PUBLIC RELATIONS AND THE UNAVAILABLE AUDIENCE

On 5 February 1988, a symposium called CHANGING THEIR MINDS – TOWARDS A NEW AUDIENCE was held in Glasgow under the auspices of the Scottish Arts Council in association with the Society of Arts Publicists (which metamorphosed into the Arts Marketing Association): text of the author's keynote address.

Where to begin?; No immediate financial benefit in pursuing the 'widest possible range'; The tools for the job exist in the commercial sector; Educational PR; What lies at the heart of Educational PR?; What are the barriers? Ignorance is one; Another barrier is the time it takes; Targets for Educational PR; Implications of Educational PR for arts organisations; The importance of teachers; The job of the Education Officer; The status of Education Officers; What happens when they leave school?; National campaigns; And meanwhile television goes on doing what it is doing.

PART FOUR

The *Arts Management Weekly* articles. A series that appeared in the magazine from 1992 to 1994.

PART FIVE

APPENDICES

PART ONE

THE AVAILABLE AUDIENCE

CHAPTER ONE

INTRODUCTION

WHY *ARTS* MARKETING?

Is there a difference?

Is there a difference between common-or-garden marketing of the kind that profitably places products in your home or provides you with services necessary to a comfortable life and the marketing of the experiences offered to us by the arts? At a day to day level where small commercial businesses are concerned there is probably not a great deal of difference between how their products and services are marketed and how the experience of, say, theatre is marketed by the local playhouse – both are essentially concerned with getting good results with the minimum expenditure of time and money, methods used being essentially practical ones. However, if we look at how large commercial organisations practise marketing and if we examine what is said and taught by academics who teach the subject of commercial marketing and who inevitably see things in terms of a strict analysis with precise definitions of objective and function we begin to see differences that become more significant the longer we study them.

These differences are fundamental and cannot be ignored. They forbid one to assume that the theory of commercial marketing can simply be transplanted into an arts environment. They make it positively dangerous to allow people whose training and experience lie only in the commercial sector to have unfettered influence over how the arts are to be marketed.

Differences of Objective and Philosophy

The arts industry has long recognised the importance of learning how to market effectively the experiences offered to the public by artists and arts organisations. There was once resistance to this notion – the 'religious' school of thought that held art to be sacred, that audiences were made by God and any attempt to improve their sizes was profanity – but that now holds little or no sway. We have tried to develop our own skills in this area and we have, over the past twenty or twenty-five years, become quite good at it. In our eagerness to do even better we have looked to the commercial sector and asked for help and we have been, more often than not, disappointed with the results. The reasons are not too difficult to fathom. Commercial marketing has a different objective and a different philosophy and these two factors influence almost everything that is planned and acted upon; furthermore, it being an activity that is fully evolved, matured as it were, it claims to offer answers to almost every question and this breeds a level of self-confidence amongst its practitioners that rules out the self-doubt that we arts practitioners experience every day and would certainly experience in their world. 'Why should the arts situation be different?' they seem to be saying; 'Why should its problems not vanish as ours do?' Of course, their problems do not always vanish but it is not always good business to admit this.

Can a scientific approach help?

Commercial marketing, when practised on a large scale, frequently bases its actions upon the findings of research and the practice of statistical analysis. This is a sound approach – but only up to a point. It is very dangerous indeed to believe that science can predict the outcome of events that are intrinsically unpredictable – and any activity involving human beings may be so described. In an area like this science can detect and describe trends, possibilities, probabilities even, but it cannot guarantee results.

Products that are out of control

It could be said that this faith in science is the main distinction between our world and the 'real world' (as a senior civil servant in the old Office of Arts and Libraries once described it to me). Commercial marketing abhors the idea of having to deal with products that are 'out of control' and wants to keep them firmly in their place, rigidly conforming to what the researchers and analysts say the public wants and, of course, what the public demonstrates that it wants. *Arts* marketing accepts that it is in a risky business and frequently does no more to influence the choice and quality of its product than to keep those who make it or choose it close to the results of their decisions in the hope that this will keep their feet on the ground. In extreme cases, of course, they may move to dismiss those whose results in terms of audiences and income are beyond the organisation's limits of tolerance.

In *arts* marketing we know ours to be a harder field to plough. We need and accept public subsidy because the income and expenditure equation, no matter how we try, no matter how good our product, no matter how large our audiences, no matter how economical we are in what we pay ourselves and what we spend on our product and in our attempts to persuade people to experience it, mainly ends up with a loss. If we take the commercial road and try to make the product subordinate to the need to make a profit by making the marketing process as risk-free as possible we know that we would end up with something that wasn't quite right; we might be cheaper to run but we wouldn't be worth running.

Who forgot to pack the Sales manual?

If you read annual reports of major commercial companies you will frequently see references to 'marketing and sales' which suggests that these are two separate – and hence different – functions. A large company which earns its way in the world by what I would term (and will in a later chapter explain) *active* selling, requires a complex structure of management, personnel and systems to achieve its vital targets of income and so must have its Sales department to handle the 'sharp' end of its business. Decisions concerning products and their markets, the prices of the products and the means whereby the markets are persuaded to want to buy the products at those prices are made by the Marketing department within which there are many different kinds of specialist and which has relationships with many kinds of independent specialist service providers. There may be other departments, concerned, for example, with Research and

Development, Manufacturing, Finance, Law and a department concerned with the selection, training, assessment and welfare of personnel and the other areas collectified under the title Human Resources. The general feeling in business is that all these departments should work together to achieve the common goal but as human beings are employed in them this is not always achieved.

At this stage it is the distinction between Sales and Marketing which should attract our attention for when people have attempted to borrow ideas from the commercial world they seemed to have said, 'We need marketing in the arts, let's see how they do it in the real world.' They brought the ideas of marketing over to our 'unreal world' but they did not at the same time bring the ideas of Sales over to us – although, it must be said, those ideas were not unknown to some of us. It is hard to believe that this could have been the case but it is the only possible explanation I can find for the curious failure to recognise the importance of this other function. However these matters are handled within a company, whether departmentalised to be separate or not, the function of marketing is wholly impotent in the absence of its companion function, Sales.

So it was then that when in 1988 the Office of Arts and Libraries and the Arts Council of Great Britain financed the production of a marketing training package comprising workbook and video in association with the Institute of Marketing there was but the briefest mention of Sales and of its close companion, Sales Promotion, mention not at all. This was a singularly sad omission and to this day these vital concepts and activities are often missing from what is said and written on the subject of arts marketing.

Marketing is an organisational function

In the arts world there are rarely sufficient staff to warrant a breakdown of management into all the possible departmental responsibilities. Finance, Law and Human Resources are almost always the job of a senior manager along with changing the light bulbs. What is to be offered to the public is usually the responsibility of an artistic director. The rest of the work usually gets done by a person or persons who used to have the word Publicity on their door and now have the word Marketing in its place.

Marketing is an organisational function; that is, it is what the business does rather than what a person or a department does. A large company needs to organise by departments but it has a ringmaster in the form of a managing director, answerable to a board of directors and ultimately the shareholders, to ensure that all work together towards a common aim and here – notwithstanding the presence of a marketing department which suggests that marketing is a departmental function – marketing is still what the business does. Everyone is involved in marketing in some way or other.

In the arts world the most influential people in a company are the artistic director and the chief executive or general manager with perhaps, or perhaps not, someone responsible for finance. With control in the hands of two or three (sometimes conflicting) interests the need to establish the concept of marketing as an organisational function, the responsibility for which cannot be denied by any of those controlling hands, is vital. Marketing cannot be delegated to one person or one group if they are not influential in the overall running of the organisation – otherwise the panel on the door might just as well read 'Scapegoat.'

A wise arts organisation might therefore decide to appoint a marketing director or manager and to give this job the status that allows the post holder significant influence on the decisions made by the management team. But what are the specific responsibilities of such a job? To contribute to decisions on matters of artistic product and policy, administration, financial planning, fundraising and so on? Yes, of course. But what is done when that door, however labelled, closes?

It certainly must involve Sales, that vital piece of baggage left behind when marketing moved over from the 'real world'. Sales as a concept and an activity is absolutely fundamental to arts marketing as it is in the commercial world. In such small businesses as ours Sales must be embraced by marketing; there will certainly be people employed with specific Sales duties (in the box office, for example) but they must be responsible to marketing so that what they do is wholly integrated into the organisation's marketing strategy. This is, of course, how most small commercial businesses are structured.

Then there is the matter of how people are to be persuaded to want to buy what the organisation has chosen to offer them, and the matter of finding out where the people live who are most likely to take the trouble to come and experience what is offered and what things they like most and like least and in what areas they are open to new experiences. How much should these people pay for their experiences? – Yet another area where decisions must be made. And what about the people who live close enough to benefit easily from these experiences but won't have 'em, not at any price? And all of these matters have to take place in the context of management that is concerned with artistic policy and with making ends meet.

We are small businesses

Small commercial businesses are much more like us. They choose their area of business because it is something they know about and like. Whether it is selling shoes or vegetables, making wrought iron gates, building boats, running a guest house, selling household products door-to-door or farming, they try to provide what people want and they try to make a living out of it. They do this by being well organised, creative, responsive, disciplined and flexible. They have different goals, much less ambitious goals in one sense, but in terms of how they set about their business they are much more like the arts business than are the large companies that most frequently seek to influence us and – equally seriously – influence the politicians that control the financial support we need. If only these well intentioned folk, who must have time on their hands, would take some of that time to see what makes us tick they would understand that although we have financial objectives we do not set out to make profit, we do not put the interests of our shareholders (unless you count the population at large) first, satisfying demand that exists today is not enough for us and we are usually not prepared to modify the experiences we are offering to people in order to attract more people.

Our rôle model is the impresario

We have a long tradition of knowing how to cope with the uncertainties of our marketing situation. We have never believed that there is such a thing as a sure-fire hit nor that we can guarantee the response of members of the public to any of the offerings we put before them. For centuries we have relied upon people known as impresarios and to this day most promotional success is owed to individuals who possess the 'nose', the 'gut-feeling' and the 'hunch' for what can be made to succeed. Receipt of public money means that our arts bodies must be publicly accountable and this inevitably demands the involvement of some democratic process in our management. Committees control those who are paid to run the organisations, those who are supposed to develop the talents of the impresario, and frequently there is tension between the two levels of management. It is impossible for a committee to be an impresario and sometimes hard for one to live in happy harmony with an impresario but the problem must be overcome if the organisation is to make progress.

Successful big businesses rely on impresarios too, but they don't like to admit it. Once one is at the helm of a major international company one has to project *gravitas*, wisdom, power and trustworthiness. Armies of marketers, researchers, analysts and corporate affairs advisers support the image, for how can a share price stay high if the person in charge is seen as someone who backs hunches?

Within our various personal limitations we try to develop some of the instincts and skills of the impresario and we usually end up with a balance between what is artistically adventurous and what is likely to receive a more predictably good response. As I said in *Guide To Arts Marketing*, 'The whole art of programming for an arts organisation is based on a sensitive appreciation of who the market is, what it wants now *and what it may be persuaded to want in the future* and the relating of those perceptions to what the organisation is capable of delivering'.

Getting the right starting point is essential

When attempting to define a subject like ours, which is so apparently close to large scale commercial marketing yet so intrinsically different, it is impossible to overstate the importance of getting the starting point, the fundamental concept, right. Whatever we accept as being our starting point it must embody the elements we know to be crucial and it must be clearly different from that which guides those who market commercially on a large scale. The concept of *arts* marketing to which I have always adhered, which has influenced everything I have thought, written and spoken is, I believe, the one that most accurately reflects the job we do and its philosophy. It has led no-one up the wrong garden path and it probably has helped to direct many people up the right garden path – but I am not at all certain as to how far up the hierarchy of arts politics and arts bureaucracy it has penetrated. I still have a letter written to me on 8 April 1988 by the then secretary-general of the Arts Council of Great Britain, Luke Rittner, who was at the time busily involving in the development of marketing of the arts people whose experience and achievements lay some considerable way outside the arts; referring to those who were creating and presenting the arts as 'asking for help' and seeking 'to be engaged with the mainstream of marketing thought' he said of my work, 'I am sad that you appear to wish to place marketing the arts in a ghetto it does not deserve'.

Although it would be ridiculous to want to put up barriers against outside influences, which is what the word 'ghetto' can mean, there is nothing wrong at all with holding fast to what you believe in. And, to extend the metaphor a little, if people want to enter the ghetto there is nothing wrong in laying down a code of conduct for them. My concern at the time of Rittner's letter was with the undue influence, even overwhelming influence, of people from commercial marketing and academics who saw the arts as an interesting – and perhaps even profitable – new avenue to explore but who would not spend the time necessary to find out just why *we* found the business so difficult. *They* assumed, I think, it was because we were stupid.

Those who have not worked in the arts are usually slow to notice that in this business people are as important to us as money; the 'people element' must be woven into any approach to marketing. They also fail to perceive that the scope of arts organisations, the field of interest, is universal, embracing the artists and arts organisations that produce the work we are to market. Of course theatre managers are concerned with what happens in their theatres but those same managers have a global concern for all theatres and the people who work in them. 'People', in this context, means more than audiences, it means artists too.

Perhaps the fault has been in the expression of the idea rather than the idea itself. Although it has always been very clear in my mind, perhaps I have taken too much for granted in my expression of that idea. For people who have worked in the business for a long time, who subscribe to the underlying philosophy of the job, who have engaged in the inevitable metaphysical discussions on 'why we are all here', I do not think there is a major problem, but for those who are new to it, those who are enjoying some form of vocational training, those who are doing the training without having had any direct practical experience of doing the job and thus engaging in those inevitable discussions and those who are bringing to bear 'outside' influences on how the arts should be marketed, the absence of a clearly stated, unequivocal and comprehensive starting point – a policy statement, if you like – may account for some of the disagreements I have encountered over the years.

The objective/definition that I gave in *Guide To Arts Marketing* has a number of virtues but it is not in the complete form that I now believe it should be if it is to lay claim to being the starting point, the fundamental concept upon which we should all agree and which should inform all subsequent theoretical and practical developments. The thought was right but the expression of it was, I now realise, incomplete.

This is the form which I now suggest should be acceptable to all who work in our business and should be accepted by those who would enter or influence it.

ARTS MARKETING

The aim of *arts* marketing is to bring an appropriate number of people, **drawn from the widest possible range of social background, economic condition and age,** into an appropriate form of contact with the artist and, in so doing, to arrive at the best financial outcome that is compatible with the achievement of that aim.

(The emboldened words form the addition to the 'old' definition that appeared in *Guide To Arts Marketing*).

This then is the starting point for *arts* marketing; it covers objective and philosophy. Is this the only way in which *arts* marketing is different from commercial marketing? I believe that you will see from the following chapters that if you *really* come to understand marketing the contents of Parts One and Two will not conflict with how you see marketing being practised by smaller commercial organisations but when you come to Part Three *The Unavailable Audience* you will be in a land rarely if ever entered by people whose goals are entirely based on the profit motive.

We must base everything we think and do upon this starting point for if we do not then not only will we fail our artists and our audiences – and hence ourselves – we will leave our industry wide open to the pressure that stems from government's desire constantly to chip away at the level of financial support that goes to our industry. This pressure will force us to go for the fast buck, to mould our artistic programmes to meet only the tastes manifested by the largest number of people *now*, to behave like the large scale commercial businesses of the 'real world', to ignore the 'Unavailable Audience' for whatever it is our job to present and, thus, by making that fast buck to accept a lower level of public financial support.

Everything that follows in this book is based upon the conviction expressed in this earlier statement, the definition of objective and philosophy. It is reinforced by my own practical experience of working in the subsidised arts sector for many years both as employee and as consultant. It is confirmed through my involvement as a shareholding executive director of a small commercial business for more than sixteen years during which time I have been conscious of almost no difference between my company and the subsidised arts organisations I have known and aware of a vast chasm between us and the world of large scale commercial business.

Marketing the arts today – two schools of thought

Now, many years after the influences of commercial marketing were brought to bear on our industry the after effects are still visible. There is still a failure amongst practitioners to include the ideas of Sales and Sales Promotion in their thinking and in their actions: this is a matter that is fairly easily put right once the holistic and comprehensive view of *arts* marketing is accepted. What will be harder to combat is a view of the audience potential within any community that sees it as something pre-determined and unalterable. This most definitely has its roots in the 'scientific' approach to which I have already referred and is widely subscribed to.

This view sees a community wholly, if not entirely, in terms of its behaviour in relation to what is to be sold; the behaviour is the act of purchase. If someone has bought a ticket for some form of performing art then that person is the target for all future campaigns involving that form of performing art. The target for the future is defined as those who have bought in the past. The development of box office systems which record details of customers, their names, addresses, what they have bought and how much they have paid, encourages this view; it makes the marketing of future events look very simple. It is a dangerous path to follow.

In this book you will be encouraged to think of the audience potential within a community not only in terms of its behaviour but also in terms of its attitude for it is this that determines behaviour and it is this, the *attitude*, that determines the potential for us. If there is one hypothesis upon which *arts* marketing rests it is that the potential audience is not a fixed quantity but is rather an ever changing mass of people who are favourably inclined (in varying degrees of enthusiasm) towards what it is we have to sell, some of whom have actually made the act of purchase in the recent past. Past behaviour is, of course, extremely important because it defines what we may reasonably expect *now* but attitude defines for us the scope for expansion in the future.

The underlying notion of the 'Available Audience', which is defined by its attitude as well as its behaviour, leads one inevitably to the conclusion that for every customer who makes a purchase there must be many, many more who *nearly* make a purchase or who are stirred in some way by the idea that they might experience what is offered. *Arts* marketing asks why those favourably inclined people do not get around to buying and offers ideas and techniques for turning the favourable inclination first into a buying desire and then into an irrevocable commitment, a purchase. *Arts* marketing also spares more than a thought for those whose attitudes do not yet bring them within our range of possibility and offers some suggestions on how we might approach what I have termed the 'Unavailable Audience'.

One can see how the 'finite' market approach based on past behaviour leads one to a simplistic view of marketing. 'They have bought in the past so they will go on buying – all one has to do is tell them what is for sale and they will do the rest. Bigger audiences? Easy. Find more people who have already bought'. Marketing thus becomes a matter of mailing lists and printed advertising matter. It really cannot be so simple.

It is my sincere belief that the *arts* marketing approach does more than take into account our philosophy, important as that may be; it offers a logical way of building audiences that is founded on a view of people that is wholly realistic, seeing them as reacting to our propositions as they do to all the others that are put before them, with varying degrees of interest depending on their attitudes and tastes and subject to all the other demands on their time and money and the human tendency to procrastination.

(Having rather laboured my point by referring constantly to *arts* marketing I shall assume that it has by now been well taken and employ the rather less intrusive 'arts marketing' in future chapters).

CHAPTER TWO

AUDIENCES

Within your catchment area
there is an Available Audience
and an Unavailable Audience –
aim for your Available Audience
now and your Unavailable
Audience later

'Our' audience

Wherever and whenever you start on the business of attracting an audience your success will be governed by two things: the audience potential that exists within your community and your ability to draw out and make use of that potential. You can do many things to improve your ability; you can go on a training course, you can work in a variety of arts jobs gaining experience as you go, you can learn to exercise your creativity as you gain experience – and, of course, you can read this book very carefully. And you can include in your approach a way of looking at your community that is most likely to help you market your events.

Your arts organisation will have its own *ethos*; it will exist to create and/or present certain kinds of art. Your organisation will probably have a view as to what kind of audience it wishes to attract. Some do not have a very specific type of audience in mind – just get the maximum number of bottoms on the seats is the aim – whereas others really want to attract people who are defined by their social and economic class, or by their age, or by their taste in a particular manifestation of an art form. No matter how broad or how narrow their target, most bodies that present arts events have a notion of what 'our' audience is like.

The major orchestra that is regularly playing in a hall of 3000 seat capacity in a city that has suffered economically, will say that it is happy enough to fill the place just so long as the audience pays for its tickets and doesn't clap in the wrong places. The contemporary music society in the same city, using a hall with 300 seats, may very well aim only for people with enough experience and knowledge to make something of the music that is being presented. 'Our' audience is often not easily defined but the idea of some kind of an audience profile quickly develops in the minds of those who are presenting the events and it is this audience that is the target of our ambitions.

The arts marketer must assess this view of 'our' audience, by discussion with colleagues within the organisation and by observation, and relate this to the marketing approach and style being used. It is important that the organisation as a whole is comfortable with the kind of product it presents, its view of 'our' audience and the techniques used to bring the two together.

Once you have this view of 'our' audience do not be swayed from it unless you have extremely strong evidence that you have it wrong.

The catchment area

Your audiences will be drawn from the community in which you are based. You may define that community in terms of geography. How far can you reasonably expect people to travel? Is there any evidence as to how far they have been travelling before you came on the scene? This is where a very simple form of market research can help – one simply looks through earlier postal and telephone orders and makes notes. However you arrive at it you should have some idea of how far afield you should set your sights. It is more than a matter of geography: transportation – the existence of good roads, the adequacy of parking facilities, the reliability of and service offered by public transport systems – will help define the scope of your audience potential and so too will the reach of local media of communication as well as the presence or otherwise of other arts organisations offering similar events. Within this limit, within what is perhaps no more than an irregular shape drawn on a map on your wall, there are the people whom you may persuade to buy tickets from you.

So, define your catchment area using simple physical criteria and keep it very fluid, changing your view of it as evidence of where your customers are coming from presents itself.

The first question one asks oneself in any marketing situation is 'Where are my customers?' and the second, 'Who are my customers?'. Now that the catchment area has been defined there is a very approximate answer to the first question (albeit one that you may well reconsider in times to come). But *who* are these customers?

Arts organisations choose the art they are to present and this defines their audience

A superficial reading of the first chapter may well provoke the opinion that everyone within the catchment area is to be seen as a potential customer. Doesn't the definition of arts marketing speak of people 'drawn from the widest possible range of social background, economic condition and age'? Doesn't that put everyone in the target?

Well, yes and no. If you mean now, if you mean that the arts marketer must set out to attract everyone in the catchment area into the audience net today, or this week, or next month, the answer is clearly no. It obviously cannot be achieved and even if it were achievable there wouldn't be room for them. But for an organisation that is supported by public money is there not a moral obligation to set one's sights on the public at large? And isn't that part of the arts *ethos*? Are we not all missionaries?

Indeed we are missionaries – but we also have to survive today, and this week and next month, and we must temper our missionary zeal with realism. We know that no matter how much we might want to bring our wonderful events before the eyes of all, we cannot.

But how do we determine who are those who could and should be our customers and those who are to be denied the light; who really makes up 'our' audience? The choice is not yours to make. Your choice, the choice of the arts organisation, is in the matter of what kind of product it is to offer; it is this, the range, the style, the *artistic content* of your programme, that you choose – and the way you present this – that defines your audience.

There is a fundamental truth about this aspect of arts marketing, where we are considering who is to experience what we have to offer, who we are going to aim for; it is that we have very little influence over who is a potential customer and who is not. Essentially, they make up their own minds. I am talking of *potential customers*, those whom you are capable of persuading to become real, ticket-buying customers before the show has packed its bags and left town. Potential customers have made up their minds before you get to them and so have those people who are not potential customers.

If the audience has made its mind up why bother with arts marketing?

Why then, in the face of what seems to be a situation which is beyond our influence, do we bother to try to change things, do we concern ourselves with something called arts marketing? The first reason is that *potential* customers abound, there are lots of them, but potential doesn't put fill seats and put money into the box office. Potential customers have attended similar events to the ones we present or they have attitudes that are favourable to the events we present but this does not mean that they will automatically fall into our laps. Arts marketing is capable of reaching the potential and turning it into actual. Arts marketing can create audiences today out of those potential customers.

Arts marketing can also change people's minds

We also turn to arts marketing because it is a process that can deal with matters over a long as well as a short term and is capable of effecting change. People do indeed make up their own minds but they do so according to the influences that are brought to bear on them; part of marketing is to influence. We have very little say over who is to be a potential customer *today* and who is not but give us time, time to bring to bear our influence, and we may see a different picture.

Marketing is very much concerned with the process of persuasion, the means whereby people are given information about something in such a way that they are encouraged to want to experience it but it has to work within a time scale that is frequently decided for it by outside factors.

Suppose that researchers and advisers had strongly recommended to the government that the holding of personal identity cards was the only way in which the incidence of crime could be effectively reduced and the government decided to conduct a nationwide referendum on the issue. Would it arrange for the voting day to be arranged in a very short time, no longer than it takes to arrange for polling stations to be set up? Or would it give itself time, say three or four months, in which to organise its campaign of persuasion? Referenda usually favour the *status quo* so if the views of the population are sought now, without there being brought to bear any other influences, the government would not get the support it needed to introduce the new measures. However, if it gives itself time it can marshall its arguments and its spokespeople and it can make its case the length and breadth of the land. To the persuader, time is always of the essence.

Meanwhile, concentrate on today's audience

While we are thinking about a wider audience at some time in the future there is the potential audience of today to consider. An attitude that is favourable to what you have to sell does not guarantee purchase by any means; there are many other things that compete for the potential customer's time and money. It takes talent, resources, time and money to get the most out of this potential audience and how we do this will occupy a large part of this book.

The Available Audience and the Unavailable Audience

It helps to think of your community as consisting of an *Available Audience* and an *Unavailable Audience*, the difference being essentially their potential to you within the time scales in which you are able to work.

The *Available Audience* consists of those people who, for reasons to do with education, upbringing, and any number of other influences which could include, for example, things seen and heard in newspapers, magazines, books, radio and television programmes, have already experienced the art form you and your organisation are presenting and include such experiences in their regular diet of activities – they like it and they buy it. It also includes people with the same basically favourable views towards the art form and who aspire to include it in their lives but are either prevented from doing so by other commitments, lack of money, lack of opportunity – or failure to be persuaded to do so by the arts organisation. The Available Audience is defined in terms of its behaviour in relation to the events you are presenting and in terms of its attitude – again in relation to the events you are presenting, and to the art form in general – which is favourable. The Available Audience *attends* or it would like to attend – or, perhaps, the idea of attending has not yet crystallised but it reads about the subject, watches TV programmes about it and occasionally even talks about it. The Available Audience is available to you *now*.

The *Unavailable Audience*, seen in those same terms, is made up of those people who do not attend events of the type you are presenting, do not feel any particular need to attend such events and, in many cases, are antipathetic to the notion that they might attend them. Defined in terms of its attitude and its behaviour this section of your community is beyond your reach within a realistic time scale using the methods that will enable you to reach, persuade and ultimately sell to the Available Audience. But do not give up all hope, some potential does lie within this group and there are ways of reaching it but they are not the ways that should be used for the Available Audience.

How this book is structured

This book is intended to help people actively working as arts marketers (and those who would have it as a career) face the challenge of finding, building and holding onto audiences for their organisations. The pressures are always those of today: there are seats to fill and box office income targets to achieve; resources are always limited so the concentration must be on the application of arts marketing to the sectors of the community where the opportunities for success exist. Too much time and money is wasted in chasing impossible dreams of audiences by organisations who fail to realise that there are audiences for what they have to offer right under their noses and only when they have secured a firm relationship with these people is it time to turn missionary.

Part One of this book offers an holistic approach to the marketing of the arts that keeps this practical and realistic view firmly in focus. Part Two looks at Publicity with the Available Audience in mind and Part Three considers ways in which the attitudes of the presently Unavailable Audience may be changed. Part Four consists of articles on various aspects of arts marketing that were originally published in the magazine *Arts Management Weekly*. Part Five contains reprints of two 'historic' documents recording how the ideas of arts marketing have developed since 1971.

SUMMARY

Define your catchment area using simple physical criteria and keep it very fluid, changing your view of it as evidence of where your customers are coming from presents itself.

Within your catchment area there is an Available Audience and an Unavailable Audience, the difference being essentially their potential to you within the time scales in which you are able to work – aim for your Available Audience now and your Unavailable Audience later. The Available Audience is defined in terms of its behaviour in relation to the events you are presenting and in terms of its attitude – again in relation to the events you are presenting, and to the art form in general – which is favourable.

The Unavailable Audience is made up of those people who do not attend events of the type you are presenting, do not feel any particular need to attend such events and, in many cases, are antipathetic to the notion that they might attend them – this section of your community is beyond your reach within a realistic time scale using the methods that will enable you to reach, persuade and ultimately sell to the Available Audience. But do not give up all hope, some potential does lie within this group.

No matter how broad or how narrow their target, most bodies that present arts events have a notion of what 'our' audience is like.

Once you have developed a view of 'our' audience do not be swayed from it unless you have extremely strong evidence that you have it wrong.

Your choice, the choice of the arts organisation, is in the matter of what kind of product it is to offer; it is this, the range, the style, the *artistic content* of your programme, that you choose – and the way you present this – that defines your audience.

CHAPTER THREE

PRODUCT PUBLICITY

Product Publicity aims to persuade people to *want to buy*

Sheep today, goats tomorrow

Thinking of your community in terms of whether individuals are favourably inclined or unfavourably inclined to what you want to sell them, which defines whether they fall into the camp of availability or unavailability, is a first step in hacking a way through the jungle of confusion that faces the tyro arts marketer. We must start by mentally dividing people into sheep and goats; into those with whom we can get results in the short and medium term and those who will take much longer to bring into the fold.

We are unusual in seeing our work in these terms. Our definition of objective and philosophy makes it clear that we have a duty towards the goats as well as the sheep. Few commercial businesses, if any, see their work in this way; for them markets consist of people who need what they are trying to sell and market growth comes mainly from attracting other people's customers who need what *they* are trying to sell. Our concern lies with *arts* marketing which, in reflecting our *raison d'être*, has a different objective and philosophy. We have to believe that we are capable of making people one day want experiences to which they are, at present, indifferent or even hostile – no matter how unlikely our chances of success appear.

The Available Audience - Attenders and Intenders

So much depends on your target and how you regard it. I have found it very useful to think of the Available Audience as dividing into two categories: those who who are already buying what you have to sell or, at least, buying very similar things and those whose attitude and interest are not, presently and for whatever reasons, translated into actual purchase. I think of them as *Attenders* and *Intenders*. It is a good mental model but it must not encourage you to believe that your task of persuasion is going to be a walk-over from now on for there are many, many reasons why these people will resist your honeyed words. And even if they are persuaded by you to want to experience what you are presenting it by no means follows that they will take the action necessary to experience it.

I have referred to arts marketing as being to do with persuasion. We try to persuade people to want to buy experiences from us. Our powers of persuasion are limited so we concentrate on those people in the catchment area who know something about what we want them to experience and quite like the idea of going to experience it. This idea is important because it influences the whole basis of our approach to the process of persuasion in all kinds of ways. At the very least it will stop our missionary zeal getting in the way of tomorrow's box office returns.

PRODUCT ADVERTISING

The most commonly used tool of persuasion is Product Advertising: pieces of paper carrying printed words and pictures; television that carries words written and spoken, pictures that are both still and moving – with music and other sound effects; broadcast sound messages with spoken words, music and other sound effects. We see and hear commercial Product Advertising every day. We read about it. The advertising industry projects itself as being capable of moving mountains – or bars of chocolate, motor cars or holidays abroad. Can nothing stand up to the power of Product Advertising? People worry about the wider implications of all this and believe that advertising will one day control the world – not so.

Product Advertising needs needs

Control of the media of communication may have considerable potential for shaking present power structures but Product Advertising is weak and can only exploit needs that are already formed. If you need something and that need is fairly close to the surface then Product Advertising can probably make you want to buy any particular product that can lay claim to satisfying that need. If you don't have a lawn Product Advertising cannot make you want to buy a lawnmower. Of course, if your need is for a nice present for grandfather, who does have a lawn and doesn't have a lawnmower, then the advertising industry will happily satisfy your need by making you want to buy a lawnmower and a specific lawnmower at that. Really clever Product Advertising might even make you wish you had a lawn. So Product Advertising needs needs if it is have a chance of success.

Attitudes are more helpful to us than needs

Consider for a while this word 'need' the meaning of which can be stretched in all kinds of directions. Dig deep enough into someone's psyche and you will find enough needs to give hope to virtually all advertisers of all products. There are needs we have that we know we have: I have a hole in my shoe therefore I need to have my shoe repaired. There are needs, just a little less obvious but still present, the existence of which we acknowledge when their presence is made known to us or we are reminded of them. We need to make financial provision for the future but we often sublimate the need, covering it up with reasons why we must spend every penny we have on living today; the advertiser of pension schemes can bring this need to the surface quite easily and then offer a way of satisfying the need by presenting a pension scheme.

You may argue that everyone needs the art that you are presenting. Of course they do! But unless that need may be tapped or, one could say, unless people know the need exists in them or will recognise the need when you refer to it, there is little that you can do to exploit that need with the tool of Product Advertising.

That is why I prefer to think in terms of the attitudes people hold towards the various art forms rather than their needs. People are generally much more aware of their attitudes than they are their needs and the people you are aiming for in the short and medium term hold attitudes that are favourable towards what you want to persuade them to want to buy. Once you base your approach on this you will find you may safely make certain key assumptions. For example, you may assume a certain level of knowledge about the art form and its leading practitioners. You may assume a level of literacy. You may even assume a certain congruity amongst these people on matters of style and taste. You may assume that you do not have to argue the case for the art form itself, you do not have to justify it.

This enables you to be consistent in your language

Above all, you may be consistent in your language of communication. If you attempt to speak to the broad range of people you always run the risk of communicating with none; only if it is very simple will your message get through. So the complex language of communication which involves words, pictures, colours, typography and design may be directed at 'our' audience and need not be modified in pursuit of people who do not yet speak and understand 'our' language. This simplifies the whole business of communication and makes it effective.

Advertising is intrinsically weak

But advertising, even when aimed at the most responsive sector, is still intrinsically weak because the media of advertising are capable of carrying and delivering only the briefest of messages. Consider a poster situated at the side of a road. What can it say to the person walking by? What can it say to the driver of a car that is passing by? The most it can do, even if its message is carefully considered and brilliantly conveyed by means of design, is to shout the briefest of brief messages. Product Advertising is supposed to be persuasive. How can a poster persuade anyone of anything if it has only a few micro-seconds exposure to the eye? The provision of more posters assists in the persuasion process by delivering the message over and over again but the effect must always be strictly limited. This does not mean that the poster – or its contemporary equivalent, the brief shout of a simple television visual, usually static, accompanied by encouraging words and appropriate music – has no part to play in the process of persuasion.

Add to the medium of the poster a more intimate form of communication, a piece of paper with a much more detailed persuasive message written and designed to draw the reader in, to hold the attention and excite and ultimately to persuade. This will complement the effect of the poster, the televised advertisement (or radio advertisement) by taking advantage of the awareness created to add more persuasive information. So the brief shout of poster, television or radio is asked to start the ball rolling, and keep it rolling as it reminds people of what is being offered, while the leaflet attempts to deliver the goods. The power of this Product Advertising is now increasing and may be effective, provided that the leaflet is put into the hand of someone who is very favourably inclined towards what you want to persuade them to buy.

Add to this Product Advertising in newspapers that repeats and reinforces the same essential message and there is now something of a campaign the totality of which may contribute to achieving the effect you need but the very brevity of all advertising will work to limit its effectiveness. Posters, television and radio – fleeting moments amidst a host of competing stimuli; pieces of paper, no matter how cunningly contrived, whose power is lost as they are dropped into the waste bin.

Product Advertising works best on the 'hottest' Attenders

Such a campaign of Product Advertising will have greatest effect on those who are most enthusiastic and knowledgeable about the art form and the specific event you are presenting – the hottest of your Attenders – but for the majority of your Available Audience you will need to do much more to make them aware of the event and to supply them with information that Product Advertising cannot convey.

PRODUCT PR

Advertising is intrinsically weak because of the limitations of the media used which restrict the amount of information that can be conveyed. Another means of delivering information is needed to back up, to supplement the advertising message, to put it into a more comprehensive context.

If you decide to go to a film or buy a book the odds are that you made the decision before seeing any Product Advertising at all. You probably read a review in the newspaper or magazine. You may have read an interview with the director of the film, or an actor or the author of the book. Of the film you may have seen some well illustrated image drawn from it on a poster or you might have seen a brief note in a listings magazine giving the name of the cinema and the times of showing. Books are often hardly advertised at all.

Information of this more general kind that is put before you in various media in the form of articles, reviews, interviews, profiles and so on is the result of an activity we may term *Product Public Relations*. The term hardly trips off the tongue but through long usage we are stuck with it and we must get used to it. The term is not so important as the need to understand precisely what it does and what it is meant to achieve.

Product PR creates a climate of receptiveness

Product PR aims to convey to your Attenders and Intenders information about the event you are presenting that will create an atmosphere, a climate of receptiveness, in which Product Advertising can flourish. No form of advertising could do the job of, say, a well written and illustrated article about a dance company, its latest work, its new choreographer, its exciting new dancers, its astoundingly successful world tour from which it has just returned, written by someone well known and respected and published in a newspaper that is well known and respected – that you are presenting in your venue in two weeks time.

Product PR can rarely do the job of persuasion entirely by itself but it is, without doubt, enormously potent, capable of making people and events of all kinds famous, if only for a little while, focusing the attention of your Attenders upon the subject and making them feel that this is something they *must* experience, tempting *Intenders* into making the special effort to make the commitment.

PR is a highly competitive industry

Being so potent in its effects there is inevitably much pushing and shoving involved in the process of putting information of this kind before the public. There is an industry of people, some self-employed, some working for PR companies, some working for arts organisations, dedicated to the delicate manoeuvres that bring writers into contact with their subjects. The competition for attention is with all the other people and organisations trying to catch the eye and then the pen of the writers. Media coverage of this kind is worth a lot because it can achieve a lot and so it must be fought for.

How Product PR works

Let us look briefly at how Product PR works. How did you make a decision to buy a recently published book? At the moment you made the decision, you had already received enough information to enable you to decide; this information will have been absorbed very recently and also in the near and probably distant past. You have read and enjoyed earlier works by the author. You saw a profile of the author in a newspaper whose literary coverage you respect. You heard the author interviewed on radio. Friends have said how much they too have enjoyed the author's work. You have developed a favourable inclination towards the writer. Now you read a review of the new book in a daily newspaper and another in a Sunday newspaper. You may see another review in a magazine. The reviews you read are favourable.

Then you see an advertisement for the new book or perhaps you are in a bookshop and suddenly there before you is the book itself which creates its own encouragement and is something which crystallizes everything you have heard and read about it; it focuses your attention and simultaneously offers you an opportunity to buy. The advertisement may tell you all kinds of wonderful things about the book – and so may the book's jacket – but it is what is already in your mind that has the greatest influence upon you. You were favourably inclined towards the author before you even knew about the new book. Then you heard about it and what you heard reinforced your attitude. Moving from this state of mind to actual purchase is no great step – provided, of course, that the book is there to be purchased or the means of purchase is there before your eyes and the process of buying is easy and simple.

No-one can predict how you will react to the information you pick up day by day from newspaper, magazines, radio and television but react you probably will. In the hypothetical case above your own direct experience of the writer's work will be pre-eminent in its effect but weight of media coverage combined with credible opinion from credible critics and friends will also have a strong influence upon you.

Book marketing provides a good example of how product PR works because the advertising element in the overall publicity is often small or non-existent; books are frequently promoted with Product PR alone.

The film industry takes Product PR to the ultimate

The film industry also offers an excellent example of how an effective Product PR machine can be used to create awareness of a forthcoming film in such a way that the experience of seeing it is eagerly sought. The product is scheduled to be available for viewing at some point several weeks ahead. No member of the public may sample the product ahead of this date. All that you know of the film is what you are told by the promoters and this information is skilfully chosen and skilfully presented. The film industry relies on star names for very good reason because the stars may be wheeled out well ahead of the release date and the media will jump at the chance of interviewing them. The forthcoming film provides journalists with a peg upon which to hang the interviews and so they are happy to provide Product PR for it. From the film promoters' viewpoint, these appearances on our television screens and in the pages of magazines and newspapers, are often all that it takes to create queues at the box-office when it first opens and it is well worth paying first class airfares and hotel costs to be able to put the stars in the right place at the right time. (Whoever calls Product PR 'free publicity' is a fool). Thereafter, of course, the film stands or falls on the opinions of it expressed by those who have seen it – the 'word of mouth' that publicists are so fond of talking about.

Film advertising relies upon very striking posters and very ordinary press advertising plus what is unique to our industry, the 'trailer', which is probably the most potent force for persuasion yet known to mankind. The trailer may be held up as a scintillating example of how to project a complex image of something in a way that emphasises its strongest, most appealing and compelling features, dynamically, excitingly and, above all, briefly. Trailers are always shown to Attenders of one sort of film or another who may well turn out to have the potential to be Attenders or Intenders for the film that is trailed. To reduce the wastage it is common to show several trailers, one after another, on the principle that if you cannot be hooked by one you may be hooked by another: the running of half a dozen trailers before the showing of a film is the precise equivalent of the greengrocer who, seeing that you have selected a melon, draws your attention to his mangoes, papayas, lychees, pineapples and rambutans. It is good business practice so to do.

The trailer, with its brilliant selection and arrangement of images and sounds – a work of art in its own right beyond question – regularly demonstrates that many people can be persuaded to want to see truly awful films, even if they later regret it. Study the film trailer and you will learn something of advertising.

Notice also how well the producers of films distance themselves from their products so that if one film turns out to be truly awful *no-one is to blame*. We may hold the actors – or, more likely, the director – responsible for our disappointment and wasted money but never the people who made all the key decisions that brought about the turkey and we'll go on buying tickets for their shows. Compare this with the local theatre that puts on a bad show. The film industry is truly marvellous.

Keep on eye on how these industries use Product PR

In marketing the arts we deal with different products with different characteristics. They cannot be put on a shelf like books. They cannot be offered for sale simultaneously in 100 different venues around the country. What they have in common with books and films is the need for Product PR as the instrument for providing background information that relates to what potential customers already know and is capable of making them favourably inclined to what you have to sell. Arts marketers can learn much that is useful by observing the techniques used by those who handle Product PR for these closely related industries.

Which is better, Product Advertising or Product PR?

Of the two techniques, Product Advertising and Product PR, which is the more powerful, which delivers the goods most effectively? In our world, where the product is an experience that may only be obtained if the potential customer takes some positive – and not necessarily convenient – action (nothing like as easy as popping into a shop to buy a book, for example) the answer must be that the two function most effectively when they are operated complementarily. They combine to make what we call *Product Publicity*.

What is Product Publicity and what is its objective?

Product Publicity is the term we use to describe the combination of Product PR, which creates a climate of favourable awareness about the product in the minds of the Available Audience, and Product Advertising, which delivers a specific message intended to crystallise generalised impressions into an image that is precise, clear, immediate and, above all, persuasive. Product Publicity has to emphasise the imminent availability of an experience which the Available Audience will find to its taste and to suggest that if the necessary action to secure the right to that experience is not taken promptly then perhaps the experience will not be available; it must then explain how that right to the experience may be secured – that is, how much it will cost and where and how the tickets may be bought.

Its objective is to bring as many members of the Available Audience as possible to the point where they *want to buy tickets*.

What happens then?

One of the most important ideas in arts marketing, one which I touched on in Chapter One when I referred to 'that vital piece of baggage left behind when marketing moved over from the 'real world', is the concept and function of Sales. An understanding of the part played by Sales is crucial to an understanding of what Product Publicity must set out to achieve.

Product Publicity is successful when it brings members of the Available Audience to the point where they want to buy what is being offered to them, where they are ready to make whatever is the appropriate commitment in order to secure it – this may be the purchase of a ticket but it may just as easily be the acceptance of an invitation to attend a private view.

Product Publicity has the duty of making people want to do something and there its responsibility ends. It is the Sales function that makes them actually do it.

I cannot give enough weight to the importance of this part of the arts marketing idea for if one believes that Product Publicity sells tickets, then that's it, that is all we need, it's time to go home. It was the failure to understand the objective of Product Publicity that led to this vital piece of baggage being left behind in the mid-eighties, just when government, the Arts Council of Great Britain and our industry as a whole were at one in wanting to advance the knowledge and practice of arts marketing in the UK. There was, of course, at least one book in existence at that time, which spelled it out fairly clearly but how could an author who had only worked in the arts know anything about marketing?

Further thoughts

Is that all there is to Product Publicity? No. It helps to understand arts marketing if the basic building blocks are described mainly in terms of what they are intended to achieve and the basic ideas that help them achieve it. When we have seen how Product Publicity relates to Sales, Pricing and Sales Promotion in following chapters, I will return to consider aspects of Advertising and Public Relations in greater detail.

What about the *Unavailable* Audience? Doesn't Product Publicity work for the Indifferent and the Hostile sectors of the community? No, it doesn't. For Product Publicity to succeed attitudes unfavourable to the art form must be changed, must be made favourable – or, at the very least, open to suggestion, susceptible. So, the Unavailable Audience must be approached using techniques that are capable of changing attitudes and only then can Product Publicity stand a chance of success; we will examine approaches to this problem in Part Three.

In the following chapters we shall see how Product Publicity Sales, Pricing and Sales Promotion; then we will return to consider aspects of Advertising and Public Relations in greater detail.

SUMMARY

Think of your community in terms of whether individuals are favourably inclined or unfavourably inclined to what you want to sell them, which defines whether they fall into the camp of availability or unavailability.

Think of the Available Audience as being made up of *Attenders* and *Intenders*.

Product Publicity has the duty of making your Available Audience want to do something and there its responsibility ends. It is the Sales function that makes them actually do it.

Product Advertising will have greatest effect on those who are most enthusiastic and knowledgeable about the art form and the specific event you are presenting. For the majority of your Available Audience you will need to do more to make people aware of the event and to supply them with information that Product Advertising cannot convey.

Product Publicity is the term we use to describe the combination of Product PR, which creates a climate of favourable awareness about the product in the minds of the Available Audience, and Product Advertising, which delivers a specific message intended to crystallise generalised impressions into an image that is precise, clear, immediate and, above all, persuasive.

CHAPTER FOUR

THE FUNDAMENTAL IDEAS
OF SALES

Product publicity makes them
want to do it. The job of Sales
is to make them do it.

Sales suffers from a bad press

The function known as 'Sales' suffers from a bad press. The very word conjures up images of unsavoury characters (driving red Cavaliers with jackets hanging in the back) who will resort to any trickery to clinch the deal. Films like *The Tin Men*, plays like *Glengarry Glen Ross* and newspaper accounts of how bad pension schemes and insurance policies are foisted onto unsuspecting members of the public, reinforce the popular image of Sales personified in the form of the unscrupulous salesperson.

There is indeed a sharp and unpleasant end of the Sales function which can take the form of extreme pressures exerted on individuals in order to get a desired result but this no more invalidates the ideas of Sales than motorway crashes invalidate driving motorcars. High pressure selling is one end – the very active end – of a spectrum that has at its other end no need for pressure at all, merely a recognition of what it is that stops people from acting on the impulses created by Product Publicity and building into the marketing system a means for reducing or eliminating those barriers.

(Does Product Publicity create only *impulses*? In the context of a specific campaign that is certainly what one must hope it does and it is all that one may prudently hope for. It is rare indeed for an organisation to be able to create a deeply seated, long lasting, passionate desire in the minds of its target public and if it is so successful then the organisation is most certainly in a Seller's Market and may, for a while at least, forget the cares of Sales. An impulse to buy, the momentary thought that *this* experience would be worth having and worth paying for, is as much as ordinary arts marketers can hope for. If one accepts the essential weakness and temporaneity of the effects of Product Publicity one begins to understand the importance of Sales.)

The ticket – something to buy

Arts marketers develop the idea of 'our' audience, the Available Audience (the Attenders and the Intenders) and, by speaking the right language and saying the right things to these people, brings them to the point where they want to experience the products they have told them about and create something – a ticket, the proxy-product – that they can buy at the time they feel inclined to buy rather than at the time the product is ready to be experienced. Putting the proxy-product into the system is one of the fundamental ideas of Sales because the presence of the ticket helps the transition from wanting to buy to buying. Don't ever think of the ticket as being merely a receipt for money paid.

Barriers to purchase

Having created something that can be bought – that is, the ticket rather than the experience it promises – the marketer must then ask what other barriers there are that come between wanting to buy and actually buying, knowing that the buying desire is extremely volatile and evaporates very quickly. The principal barriers are those of time and distance. The cost of what is offered for sale must also be considered as a potential barrier; there is some disagreement amongst practitioners as to how influential price is upon that movement from wanting something actually to securing it but at this stage we must see it as a potential barrier at the very least and we shall return to the matter later in this book.

Barriers of time and distance are indisputably the principle reasons why the motivated person does not actually buy: the barrier presented by the time it may take to buy a ticket, the barrier of the physical distance between the motivated person and the place where tickets are sold. Distance involves travel which takes time and costs money. Taking a trip to buy a ticket is something most easily put off until later. If a person experiences the impulse to buy at, say, 10pm in the evening and there is no way to consummate the buying desire at that time then delay has been introduced into the process and the purchase may very well not take place no matter how well motivated the person is (unless they are one of those passionate desirers upon which Sellers' Markets are based). In our world most arts experiences are felt to be generally and widely available and rarely does the would be customer feel that an opportunity to have an experience must be secured *at that time*. Probably more sales are lost through procrastination than for any other cause and it is almost always our fault because we fail to detect the barriers and those responsible do not do enough to reduce or eliminate them.

The box office and its potential

The box office is at the heart of Sales. Not a place of high pressure arm twisting, confidence tricks and psychological chess playing but a place where the wanting is converted into buying. It is a place where a very passive form of Sales is most usually practised but within it there is potential for more once the potential of Sales is understood.

It is within the box office that steps may be taken to move from a passive role to a more active one. The would be customer, entering the box office area may simply be provided with the type of ticket requested but experience tells us that often those potential audience members are uncertain about what they want; they may be sure of what evening of the week but unsure as to the seating area, the price and the relationship between them. They may gently be guided into choices that are more suited to them if the Sales staff are skilled at finding out what they really want. It is quite possible that the person wanting a certain seat area on a Thursday evening may accept a Wednesday evening performance if choice within the favoured seating area is restricted on the Thursday, but someone has to determine what is the most important factor. This is hardly high pressure selling but it is more than passive and certainly more than the traditional blank face behind the glass snapping out information only when prompted by questions.

When the would be customer is in contact with the Sales staff there is an ideal opportunity to make more of that contact – to sell them more. When one thinks of how hard it is to extract the Available Audience from the broad public mass – and how expensive it is to do this – when one such member emerges and identifies itself, the need to make more of the opportunity becomes an imperative. This person, who is in the process of moving from the state of 'would be' to *actual* customer, must surely be told of some of the other wonderful experiences that may be secured. And if time is short and the customer is unwilling to stay then at least the name and address may be obtained so that the organisation's carefully conceived, highly persuasive and Sales orientated, literature may be sent to them. This is much more into the active mode and it still does not enter into the high pressure area.

The Sales team must be brought to understand that every contact they make, whether it is personal visit to the box office, telephone call or posted order, must be exploited to the full. Each and every customer is worth considerably more to the organisation than the value of the money they have just parted with; they represent a contribution to the audience attendance target as well as the financial target over months and years ahead. If for every event and every campaign the arts marketer has to start afresh looking for yet another audience the process will consume large sums of money and the demand on energy will be huge. Better by far to capitalise on each campaign, building up the list of known attenders and establishing relationships with them.

Over recent years much work has been done on the management of box offices. It is now widely acknowledged that Sales staff need training and need to be well motivated just like other working persons if they are to fulfil the ambitions of the organisation. Their working environment must be taken into account as well and so must the pressures on them created by inadequate staffing. The potential within such Sales teams is huge once it has been recognised and once the organisation sets out to build it into a truly effective force. If this is not done, if box offices remain the province of bored timeservers who protect themselves from the public with stony faces and unanswered telephone calls, then arts bodies will go on believing that success or failure is a matter only of booking 'stars' and having someone to handle the press.

The marketplace

For those who are interested in comparing orthodox commercial marketing with arts marketing what we are considering when we talk of box offices is the last of the famous four Ps – Product, Price, Publicity and Place – so often referred to by commercial marketers. The word 'Place' is not self-explanatory in this context. Better by far to say *marketplace* and take it to mean the place, or more appropriately these days, the system, where or in which, the purchase takes place. For example, where the principal tool of a campaign is a leaflet conveying a Product Advertising message and a ticket order form for completion, then the marketplace is the leaflet's coupon. However named, the concept is an important one; if you want to achieve sales you must have a good 'marketplace.'

Credit and charge cards create a new marketplace

The progress we have made in acknowledging the importance of Sales can be seen if one examines the theatre listings in a newspaper of ten or fifteen years ago. Then the use of credit and charge cards was widespread in the world at large yet they were not accepted for telephone bookings at theatres. The theatre listings make no mention of the facility at that time. During my work as a consultant in the early eighties I regularly proposed the acceptance of credit and charge card bookings both for calling customers at box offices and for those who wanted to book by telephone. Invariably there would be someone in the management hierarchy who would point out that the credit and charge card companies demanded a percentage of the payment and protest that this could not be afforded. This not only revealed a failure to understand the role of Sales but it epitomised the negative approach to arts marketing which bedevilled the business then and still has an effect today. Credit and charge cards may appear to be devices that enable people without money then and there to buy things, that is they appear to be instruments of credit – but they are really Sales tools, implements that bring the wanting and the doing close together, particularly when used in conjunction with the telephone – they create a new marketplace.

It can hardly be doubted that the telephone combined with the acceptance of 'plastic payment' is almost the perfect Sales system but the combination only really works if the organisation and its staff do their stuff. There is no sadder example of wasted effort and money than to have a highly motivated potential customer, card in hand, hearing the telephone ring out minute after minute.

Other methods of payment

The creativity of the financial sector seems boundless and each step forward in systems of credit transfer can make our goal of the 'seamless purchase' easier to achieve. The good, old fashioned cheque is still a firm favourite with the older, better-heeled customer and the relatively simple handling involved makes it popular with box office staff. For many, particularly younger people who cannot yet get clearance for charge and credit cards, the cheque also still possesses the odd quality of not seeming to be 'real' money and is thus easier to part with. For postal bookings the cheque offers no disadvantages to the organisation apart from the occasional one that bounces but as the item being purchased is most usually a written promise of an experience the organisation can always break its promise if the customer breaks the contract by issuing a dud cheque. More difficult is the person at the head of a busy box office queue who takes too much time finding the cheque book, then finding the pen, then slowly and meticulously filling it in – not all barriers to purchase can be eliminated.

Charge and credit cards are likely to stay favourites with our industry because they also allow the customer a period of grace before actually passing over the money. The 'switch' card which makes an instant debit of the customer's bank account is increasingly popular for face-to-face transactions particularly with people who like to know just how their finances stand at any time – the other forms of plastic can create a feeling of uncertainty. In both cases there is the risk of adverse publicity and the systems going out of favour with the public as crooks discover ways of stealing money through obtaining people's personal details and card numbers. It is important therefore that managers take precautions to ensure that their customers' data is handled in a secure manner and their fears are allayed.

Standing orders and direct debit arrangements are particularly appropriate when payment amounts are large, as they often are with subscription schemes and they have the advantage of tending to keep customers because they require a conscious effort to cancel. This fact has been used to good effect by publishers of magazines who can offer quarterly payments of annual subscription charges by, say, direct debit which has the effect of reducing the apparent price barrier so that the price to be paid is one quarter of the annual charge and, by making use of the 'inertia factor', keeps people subscribing for much longer than they would if they were faced with an annual decision whether to renew or not.

Plastic cards offer a similar facility and it is fairly common these days for a magazine subscription form to offer the option of payment by, say, credit card which the publisher is to act on in the usual way but with a few extra words which authorise the publisher to go on drawing the annual or quarterly payment until countermanded by the subscriber.

It is the job of the arts marketer constantly to assess the effect of such payment methods upon the customers. Methods which exploit the tendency of the customer not to cancel payments can work against the organisation's interests if people begin to see them as unfair attempts to gull them into paying more than they originally intended. Watch out, therefore, for newspaper articles that say the methods are wrong for there may then be a backlash that will do harm to sales figures and customer relations in the longer term.

The linking of television channels with the advertising of products which may be bought there and then by electronic means is already well on the way. It will prove to be too expensive for most arts organisations but for those with high ticket prices, such as the 'blockbuster' opera and ballet events that have come about in the past decade, the method will be used – because it allows the would be customer to act on the impulse to buy and puts no barrier between wanting and buying.

One superb idea, originating from the mind of the late Richard Condon who was one of the great impresario arts marketers, (based for the latter part of his career at the Theatre Royal, Norwich) was to encourage his customers to open accounts with the theatre as one might with a local butcher or garage. The customer then simply ordered tickets as required, receiving a bill at the end of the month which was to be paid within, say, thirty days. Of course care has to be taken with such schemes but the incidence of people failing to pay is low and the more general benefits are very high. The method simply eliminates one of the barriers to purchase – as well as establishing a special status for the customer which is likely to produce more attendance and, in all probability, encourage purchase at a higher price.

The effect of Sales ideas upon arts marketing

The creation of an effective arts marketing system requires an intense scrutiny of plans to see if all that can be done has been done to push the sales barriers down to their lowest possible level. When a Product Advertising campaign is being planned the Sales implications must be considered at every stage with the question, 'How do they buy?' being asked.

A newspaper display advertisement? Large enough to carry the motivational message? Of course. Large enough to carry basic sales information such as box office opening times and telephone number? Of course. Large enough to carry a ticket ordering form? Ah, perhaps that had not been considered, yet there is much evidence that people respond more readily if there is a coupon, an order form, to complete and send off. Do you want to encourage telephone booking? Of course. Can the organisation cope with demand? What steps need to be taken to make sure that it can? Postal booking? Yes. Will you supply a Freepost address or will you send a Business Reply prepaid envelope? Surely they can pay their own postage. They may be willing to pay but what if they cannot lay their hands on a stamp *at that time*. (My own evidence, obtained from questioning seminar attenders over more than twenty years, is that some 60% of any group of people cannot find a stamp either on them or in their immediate surroundings – so could not *at that time* buy a ticket by post – of course they could always obtain a stamp later but other matters will interfere, as they inevitably do, and the stamp will be forgotten and so will the purchase).

If purchase by person at the box office is to be the main Sales marketplace, as it often is with smaller organisations in small places, then are the times of opening convenient to the arts organisation or to the public? If you want to sell then you must behave as though you want to sell. How early can you open? How late can you stay open? Must you close for lunch?

If the box office is within the venue itself then is it open after performances so that customers thrilled by one experience can rapidly and easily secure another one?

Implications for Copywriter and Designer

Another barrier to purchase usually lies outside the direct responsibility of the people with Sales responsibilities and the need to reduce this barrier illustrates once more how important it is for Sales to be fully integrated into the marketing of the organisation – it is to do with those parts of Product Advertising that are supposed to carry the motivated person through to making the purchase, whether it be by making a telephone call, completing and posting a form or travelling to buy a ticket. Later in the book we will see how Product Advertising is intended to blend into Sales by leading the potential customer into some form of action; it is this part of the process that is frequently executed badly. Why should this be so? Inevitably it is because the idea of Sales has not been fully integrated into the thoughts and actions of the personnel concerned.

When creating a piece of Product Advertising material, whether it be leaflet, poster, brochure or full-scale booklet, the part which is most exciting to do is the decision as to what is to be said about the experience that is being offered and the expression of it in an exciting, engaging and persuasive way. The arts marketing officer conceives the heart of the message, what it is about the event that is most likely to motivate, and then, working with a designer (and perhaps a copywriter), sketches out ideas for expressing these thoughts and, perhaps, if the designer is not a megalomaniac, how they are likely to look. The designer takes over usually going away to return some days later with the fruits of her or his creativity. It has become a fully creative process and the risk here is that the true intention of the work may be overlooked. The intention is to spur people to action not only to please them or excite them or to motivate them; they must be brought as close as possible actually to buying so the means of buying must be made very evident and clear.

Sales information needs space and first rate typographic treatment

So often have we seen this vital Sales information treated inadequately. Would be customers almost always need explanation and guidance. They need to know how much the experience costs and where in the auditorium their money will put them. They need to know dates and times. A clear explanation of how payment may be made is needed which includes not only the range of acceptable methods but also the place where payment must be made. This part of the piece of printed material is the marketplace, it is where the transaction is occurring. Such information must be conveyed with maximum clarity and, before commitment to printing, must be minutely scrutinised for it is every bit as important as the creative work that has preceded it. From the design viewpoint the material needs space and first rate typographic treatment; it should not be considered as of secondary importance meriting only 'small print' treatment.

The application form is just as important

If the purchase involves the completion of a form then it too should be afforded the same level of respect by the designer. The layout should be tested by the arts marketing planner. Fill out the form yourself. Is there space enough for a normal address? Have you asked for the postcode? Telephone number? Should it be work number and home number?

How is time and date of performance to be specified? (Check to see how well these are stated in the main body of the material). What will you do if you cannot supply what the customer has specified? Do you want second and even third choices to be given? Does the form reinforce your intentions in this regard?

And when you receive the order and payment?

And what will you do when you receive the order and payment? Tell your customer when tickets will be sent and the circumstances under which you would prefer to hold them for collection before the performance (one hopes that in these enlightened times the customer will not be asked to turn up an hour before the performance to collect tickets; this used to happen in the early days of credit card booking by telephone). This information may be given in the explanatory guidelines but there is no reason at all why it should not be repeated on the form itself. When communicating information never shun repetition.

Even check the type of paper to be used

Today people use a wide variety of writing instruments. The fountain pen is still in use and there are ball point pens, felt tip pens and so on. Check that the paper you plan to use for the printing will accept all kinds of ink. (At the time I was writing this book I was asked to complete an 8 page application form issued by a financial institution which asked that the entries be made in black ink – unfortunately the paper used repelled the black ink in my fountain pen and proved extremely resistant to the ink of a roller ball pen – I laboriously scratched my replies into the paper coating eventually making my mark on the paper beneath). Had the application been for theatre tickets I am not sure I should have persevered.

See the guidelines and application form as the culmination of the process of persuasion

There are many occasions when the ability to imagine oneself in the role of a customer helps the arts marketer and no less when planning guidelines and application form. Remember how you feel when you have decided you want to buy something from, say, a mail-order catalogue or, to give a case where one may be really quite excited by the prospects ahead, a holiday brochure. Completing the form, writing the cheque and posting it is the culminating point of a process where you have taken in information, weighed up options, related prices to your own personal scale of values, and fought with the feeling of guilt that you are perhaps spending money which should be devoted to more prudent things, such as your savings account or your pension. If you have not quite enough money at the time then you may also have to promise yourself that you will restrict other spending in the weeks ahead so that you may stay within your spending limits.

So putting the finishing touches to the decision to buy and making the final commitment is a kind of release from the conflicts I have described. To put hurdles in front of a would-be customer at this stage is most unwise.

To illustrate this point further: on many occasions, when conducting seminars, apart from asking my 'stamp' question – that is, do you have one on you at this time so that you may respond to a piece of Product Advertising *now*? – I ask if when people have booked a holiday from a brochure whether they then post it using a first class or second class stamp. No-one has ever said that they use second class mail. This is, I think, a useful illustration of the state of mind of the well motivated customer who, having made the decision to buy, now wants to clinch the deal and does not want to be disappointed. Such an insight into how we feel should guide us when integrating Sales ideas into arts marketing. It may even give us cause to think again about the wisdom of offering people Freepost or Business Reply envelopes without due regard for the need people have to feel relieved that their purchase will be confirmed as soon as possible. Freepost replies are treated in the UK as being second class at best and when they arrive on the second day after posting come on the second delivery. It is possible to have a First Class Business Reply arrangement with Royal Mail and, if my assumptions are correct, then this would be a better option.

An alternative, which may well have even better effect, is to state in the guidelines and on the order form what is the Freepost address and then to add words to the effect that customers wanting to ensure that their orders arrive promptly – and thus by implication to receive preferential treatment – should use a first class stamp and use the full postal address of the organisation rather than the Freepost address. An improvement on this is then to give a special telephone number which will enable bookings to be made immediately. The person who does not understand the ideas of Sales will wonder why one does not simply give the telephone number or will assume that the information about postal booking is for those without telephones. The person who does understand will recognise the thought processes that the nearly-customer is being taken through and will see the importance of giving postal information, including the reference to using a First Class stamp, as a way of creating an impetus to buying as soon as humanly possible – by telephone.

It goes without saying that an undertaking to deal with all orders within a day or so – better, on the day they are received – will encourage the customer to act more swiftly.

The aim is to promote swift action

The influence of Sales ideas upon arts marketing is therefore to identify as many barriers to purchase as possible and by reducing or eliminating them to smooth the path to the culmination of the desire to buy. All Product Advertising should have a Sales element which should be explicit and uncluttered and, if well conceived and designed, will actually contribute to the customer's desire to move quickly in order to secure the object of desire. Underlying everything is the thought that if the customer hesitates then the sale may be lost.

Sales Budgets

There are cost implications in many of these suggestions but expenditure is inevitable when one is trying to achieve sales and the income that derives from sales and it must be budgeted for just as any other expenditure. Often arts organisations do not budget for Sales expenditure. They have allocations for Product Publicity but they do not see Sales as requiring separate treatment. If an organisation does not acknowledge through its budgeting system that the Sales sub-function needs money just as Product Publicity needs money then each Sales activity will involve an internal battle; better by far to establish the right of Sales to a share of the cake.

Use the right terminology

I have already referred to the need to identify staff with Sales responsibilities as *Sales* staff and to establish the work in the management budgeting and accounting by using the title Sales for expenditures made under that heading. Also introduce the use of the word Sales into arts marketing planning. Get people used to it. Do not accept loose terminology such as calling the process simply 'Publicity' when you know that much more is involved than this. We have seen how easy it is for the ideas of Sales to be completely overlooked (see Chapter One) and if they are then they will not be taken into account in the overall arts marketing work. In a perfect world every arts organisation will employ a person or persons whose principal responsibility is to contribute the Sales perspective to arts marketing decisions and to take responsibility for all activities with a Sales element to them, most particularly the box office. Such a person would control a Sales budget and would have the word Sales in the job title. Only by so enshrining it in the entire system of the organisation will its importance be recognised and not forgotten.

The relationship of Sales to Price and Value

Price can be a considerable barrier to successful Sales and not always in the way one might first imagine. You charge for the experiences you are selling and as everyone knows if you pitch the price too high you may create a barrier too high. We also know that if the price is too low there may be created a barrier of credibility along the lines of 'If it's that cheap it can't be much good.' Often managers respond to the matter of how much to charge by charging many prices and this in itself can be counterproductive for the act of presenting people with a decision to make which mostly cannot be made according to rational criteria creates a confusion barrier for them and while they ponder the desire to buy evaporates.

When a price is put on anything it makes an implicit statement about its value and it is value, that is, the perception of value and how it relates to the individual potential customer's own scale of values (this term should not be taken to mean anything more than the order of buying priorities a person has), that has a major influence on whether the person will be more motivated to buy or less motivated. There is very little one can do about the potential customer's hierarchy of scales of value – one person rates going to the theatre once a month as being more important than buying new clothes, another would rather have a good holiday once a year than spend money on concert tickets – so all the marketer can do is make the experience offered appear to be the best value possible.

The best way of presenting value is through Product Publicity which presents the experience offered as being worth having and through a Pricing approach that will not jar with the potential customer's feeling about what is the 'going rate' for similar products offered by other organisations or, more important, what it is worth paying to have the experience. There is very little science that will help in this process and it is an area where the instinct of the impresario is needed. In April 1994, Barbra Streisand appeared in Wembley Arena, London and top price tickets sold out very quickly at £260 each. No market research could ever have predicted a price to be charged that would be so high and would be paid by so many people.

So the idea of value must be established in the minds of the Available Audience so that the barrier of price is reduced; it cannot be entirely eliminated, of course, because there will always be people who have, on the day you contact them, received their tax bill or have just lost their jobs.

Sales Promotion

Then *add value*. This is a most important concept in arts marketing. It is closely allied to Sales. When you *add value* you try to make the potential customer jump what remains of all the barriers to purchase – not just price. This process is called *Sales Promotion*. Having established in the minds of your Available Audience the impression that what you are offering is well worth the price you are charging you then offer to improve the deal by either giving more for the same stated price or by charging less for the same experience – provided the nearly-customer does what you want, which is to move promptly to make the purchase. One must always try to reduce the gap between wanting and buying and Sales Promotion is the most effective way of doing this.

'You may have this experience in six week's time. It costs £20. Tickets are available now (by telephone credit card purchase) and if you buy before Friday you pay only £18. Or you have the choice of any seat in the house. Or we'll send you a £10 voucher that you may use when you next buy a double ticket from us. Or – if you have established the atmosphere of a Seller's Market – you get nothing more than your ticket. You are one of our club members/subscribers/regular customers and we won't sell tickets to anyone else until after Friday. The real impresario arts marketer can make the simple right to purchase into a privilege and hence into a Sales Promotion.

So, when the ideas of Sales are brought into arts marketing they do not work in a simple linear way with Product Publicity bringing people to the boil and then Sales stepping in the clinch the deal. Sales works directly on the barriers of time and distance. Product Publicity works with Pricing to establish value. And then Sales Promotion works on value to reduce even further the negative effects of price and to accelerate purchase by enhancing the value in the minds of the available audience. The process illustrates how important it is for arts marketing to be fully integrated into the decisions made by the organisation.

At a practical level where organisation of personnel is concerned then Sales Promotion is better handled by those with specific Sales responsibilities with their input being taken by those making Pricing and Product Publicity decisions.

What next?

The next step is to take a look at Pricing and then, with the ideas of Sales and Pricing together in mind, to examine Sales Promotion in greater detail.

SUMMARY

Product publicity makes them want to do it. The job of Sales is to make them do it.

Sales attempts to identify what it is that stops people from acting on the impulses created by Product Publicity and building into the marketing system a means for reducing or eliminating those barriers.

Putting the proxy-product – the ticket – into the system is one of the fundamental ideas of Sales because the presence of the ticket helps the transition from wanting to buy to buying. Don't ever think of the ticket as being merely a receipt for money paid.

Barriers of time and distance are indisputably the principle reasons why the motivated person does not actually buy:

Probably more sales are lost through procrastination than for any other cause.

Credit and charge cards may appear to be devices that enable people without money then and there to buy things, that is they appear to be instruments of credit – but they are really Sales tools, implements that bring the wanting and the doing close together.

When a Product Advertising campaign is being planned the Sales implications must be considered at every stage with the question, 'How do they buy?' being asked.

All Product Advertising should have a Sales element which should be explicit and uncluttered and, if well conceived and designed, will actually contribute to the customer's desire to move quickly in order to secure the object of desire. Underlying everything is the thought that if the customer hesitates then the sale may be lost.

If an organisation does not acknowledge through its budgeting system that the Sales sub-function needs money just as Product Publicity needs money then each Sales activity will involve an internal battle; better by far to establish the right of Sales to a share of the cake.

CHAPTER FIVE

PRICING

Charge as much as you can get

The best financial outcome

Let us start this chapter by reminding ourselves of what arts marketing is meant to achieve – *to bring together appropriate numbers of people, drawn from the widest possible range of social background, economic condition and age, into an appropriate form of contact with the artist and, in so doing, to arrive at the best financial outcome that is compatible with the achievement of that aim.*

The *best financial outcome* is the part of the aim that has most obvious relevance to Pricing but if we are to set out to achieve the objective in full consideration must also be given to the 'people element' contained in the statement. We want to earn money from our sales but we also want to earn it from as many people as possible, drawn from as wide a range as possible.

Given that in most performing arts situations there are unalterable physical limitations that make it hard to exceed what are 'appropriate numbers', arts marketing is concerned almost all of the time with achieving the maximum number of people within those confines. So, out of any arts marketing situation the simple, short term objective is to attract as many people as possible and to get as much money as possible from them in exchange for the experiences you are providing. Which would you prefer to have in your theatre or concert hall, 1000 people each paying £5 or 500 each paying £10? Seen in money terms only the choice doesn't matter but in arts marketing terms it matters very much; the former is surely twice as successful as the latter.

How much do you charge?

The organisation considers its programme for the year ahead, or whatever period it finds convenient, and relates the cost of providing the programme to the money it is likely to receive in subsidy and thus gives itself a financial target – the money it must earn from its sales. Or it relates the cost of providing the programme to what it believes it can earn from its sales and thus discovers how much it must achieve in subsidy and from other sources of income. The stance it takes depends on how confident it is of achieving its sales targets and how well its face fits with the givers of subsidy. Either way there is a sum of money to be earned over the period. The programme is then broken down into appropriate units, individual performances or groups of performances, and sales income for each is estimated; the total of the items of sales income obviously must equal the sales income needed to balance the figures over the period.

The target sales incomes are then related to the number of experiences that are there to be sold – the number of seats and so the number of tickets.

Divide the sales target for, say, one performance or group of performances, by the number of seats that are there to be sold and you have a median, an average, price that is to be charged. Sell all your seats at this price and you achieve your sales target.

So far, so easy.

It is at this stage that the arts marketer starts to ask some awkward questions.

****

What happens if I do not sell all the tickets? Is it wise to work on the assumption that I shall sell everything I have to sell?

No it isn't.

If I assume that I will sell less than all I have to sell then I shall have to put up the price charged to beyond the median price if I am still to achieve my sales income target. Yes?

Yes.

But if I put up my price will that not tend to reduce the number of tickets I sell?

It's possible. It doesn't always happen but it might. If you scale down the number of tickets you think you might sell to a very

68

low figure then the price you will have to charge per ticket will have to be much higher and then you might sell even fewer. If 500 seats have to yield £5,000 and you plan to sell all of them the price to charge is £10. If you think you might sell only 250 seats then your price must be £20.

This looks like the land of the self-fulfilling prophesy, doesn't it?

Indeed it does and is.

****

So how do you put a price on your tickets?

Apart from simple arithmetic, these questions have been about confidence and what is called *price elasticity*. Confidence, that of the arts marketer and the organisation, grows with time and experience of dealing with the Available Audience. Even the dullest of arts marketers can, with time, develop some of the instinct of the impresario, can develop a sense of how the available audience is going to respond to what is to be offered to them so that a reasonable estimate of likely attendance can be made. Price elasticity is a term used to describe the extent to which sales fall or rise according to changes in price. In a highly elastic situation a small movement in price results in a high increase or decrease in sales. In a less elastic situation sales figures do not respond very significantly to price changes. What evidence there is suggests that in the arts industry the price/sales relationship is not very elastic so if prices are put up the loss of income due to a fall-off in sales (if there is a fall-off at all) will be less than the extra money you take from the tickets you have sold at the higher price. It is, however, dangerous to approach Pricing without relating this notion to the practical experience gained with one's own Available Audience.

If you are beginning to develop a feeling for your Available Audience and confidence in your judgement and if you have no reason to doubt the view that the price/sales relationship is not very elastic then aim high in terms of target attendances and high in terms of the price you are to charge.

How high is high?

I have used the word 'high' in relation to price. The term is meaningless unless it is compared with something and, in any given situation, it can only mean high compared with, say, what you have been charging in the past, what other organisations like yours are charging or – and this is a very unscientific approach – it is what you think is high, what you feel is the limit to which your available audience can be pushed. It would be useful to have a more reliable system of measurement but we don't and so we have to rely on our personal assessment and on how the available audience responds to the prices we put before it. As a rule of thumb a high price is a price paid that you thought was probably pushing the limits of acceptance; a price that is too high is one that doesn't get paid.

Be more ambitious

Earlier I described the way arts organisations calculate their sales income targets; the method is essentially governed by their financial needs and the understandable wish to balance the books. In a sector which traditionally loses rather than makes money good financial housekeeping is part of the *ethos*. This simple approach should not be the dominant factor in one's approach to Pricing; it is really no more than the first step which establishes the *lowest* acceptable figure to the organisation – there is absolutely no reason why the organisation should just set its sights at this level. In arts marketing one's sights should always be set as high as possible; so set out to achieve *as much as possible*. As many tickets sold at as high a price as possible.

There is no law that says you cannot take in more money than your estimates provide for and there is no law that forbids your setting your target income higher than that needed to balance the books. Of course, if you do better than you need to do according to the level of subsidy available to you it could well be – it probably will be – that those who supply your organisation's subsidy will say that you clearly need less money and will try to reduce your subsidy next year.

What can one say about this? Arts organisations have become familiar with the shifting of goalposts by arts funding bodies and government. When arts sponsorship was in its infancy twenty years ago arts managers expressed the fear that if they raised money from commercial sources – money that could never be relied upon – their subsidy, derived from more reliable sources, would be reduced. They were assured by government and by the arts funding bodies that this would not happen. Today, arts sponsorship is perforce woven into the financial structure of most arts bodies and they are forced to rely upon this most unreliable of sources because their successes in raising such money has led to reduced subsidy in relation to the size of their needs. So, what *can* one say?

One can say 'to blazes with them' and set out to do the very best one can in terms of audiences and income from them. Arts marketing does not succeed if it takes the negative path, if it sets out merely to achieve easily attainable targets. If it does it loses its vitality and so do the arts marketers. Success is hard enough to achieve and if it is proposed to reward it with a tougher set of circumstances next year then one has the choice of either taking it as yet another challenge or raising a mighty yell of protest that calls the bureaucrats to order. At the individual level, as they affect the arts marketer, negativism and averagcism are anathema; as in life, one deals with each problem as it emerges and dull-witted bureaucrats can be racked alongside verrucas and bad weather on bank holidays.

Can our audiences afford 'high' prices?

We are frequently inhibited in our approach to Pricing by our fears that no matter how attractive are the experiences we promise and deliver and how excitingly and attractively we describe them in our Product Publicity, our available audience will not be able to afford to pay our prices. Of course there are people with so little money that their horizons cannot go beyond plain existence; this is an awful fact of life which provides a background to every situation where products and services are offered for sale but it cannot inhibit the normal processes of life. In the arts world, where most people have a keener appreciation of the plight of the poor and find poverty distressing in the extreme, it is hard to plough on marketing what are essentially luxury items – but we must and we must not let our work be inhibited by factors over which we have no control. If the prevalence of poverty is a matter of politics then let our playwrights and theatre directors, authors, poets and all artists who have the ears, eyes and respect of the public influence politics through their work – and we can express our views through the ballot box. Meanwhile, our work must continue and the only way we can bring our products closer to people with little money is by making special arrangements to assist them. The next chapter will return to this matter.

The importance of Product Publicity in creating a sense of value

Whatever price or prices you put upon the experiences you are offering they will impact on the available audience at the same time as your Product Publicity impacts upon them and it is now that the potential buyer makes an instant estimation of *value* – the perception of what is being offered is related to the person's tastes and attitudes and, if there is a tickle of interest, the matter of cost becomes a consideration. If what is being offered appears to be extremely attractive, a rare experience, something that will not be available again for a long time, then the potential customer is likely to be prepared to pay and pay highly for it. If what is being offered falls within the normal range of arts experiences – a typical concert by a symphony orchestra, a play of the type and quality customarily offered by the local theatre, for example – then the potential customer will expect to be asked to pay a typical price, a price that falls within her range of expectations. We see this matching up of product offered with price asked, which is almost an unconscious process, happening every day of our lives and we react this way ourselves in other settings. It underscores the importance of making the Product Publicity really effective in projecting value that is compatible with price.

Will our audiences pay 'high' prices?

We try to create in the minds of the audience a sense that this experience is worth the price being charged, that it is good value according to the individual's scale of cultural and material values. In most cases this process of weighing up value is not a rational one.

If we look outside the arts we see countless examples of wholly irrational expenditure taking place because the spenders believe that for them the purchase represents good value and will bring them something that will benefit them and will benefit them more than other purchases. The most striking example of wholly irrational expenditure is the motor car the industry of which succeeds in persuading large numbers of people on quite low incomes to take on credit commitments which are huge in relation to their other needs and other expenditures. Once purchased the motor car consumes money day after day and as it does so it becomes less valuable as it moves towards the graveyard. Knowledge of what is the true cost of buying and running a car is available to all yet the motor car industry still occupies a major part of our national economy. Holidays abroad, costing in total sums in the order of £1000 per individual are regularly bought by people who, if their personal circumstances were studied, would be seen not to be able to afford them. People with virtually no money often spend what they have on smoking and drinking. Rich people are no more rational – but the results are less damaging to them.

So, knowing that the impulse of purchase is not a particularly rational one we may approach the Pricing of our products in the same spirit as any other marketer and set out to *charge as much as we can get*. That is, to push the price up until we encounter resistance to it, then either pull back a little or set out to make our products seem even more attractive, even better value, so that people will rank this kind of purchase higher up their own personal scale of values. For this is what people do when they buy a ticket for one of our events; having the experience is judged to be *worth having* and therefore worth paying for, possibly even worth doing without something else for. Opera is the most expensive of arts experiences and we have all known regular opera goers of modest means, people who spend considerable sums of money indulging their passion and their habit at the expense of something else.

The total price of the experience – more than the ticket alone

If one takes the pragmatic approach of charging as much as one can get then all costs involved in leaving the home to go out to the theatre or wherever must be taken into account. If the overall outlay, including travel, eating, drinking, cost of babysitter and so on plus the cost of the ticket exceeds the would be customer's sense of what is worth having and worth paying out for, then the purchase will not take place. If, in spite of an overall cost that is in truth too high for the customer and the purchase goes ahead nevertheless (purchases often being made irrationally) then a second purchase is unlikely to take place.

The arts marketer must, therefore, take into account all costs involved in obtaining the experience. If there is resistance to paying a price even when it is believed that Product Publicity has done a good job, then other cost factors will be playing their part. In theory people can move from their homes to the towns and cities for their arts experiences using cars and rail but they often do not because rail travel is often expensive in relation to the ticket price; it seems 'wrong' to spend £35 travelling to see a show that costs £20 per ticket – the sense of what is 'worth having' is offended. And, of course, the combined cost of ticket and rail fare plus all the other incidentals, will always be pushing the individual nearer the point where it is felt that it is 'too much', that is, it has gone beyond its place in the personal scale of values.

Nuisance factors play their parts as well; not only can the cost of the rail fare be a negative influence but also the complexity of fare structures with travel on one day being more expensive than on another or travel by trains before or after certain times being priced differently, makes our would be customers uncertain not only as to cost (and not knowing the price of a rail ticket at the time one is considering the idea of travelling to see a show is another Sales barrier) but also perhaps doubtful of the system's ability to deliver the passenger to the right place at the right time. Car parking costs, fear of clamping or having the car towed away, vandalism and so on, all exert negative forces upon the would be customer and are taken into account in the few minutes after the impulse to buy, when, if at all, rationality enters into the decision making process.

What is the best approach to Pricing?

We set prices in order to achieve the best financial outcome. We have sales income targets and we must achieve them. There are two factors involved, the number of tickets we think we might sell and the price we put on those tickets. If we are optimistic about the number of tickets that will be sold then we start to feel that we may charge a lower price than if our attendance target was lower. Pessimism leads to higher prices. We are dealing with the future, we are dealing with how bullish we feel about the event and our ability to promote it well – we are dealing with *guesswork* and no gloss of phoney management speak can be put on it. This is where the need for the talent of an old-fashioned impresario comes into play.

The impresario, who has selected the event and is thus in the position of artistic director as well as marketer, uses experience and a sense of what the market will bear to set prices. Optimism can be taken for granted for the impresario would not be involved if she or he were pessimistic about the future results. Prices are determined by what it is felt people will pay. As I have already said, it is guesswork. It is guesswork supported by experience. But the impresario takes a longer term view,

The impresario is in business for life and accepts that in a risk business there will be ups and there will be downs. Failures will occur for reasons not to do with Pricing; similarly successes will occur. The trick is to make sure that the successes outweigh the effects of the failures. The impresario always aims to take as much money as possible on Monday because it might be needed to bail out Friday's event. No income is too great, therefore, for the impresario.

It is this view that should knock firmly on the head any thought that sales targets and hence price should be determined by how much the event costs to mount – particularly when this cost is low. At the beginning of this chapter, under the heading 'How much do you charge?', I described the way in which most sales targets are established and I referred to what the organisation 'believes it can earn from sales' as being a factor in the process. The arts organisation must take a confident stance at this point; it must go for the maximum it thinks it can take. The cost to the organisation of providing the product is mainly irrelevant. The arts organisation, just like the impresario, has to live to fight another day and needs maximum income from every event. If sales targets are tied to the cost of the specific event according to some formula that takes into account fees, overheads and so on, then opportunities to maximise income will be lost. So, if one has the opportunity of promoting a low cost event, taken on, perhaps, because it seemed a bit of a gamble, and making lots of money from it, it must be taken and, indeed, this approach should be woven into the arts marketing philosophy of the organisation.

There are times when the organisation would wish to promote high cost events and where sales targets based on those costs would put seat prices beyond what the market would probably bear. Does one then back out of the situation? If an organisation is seeking to build a strong relationship with its Available Audience then it must, if only from time to time, offer something extraordinary and this may well cost a lot to provide. The organisation that practises 'free floating' Pricing, always going for the most irrespective of the cost of the event, will have money in hand to make such eye-catching, exciting promotions possible – at a (temporary) loss, if necessary.

There is, in the subsidised arts sector, a tendency towards a negative approach which is the antithesis of that of the impresario who must stand without support. Once, when I was advising a small music body on the promotion of a series of concerts it became obvious that a small amount of sponsorship income would be necessary to make it possible. Of the eight concerts planned one was likely to be a sure-fire box office success and the confident forecast was that its income would exceed its costs. Another, at the other end of the spectrum in terms of appeal, was forecast to lose quite a lot of money. According to the manager this latter event was the one for which sponsorship should be sought – because it needed it. I pointed out that sponsorship should be sought for the first event because, being highly attractive it was much more likely to attract sponsorship and the money could then be used to support the latter concert. The manager was focused on the need for money and on the event that needed the money in the same way that arts managers, when deciding sales targets, set low ones when the need for money appears to be lower. Always think of the totality, the organisation, the series, the festival, the season, when setting sales targets, rather than the individual event.

Do not establish a 'going' rate or allow one to become established

Price resistance is more likely to be met with when prices are *seen* to be increased. When you make your offer of an experience at what is your customary price or if it falls within your normal range of prices the potential customer may relate that price to some other price charged by some other industry or organisation and may react adversely to the comparison – but like is not being compared with like and the chances are that if the impulse goes against you it will be on grounds other than those of price. When you have established a 'going rate' for your type of product by charging the same price, or very close to the same price, for a long time you will have established a price/value relationship in the minds of your customers and when you increase your price you automatically damage the perceived value of your product. It may be that the damage is only slight and the customer may quickly recover from it but relationships are strange things and sometimes people may react quite irrationally to a price rise that they can, in fact, easily tolerate. Such a response is usually more emotionally based than rational with the refusal to buy at the new price having at its root the desire to 'get one's own back' in some perverse way. In a society like ours, where consumers are constantly being reminded of their rights and to be on the lookout for sharp practices on the part of all businesses, it is only too easy for a minor matter such as a 50p increase on the price of a ticket to be seen as yet another rip-off in a heartless world perpetrated by soulless bureaucrats or get-rich-quick merchants.

If you vary your prices event by event then you will have greater freedom to introduce a trend upwards without there being an adverse reaction because comparisons cannot easily be made. Provided the overall range of prices charged event by event does not strike your available audience as being unduly high you should be able to project your organisation as offering good value for money *in general* rather than being pegged to a particular price.

Small increases introduced frequently

Against the background of projecting your organisation as offering value within a realistic price range only a very large increase in price is likely to cause a backlash. If you fear price increases – and many do because they believe the pricing situation to be very elastic and so sales will fall – then putting up prices is something to be put off until the last minute. The last minute is when the financial director, in the eleventh month of the financial year, observes that the organisation's income is well below what is should be and the management committee panics into a swingeing price rise. Then an adverse reaction is predictable.

It is almost inevitable that you will have to increase prices as times passes. Even in a non-inflationary economy the lively arts organisation wants to do more and to do better and thus needs more money. The sources of non-earned income rarely recognise this endearing fact about our industry and turn blank faces to our enthusiasms. So we must obtain more money from the sale of tickets.

Little but often is the way. Not only will you avoid adverse reaction but you will also take in more money than had you waited a year and introduced one big increase. In *Guide To Arts Marketing* I gave examples based on a theatre that was charging £2 a seat (those were the days!) and aimed to increase the price to £5 by the end of three years. The assumption was that the theatre gave six performances a week and the average number of tickets sold per performance was 500. Four different ways of approaching the price increase were considered: the first had the theatre increase its price by 50p every six months, the second had the price increased by £1.00 every year, the third had the price increased by £1.50 after eighteen months so the prices went from £2.00 to £3.50 and then, after a further eighteen months, pushed up to £5.00. In the fourth case the theatre waited for three years and then put up the price from £2.00 to £5.00. The first approach gave the theatre £585,000 more than the final, 'let's delay the fateful hour' approach. Even the difference between the first and the second cases gave the theatre £117,000 more. And these were, by today's standards, very, very low prices. And, of course, a negative customer response became more likely as the frequency of price increases decreased and the size of the increases went up.

Multiple pricing – a barrier to Sales

In the previous chapter on Sales I referred to price as being a barrier to purchase. Clearly a price that is too high or a price increase that is ineptly applied can impede or arrest the impulse to buy but there is another barrier to be considered; it concerns the range of prices that are charged for tickets to the same event.

I have often asked those who attend my seminars, some students, some experienced managers, why in our industry we very frequently charge different prices for what are essentially the same experiences. I point out that we go to great trouble and expense to convey a promise of the experience that is to come that is persuasive and leads many members of our available audience up to the point where they are ready and willing to buy. What we are offering through our Product Publicity is an experience not a variety of experiences and we say very clearly that this experience has value; it is an experience that is worth having.

Then we say 'You may have this experience for any one of six different prices'.

Does this not harm the notion of value that is so important in marketing? No longer is it one experience that is being sold, it is a wonderful experience, an extremely good experience, a pretty good experience, a not bad experience, a so-so experience and a pretty bloody awful experience.

Why do we charge many prices?

The answers I get to my question usually fall into a few different categories. The most common is that the seating of the building does offer different experiences and that one should not charge the same for a 'good' seat as for a 'bad' one. The next is based on the idea that as some customers have more money than others one should have a range of prices so that all income brackets are catered for. Another, slightly harder to winkle out of people, is that as there is no way of knowing exactly how much one should charge for the experience one should try a scatter gun approach in the hope that somewhere within the range of prices there are one or two that seem about right to the would be customer. Another, on which it is even more difficult to extract confessions, is that multiple prices are charged because multiple prices have always been charged – it's a matter of tradition.

Of these four I have sympathy only with the first – and even here I have serious reservations.

Of the others? Trying to match prices to the ability of customers to pay is naive to say the least; how can we know what a well-off person is prepared to pay and how can we be sure she does right by us and always buys the most expensive tickets? How do we know that a less well-off person will always go for the cheapest seats? And, since the numbers of seats in each price range have to be decided in advance, how do we know how many well-off people we are going to attract and how many less well-off? There is likely to be some correlation between spending power and price paid for tickets but it would be impossible to quantify it.

The idea that we should pitch a range of prices at the customer in the hope that one might be appealing – for whatever reasons, to do with money, to do with the perception of value, who knows? – is totally contrary to the way in which we should approach arts marketing. In considering the theory and practice of arts marketing we try to be rational at every stage and we should not abandon this approach when we come to pricing. We should take a similar view of pricing by tradition. We can do better than this.

Different prices should mean different experiences

Where there are significant differences in the quality of the experience offered, brought about by the seating arrangements and the characteristics of the building, then multiple pricing would seem to be logical provided we accept that each price would need to be bracketed with some description of how the seating area compares with others and how it will influence the quality of the experience we are offering. If we accept that we are trying to persuade people to buy experiences then it can surely not make sense to promise just one experience and attach to it a list of prices. One might compare what I am suggesting with a typical holiday brochure which on a two-page spread extolling the wonders of Heraklion in Crete will then itemise and price the experience of spending one's holiday in one of several hotels. The hotels are pictured and described with attention being paid to how one's holiday in Heraklion could be enjoyed in (a) a small family run hotel without air-conditioning (b) a three star hotel twenty miles away from Heraklion or (b) a five star hotel with swimming pools, jacuzzis, two restaurants and four bars in the centre of town. In fact, many holiday experiences are being offered, not just one, and each different experience carries a different price tag.

I have never seen an arts brochure that follows this logic but, if multiple pricing is decided upon, then should it not then describe, say, the pleasures of experiencing the show from a seat in the stalls? – *uninterrupted sight lines, no need for opera glasses here, convenient for no less than two bars including our famous champagne bar, why not place your order for interval drinks when you arrive? The comfort of our seats has to be experienced – and no problems for those a little long in the leg! Or the rear section of the upper circle? – We call it Valhalla, the home of the Gods! A firm favourite with our regular patrons who enjoy the uniquely friendly atmosphere that pervades. How many great artists saw their first play from such seats! Its budget price makes Valhalla the favourite seating area of some of our most loyal audience members, young and old alike.*

The idea is perhaps not quite so bizarre as it first appears.

The tradition from which multiple pricing grew

The theatre posters from the Victorian and Edwardian eras make it very clear that there were distinct areas within the auditorium with each having a different price; the difference between the areas was more to do with the implicit guarantee that one would be mixing with people who dressed and behaved similarly to oneself than the quality of the experience offered from the stage. The posters spoke to a very different society from ours, of course; a society that was as classified as were the seating areas. Indeed the range of seating locations and prices was a direct model of that society. In one sense, in the sense that people in that society 'knew their place', the specific quality of the entertainment experienced according to seating area could well have been less significant to the customer than the matching of social class with seating (or standing) area. There was no need to describe the experience of standing in the pit or sitting in a box; people knew what 'their' area was like and, because of economic and social influences choice of area was more or less irrelevant for them. We, of course, live in a very different society where working people (given that they actually are in work) traditionally thought of as poor now have much wider ranges of choice and have the freedom to indulge their tastes more or less free of social restraints; it would be most unwise to copy the ways of a society so different from today's. It is a strong argument against pricing according to tradition.

Perhaps no more than two or three prices?

It has always struck me that where different prices are offered it is always the extremes that are most significant and these extremes are thought of (by customers and arts manager alike) as the 'best' seats and the 'cheapest' seats. These are different propositions; one is based on the quality of the experience and the other on the cost of the experience. It is quite unlike the socially stratified offer of earlier times and is no bad way of distinguishing between those to whom price is less important than the quality of the experience and those to whom quality of experience is important but at a low price.

This would suggest that in the majority of cases two prices would meet the need and there is no justification in offering a wider choice. One might stretch this to include three categories: the 'best seats, the cheapest seats and a middle range, a sort of bargain category, parallelling the way in which the record companies market classical music where, whatever the price the customer's desire for recorded music of the highest quality is never doubted and the contrary is never implied. Another good example is the airline industry which has settled on three qualities of travel: Standard, Business and First classes. Two or three such price options would lend themselves to the approach I have already outlined where the fundamental reasons why people might choose to buy would be at the core of each descriptive package. Beyond this, the division of, say, the stalls alone, into four categories would defeat anyone's powers of imagination and description.

There must be significant differences between the seating areas. The 'best' seats must be capable of being honestly described as such and clearly worth paying for (by implication, paying *extra* for). The middle range seats must be in a distinctly different part of the auditorium and so must the cheapest seats (where one is asked to pay *less*). There can be no logic at all in having in one area a bank of, say, five rows at price *(a)* and immediately behind it another bank of five rows at price *(b)*. There may arguably be some difference in quality between the front row of the first bank and the back row of the bank behind it, but what of where they meet – where the back row of the front bank meets the front row of the back bank? Can 18 inches closer to the stage be worth a price differential of several pounds? The airlines solve the problem by hanging a curtain between economy and business classes but that wouldn't work in a theatre.

Choosing a price to pay can be confusing

At the heart of the co-ordinated work of Product Publicity and Sales is the idea that a highly persuasive package of information is targeted at the Available Audience with the intention of bringing its members to the point of wanting to buy. The job of Sales is to clinch the deal and it does this mainly by eliminating or reducing the barriers to purchase. One of the barriers is that of confusion. If the Product Publicity is not direct and clear, if any part of the Sales information is not direct and clear, there will be confusion in the mind of the would be customer. To ask the would be customer to make a difficult decision – and to make a choice of one price from several may very well prove difficult – causes confusion which causes delay – and delay kills sales.

Offering a customer a variety of prices will run the risk of causing confusion and delay. Using the technique of creating separate 'price/value/experience' packages as I have described earlier may help guide the would be customer to a swift decision but it cannot be guaranteed.

Everyone wants the best seats

Everyone who is motivated to buy a ticket, one way or another wants to sit in the best seats according to their own tastes and circumstances. 'Best' may mean location or it may mean price or it may, particularly on the part of regular attenders, mean seats that satisfy some personal view as to what is best value for money. The most realistic way, therefore, of defining a 'best' seat is to say that it is what the customer wants and to let this view influence how we price our seats.

When we price differentially we are making the decision as to which seats are best and are automatically defining the remainder as being less than best and this inevitably conflicts to some degree with the positive, persuasive statement about the experience we are offering made by Product Publicity. If we allow the customer a completely free choice of seating location by charging only one price then, I suggest, we will be surprised to see how many best seats the auditorium contains.

Under these circumstances the only limiting factor on the customer's choice of seat will be that created by people who have been further ahead in the queue and have already bought but the seats left unreserved will not have attached to them a label saying 'less than best'. And people are familiar with the principle of first come, first served and generally accept that one's choice will be less broad if one joins the queue late in the day. Indeed, a person who rushes into a theatre two minutes before curtain up and secures the last available seat, which has a restricted view and little leg room, will still regard that as being, under the circumstances, the best seat – the best seat that is available, that is.

Advantages of charging one price

Charging one price (or restricting the number of prices charged to no more than two or three and making these clearly identified with distinct seating areas where there are distinctly different qualities attached to them) directly assists the Sales process. It reduces confusion ('Where is the best place to sit? Can I afford it? Wouldn't I be better sitting in a more expensive, and hence better, seat?'). It reduces conflict ('It is an important event. I really should have the best seats but they are all sold. I should really buy the cheapest seats but I don't want this to mar my enjoyment'). Most important of all, it works to counter the tendency people have to procrastinate.

If the best seat is the seat the would be customer wants *and if it is likely to be available* then at the moment the decision to buy has been made it becomes very important to translate the desire into immediate action. Provided that the would be customer knows that time is of the essence and that postal and telephone bookings will be processed as soon as they are received, the desire to secure the best – or best available – seat will tend to make the would be customer jump over the last remaining hurdle to become a real, rather than a would be customer.

Of course, this desire to secure the best available seat can be used to accelerate the purchase of tickets when a multi-price structure is being used. 'Buy now while stocks last' is the essential message. But it can never work as well as when 'best' means *best* rather than 'the best of a number of categories most of which are not the best because they are lower in price'.

Not all customers can be at the head of the queue; how can they all be content with their purchase? The organisation has been selling the best available seats at the time the customer buys. It can do no more than play the game fairly and allocate strictly according to that promise. People will accept a less than ideal seat if they know it was the best available at the time and if it is priced the same as all the others then it cannot be a bad seat, can it?

What about the really bad seats?

Arts managers often accept the idea of unit pricing but have lingering doubts about certain seats or certain areas; how can they be worth the same as the others? I have said that where there are distinctly different seating areas they may be priced differently but if some seats are truly bad then why sell them at all?

Underlying almost everything I say in this book is the assumption that the arts manager needs to improve the organisation's arts marketing and this is likely to mean that it is not always selling all its seats. If an auditorium has sold 80% of its seats then 20% are not occupied. Unit pricing and a free choice of seats on a first come first served basis should make sure that those 20% of seats include amongst them the worst ones. As sales increase so does income and the organisation can feel more and more confident about simply ruling out seats that are not fit to be sold or selling them as such at very low prices at the very last minute. If the fruiterer has three bruised mangoes he does not put them out on display until all the good mangoes are sold and then he prices them accordingly.

Creating a 'rush to purchase'

When tickets first go on sale the organisation wants the take-up in the first few days to be as high as it can make it; it wants to create a 'rush to purchase'. Anyone who has ever launched a campaign knows that if the chemistry is right, that is, if the ingredients are correct and mixed in the right proportions then there will be an opening surge of demand and if that surge does not occur then in all probability the campaign will not succeed. If 1000 tickets are to be sold and there are ten days in which they may be purchased then it is extremely unlikely that orders will arrive at the rate of 100 a day; there will be more at the start and then numbers will diminish. If the Product Publicity has been good and if all the ideas of Sales have been brought to bear then on the day when tickets go on sale there should be either a queue at the box office or, better still, *far* better still, a pile of envelopes. Most arts organisations these days do as much as they can to avoid creating box office queues (which create their own frustrations and inconveniences for would be customers) and try to stimulate advance bookings by post. The advantage of postal booking is that the customer can make the booking at any time, night or day, and the organisation can open the envelopes at any time, night or day, so can make best use of its staff resources. Another great advantage is that although tickets may not be despatched until after the stated date the envelopes may be opened and the success of the campaign assessed so that extra measures may be taken to boost demand before it is too late.

It is not easy to communicate to the Available Audience that tickets are sold on a first come first served basis and that responding promptly with an order will give the customer a better bargain. If a rush to purchase is to be achieved then this idea must be conveyed convincingly. Product Publicity must carry advice to respond immediately and a statement that bookings will be processed in the order in which they are received.

Moving onto another aspect of Arts Marketing

In the preceding chapter I described the Sales function as being more passive than active, with the focus being on the reduction and elimination of barriers to purchase. In looking at Pricing we have seen that when approached in a certain way it can be used to encourage the would be customer to take positive and immediate action, to close the gap between wanting to buy and buying. I have suggested that the combination of unit pricing and the offering of a way to secure better value (that is, the 'best' seat for the same price as all the other seats) will persuade the would be customer to jump the final barrier of procrastination.

This use of what might be termed 'seat preference' in return for prompt action introduces us to a another aspect of arts marketing that works in conjunction with Product Publicity, Sales and Pricing – it is called Sales Promotion.

SUMMARY

We want to earn money from our sales but we also want to earn it from as many people as possible, drawn from as wide a range as possible.

If you are beginning to develop a feeling for your Available Audience and confidence in your judgement and if you have no reason to doubt the view that the price/sales relationship is not very elastic then aim high in terms of target attendances and high in terms of the price you are to charge.

As a rule of thumb a high price is a price paid that you thought was probably pushing the limits of acceptance; a price that is too high is one that doesn't get paid.

There is no law that says you cannot take in more money than your estimates provide for and there is no law that forbids your setting your target income higher than that needed to balance the books.

Whatever price or prices you put upon the experiences you are offering they will impact on the Available Audience at the same time as your Product Publicity impacts upon them and it is now that the potential buyer makes an instant estimation of *value*.

Knowing that the impulse of purchase is not a particularly rational one we may approach the Pricing of our products in the same spirit as any other marketer and set out to *charge as much as we can get*.

The impresario always aims to take as much money as possible on Monday because it might be needed to bail out Friday's event. No income is too great, therefore, for the impresario.

When you have established a 'going rate' for your type of product by charging the same price, or very close to the same price, for a long time you will have established a price/value relationship in the minds of your customers and when you increase your price you automatically damage the perceived value of your product.

When prices are to be increased little but often is the way.

What we are offering through our Product Publicity is an experience not a variety of experiences and we say very clearly that this experience has value; it is an experience that is worth having. Then we say 'You may have this experience for any one of six different prices'.

Where different prices are offered it is always the extremes that are most significant and these extremes are thought of (by customers and arts manager alike) as the 'best' seats and the 'cheapest' seats. These are different propositions.

To ask the would be customer to make a difficult decision – and to make a choice of one price from several may very well prove difficult – causes confusion which causes delay – and delay kills sales.

Everyone who is motivated to buy a ticket, one way or another wants to sit in the best seats according to their own tastes and circumstances.

The most realistic way, therefore, of defining a 'best' seat is to say that it is what the customer wants and to let this view influence how we price our seats.

The combination of unit pricing and the offering of a way to secure better value (that is, the 'best' seat for the same price as all the other seats) will persuade the would be customer to jump the final barrier of procrastination.

CHAPTER SIX

SALES PROMOTION

Sales Promotion can help us
sell, can help us sell more, can
help us sell faster, can help us
sell further ahead.

The relationship of Sales Promotion to other Arts Marketing functions

The arts marketing activity known as Sales Promotion invites a variety
of descriptions. It can be seen as a way of enhancing the perceived
value of what is offered for sale; as a means of persuading the would be
customer who has been motivated by Product Publicity and is close to
the act of purchase to jump the final hurdle – whether it be one of
procrastination or plain old-fashioned reluctance to part with money –
or as a way of adding extra sizzle to the sausage. In truth Sales
Promotion is all three.

As we have seen, Sales has the job of bringing the would be
customer to the act of purchase and can do this in a passive way, by
reducing or eliminating barriers to purchase, and in an active way by
positively pointing out to the interested person the benefits of taking
action now rather than later. In both situations Sales Promotion
assists.

Being concerned with value, decisions involving Sales Promotion
impact directly onto those involving Pricing to the extent that most
Pricing decisions should be made with at least a thought of possible
Sales Promotion methods in mind. One example of this would be
when a price is set that is thought to be possibly higher than the

market will bear; if price resistance is met with then Sales Promotion methods may be used to improve the value/price perception.

Product Publicity has the job of making people want to buy and in order to do this must present information about the product in a persuasive way. The are few instances in the arts when the presence of a form of Sales Promotion, expressed as part of the overall message, cannot contribute by, at the very least, adding some sizzle to the message.

Arts organisations whose philosophy requires them to target lower income groups as well as the rest of the public within their Available Audience will find in Sales Promotion ways of lowering the price charged to the lower income target group without harming the price/value relationship known to be acceptable to people in the better off groups.

In the commercial world, both large and small scale, where Sales Promotion is a widely practised aspect of marketing, it is said that where publicity pushes the product to the public, Sales Promotion pulls the public to the product.

To be handled with care

Being concerned with enhancement of value and hence with money, Sales Promotion methods can quite easily lead the arts marketer into making statements that may jar with the Product Publicity message and language by appearing crude and brash alongside them. It is thus a tool that requires careful handling. Just as Sales can become counter-productive if it is too active, too pushy, so also can Sales Promotion if it is projected in an insensitive way.

Enhancement of value

Summarised very simply, Sales Promotion aims to create offers to the potential customer that will either provide more value for the stated price or will cost less than the stated price with no reduction in the value of what is being purchased.

The starting point is the implicit statement of value made when a product is offered to the public at a price; the experience being offered to the available audience has a value expressed in the form of a ticket price. In the last chapter we considered the importance of the idea of value and how an arts organisation must try always to be in a situation where the price it puts on anything actually defines the value of the experience being offered. Once value is established Sales Promotion may enhance it.

Essentially the Sales Promotion method contributes to the process of persuasion and to the Sales process; it says 'Do what I want you to do and I will give you something extra'. The 'something extra' contributes to the message of Product Publicity and the 'Do what I want you to do' contributes to the Sales process.

There must always be something that you want the would be customer to do. Sales Promotion almost always costs the organisation something and a return must be obtained (or at least be obtainable) if the exercise is to be worthwhile.

There must always be a reason for using Sales Promotion

Arts marketing may be thought of as a toolbox with its various sub-functions as the tools. Some are used all the time, such as Product Publicity and Sales; others only when there is a need. If you are achieving your audience and income targets then you probably do not need to use the Sales Promotion tool. Organisations usually develop a view as to how far along they lie on the spectrum whose extremes are, at one end, the Buyer's Market and at the other, the Seller's Market. Sales Promotion rarely has a part to play when would be customers are fighting to get to the box office.

In my personal experience I have never known what it is like to have a show or publication that 'sold itself' so, for me, Sales Promotion is an old and valued friend and I feel uneasy at the prospect of any campaign that does not contain some element drawn from its ideas within it.

What can be achieved using Sales Promotion?

What do we want to achieve from any campaign? We want to sell all our tickets for as far ahead as we can plan our programme. We want to be economic with our expenditure so that each and every Attender and every Intender who has been persuaded to cross the line costs us as little as possible. We want to obtain the maximum income so that our future plans can be made with confidence. We want to draw our customers from an Available Audience that includes as wide a range of people as our corporate philosophy envisages. We want to achieve success within our own financial and philosophical framework – success expressed in terms of people and the difference between our income and the cost of achieving that income.

The Seller's Market and the Buyer's Market

I have already referred to the Seller's and the Buyer's Markets. What do the terms mean? A Seller's Market is a marketing situation where the desire of the market, the Available Audience, to secure what is offered is so great that almost no effort is needed on the part of the promoting body to sell its tickets. A brief examination of the traditional way of marketing, say, commercial theatre, reveals an approach that is based on the Seller's Market. The product itself must be famous and so are as many as possible of the people involved in the production; the criterion for selecting the product is that before any campaign starts it is in demand. It is part of the impresario's art to judge, or guess, what is likely to be in demand. The great impresarios are capable of creating products that are going to be in demand even if, because they are brand new, they have no track record at all. A Lloyd Webber musical, where the composer is, of course, a great impresario, begins its life with no reputation beyond that is has from the association with Andrew Lloyd Webber and with his other successful musicals. The new musical will find its first audiences quite easily because before the show opens it is in a Seller's Market – albeit a slightly shaky one. Thereafter all will depend on how critics and audiences respond to the reality. If the new show is right for the market then the Seller's Market will continue for months and even years.

So a Seller's Market is a wonderful thing for the impresario and the reason why so many choose only to back favourites and to devote their energies to securing more of them from the distant corners of the globe. Naturally the sure-fire winners are aware of their status and pitch their fees accordingly. It is a game played for very high stakes.

From a customer's viewpoint the Seller's Market is not altogether pleasant because its existence brings about an attitude towards audiences which sees them as milch cows, as things to be exploited; hence the very high prices of refreshments and programmes and high charges for doing something as simple and necessary as stowing away a coat and briefcase. It is almost impossible for an organisation that is in a Seller's Market to behave towards its customers as though it might want them to return to see another show. In the London theatre scene particular shows are not linked in the public mind with particular theatres and so even if customers feel resentment towards the way they have been treated they will have no focus for it, no one to blame – although their attitude towards theatre going in general is very likely to be harmed. Where the promoting organisation is closer to its market and needs repeat business customers must be treated with much more care and respect.

The culture of many large-scale promoting bodies is to behave as though they were in a Seller's Market. If they truly are then they will have an easy marketing ride. If they are not then the assumptions they make about the easiness of their tasks and the willingness of potential customers to accept abrupt and unhelpful behaviour at the box office and to flock to buy tickets at the mere insertion of an announcement in the newspaper, will lead to disappointment. Very few arts bodies are, in fact, in a Seller's Market and they would do well to remember it.

Once an organisation gets into the Seller's Market mode it finds it hard to respond intelligently to a fall-off in audience demand. It is not familiar with the ideas of arts marketing; the tools in the toolbox are rusty. If you have been behaving as though marketing was easy then the use of, say, Sales Promotion, is alien and, if used ineptly, might even make the situation worse. I can remember, in particular, the excellent production of *Carmen Jones* at the Old Vic theatre, London in the early nineties. It was very successful for a very long time – and that success did not lead to the worse excesses of the Seller's Market I'm pleased to say – but when audiences started to fall off there was clear evidence that the organisation did not know how to cope. Sales Promotion was used, in the form of 50% discounting of the highest priced seats, but it could not save the show. A highly publicised change in pricing policy to make all seats the same price would almost certainly have kept the show running for many more months and would, incidentally, have stacked all the customers towards the front of the auditorium where they would do most good for the atmosphere of the show.

A Buyer's Market is the reverse. Customers feel free to pick and choose. They know that the organisation cannot fill its seats. The experiences that are being offered to them are seen to be so available that there is no particular reason why anyone should book to have them now – later will do. We know that procrastination kills sales.

What is the correct stance for an arts organisation to take, therefore? There are really two distinct areas to be thought about: there is the actuality – are we about to launch something that is truly a bestseller? Does our organisation have a reputation for putting on bestsellers? Are we truly in a Seller's Market? Or are we going to have to fight to get an audience for this show? And there is the mode of behaviour: is the organisation tempted to strut or tempted to beg?

No matter what the actuality, the wise arts organisation always strikes a balance between these two extremes of stance. It is just plain bad business to boast just as it is to cringe. Both are the wrong kind of behaviour for an organisation that needs to build a close relationship with its Available Audience. The tendency the staff of any organisation has to behave according to its perception of what kind of market it is in must be controlled.

We have all had experience of Sales staff (in the box office) treating customers as though a favour is being done by selling them a ticket – or keeping queue customers waiting whilst a telephone booking is taken – or, as so frequently happens, allocating the very worse seats to large groups (particularly of school children) as though they were being greedy in wanting so much of this commodity that is in so much demand.

It should be part of Sales staff training to instil a behaviour that suggests confidence – confidence in the show's ability to do well – is professional and is friendly within that limitation. As far as the outward behaviour of the staff is concerned it does not matter how well or badly the show is doing when they come into contact with the public. Sales staff in the box office facing a virtually empty seating plan do not say to a customer, 'you can have any seat you like' they say 'You are booking early, so the choice of seat is good, may I suggest you try these?'.

Cool professionalism should run throughout the organisation. Most of us know the sense of desperation that grows in an organisation when its best marketing efforts are not rewarded with high sales. It does not make us run out into the streets to pull people towards the box office but it can easily lead us into taking transparently desperate steps to attract them, which is almost as bad.

If Sales Promotion has a fault it is that it can all too easily suggest that the organisation is in trouble and is doing the equivalent of putting a notice in the window saying, 'Closing Down – Half Price Sale'. Our Available Audience picks up such clues very quickly and before you know it the word is around that your show is a turkey.

Charles Dickens, in Nicholas Nickleby, said 'It being a remarkable fact in theatrical history, but one long since established beyond dispute, that it is a hopeless endeavour to attract people to a theatre unless they can be first brought to believe that they will never get into it'. Nowadays audiences may be very slightly shrewder but this is still the essential message that we have to get across and if we feel that some form of Sales Promotion will assist us then it must not conflict with this message. Provided there is a sound reason why the Sales Promotion is there – for example, in return for making the purchase sooner rather than later or for buying more expensive tickets than one might normally do or for buying tickets not only for *this* show but also for the next one – it will not harm your image of calm confidence in the success of your enterprise.

Seat Preference is the finest form of Sales Promotion

In the previous chapter I described how the price of something makes a statement of value. One may take a wider view of what 'value' means to a potential customer. The information projected by Product Publicity will connect with that person's own tastes and attitudes and the experience offered will be related to them; so value can mean how valuable is the experience going to be to the potential customer. However, at the time potential customers become would be customers there is a simple equation in front of them; this is what is offered to you and this is how much it costs. By implication it is worth this much; this is its value.

Then, when the would be customer is about to metamorphose

into a real customer by buying a ticket, there is usually a closer examination of what precisely is to be had for the price. 'Agreed, I'm going to see this show. I'll pay the price. Now, where am I going to sit? *I want the best seat I can get*'. Unless the marketing situation is in an extreme Seller's Market, where the securing of a ticket in the face of high demand is sufficient, the would be customer will almost always have an interest in getting the best seat. As we have seen in the previous chapter, the best seat is really no more than the seat the would be customer wants. The skilled arts marketer can use this desire for the best seat to create a form of Sales Promotion that can be highly effective.

In the marketing process the bringing together of the desire to buy with the act of purchase must happen as quickly as can be; in an ideal marketing situation wanting and doing should be like a chocolate bar dispensing machine where one sees the bar of Dairy Milk through the glass, wants to buy it, sees how much it costs, puts the money in the slot and opens the tray and thus satisfies the desire. If there is a delay in the ticket-buying process – the equivalent of not having a 50p piece to hand when facing the dispensing machine on a London underground station – then a hundred and one reasons for not buying will stop the buying from taking place. The arts marketer must use every shot in the locker to accelerate the process or sales will be lost.

If at the time of metamorphosis would be customers have their attention drawn to the matter of the seat they might occupy and it is made plain to them that prompt action might very well secure for them exactly the seats they favour or there is an undertaking given that 'best' seats will be allocated on a first-come, first-served basis, then this is in itself a valuable form of Sales Promotion.

As with all such methods it must be handled carefully. If the Product Publicity gets into the hands of some customers some time after the launch of the campaign *and they can see that this is the case* then there is the risk that they will assume that all the 'best' seats will have been sold and will not take the matter further. If your campaign has been successful then their assumption will have been correct but you will have achieved success without them. If it has not been successful then you have lost valuable sales. The trick here is not to allow the Product Publicity to be too specific about dates other than the dates of performance. Announcing the date when seat allocation will start is a good way of accelerating buying activity but it also kills the effect of the material as soon as that day has past; this is a strong argument for planning a campaign very carefully, setting deadlines for production of print and for distribution and ensuring that they are adhered to so that not only is the Available Audience targeted in terms of physical distribution but also receives material when you choose.

This does not necessarily mean that all potential customers receive material at the same time. If one has built up a group of Attenders and wants to achieve a higher level of sales from it then it may well make sense to give those regular customers some priority as a reward for loyalty. In such a situation these people will be told that they are being given a priority booking privilege which ends on a stated date – after which tickets go on sale in the usual way. With such people the priority booking privilege will almost always have the desired effect, encouraging more rapid purchase and therefore greater sales and, because of their relationship with the organisation, their interest in the product offered will not evaporate when the priority booking period is over.

Usually details of the priority booking privilege can be conveyed in a covering letter that accompanies the Product Publicity but I have found it worthwhile to produce a 'Special Edition' of a brochure which is dedicated to the known Attenders. Production of the latter obviously costs more money but if the extra returns anticipated from the method are likely to be substantially higher then it may well be worth doing. Knowledge of printing methods can enable production costs of the 'Special Edition' to be kept down by, for example, changing only text that is printed in one of the basic colours of a four colour printing run. In such a situation it would not be uncommon to produce, say, 100,000 brochures for distribution within the catchment area by a variety of means and only 4000 or 5000 copies of the 'Special Edition' sent by post to known, regular Attenders.

Using the Booking Form to aid the Seat Preference method

A device I have used to considerable effect is to include a seating plan on the booking form. Seat numbers are not given. The customer is asked to ring three locations on the plan and to mark them 1, 2 and 3 to indicate choice of seating area in order of preference. Alongside this is the reminder that all seats are the same price and that they will be allocated on a first come first served basis starting on a certain day. An address to which orders must be sent is given; this may have a Freepost address or you may choose to include a first class Business Reply envelope. If Freepost is used then customers should be reminded that Freepost receives second class postal service and that if they wish to improve their chances of getting their choice they should use the full address and a first class stamp, or telephone.

Consider how this encourages the customer to act quickly. Product Publicity delivers a convincing message that creates the desire to buy. (A unit pricing policy means that the customer may secure the best seat, according to whatever criteria are important to the customer, not according to decisions made by the organisation). The best seat may be secured if immediate action is taken. Customers are asked to mark their chosen (their 'best') seat so that the box office staff will know what is wanted – but is also asked to add other choices in case ... by implication, in case the customers delays in posting the order. The advice to use a first class stamp or the provision of a first class Business Reply envelope adds to the impetus.

Of course, sales staff will have to make choices as to how tickets are to be allocated but the three labelled rings of preference help them as well as accelerating the customer's action. My experience has been that the location and size of the rings give a very clear idea of how badly a customer wants to sit in a particular area. Small rings clustered in one area say one thing. Large rings clustered say another. Rings scattered about the plan say something different again. Sales staff have told me that they rarely receive complaints about allocations based on this method; they have also said that it is surprising how wide is the choice of 'best' seats and how many there appear to be of them.

Seat Preference, Unit Pricing and Multiple Pricing and the 'Star' event

Seat preference is, in my opinion, always more effective when used alongside unit pricing – charging one price for every seat in the auditorium – but, of course, it can be used quite effectively alongside the more traditional approach to pricing. If the price sectors are few in number, say, no more than the three I have already advocated, then the method will be all the more effective.

Where multiple pricing must be used for the principle business of the organisation unit pricing may still be used as a way of accelerating purchase. One event in a season, or any convenient period of time, is chosen to be the lure, the bait on the hook. It should be the most attractive event possible, the one most likely to appeal to the largest number within the available audience in one's catchment area. All tickets for this event bear the same price and this price need not be particularly low, indeed it should be as high as possible, as high as you think the market will bear. The whole season, or festival, or whatever is the convenient grouping of the events where multiple pricing is to be employed is then offered to the available audience by means of Product Publicity. Alongside the enticing promises of delight and enlightenment and given pride of place is the chosen 'star' attraction tickets for which are available only to purchasers of tickets to two, or three, or more (you choose) of the other events. Tickets for the 'star' attraction are all the same price and tickets are allocated on a first come first served basis: this means Dear Potential Customer, if you book *this minute* you might just get the best seat in the house (which is, of course, the one you want – wherever it may be) for this *wonderful, star attraction* and, of course, you will be allocated the best available seats in your chosen price range for the other events.

Used with flair this method is almost unbeatable and, of course, may be adapted to a very wide variety of situations. Not only are sales for the generality of events accelerated and hence increased but it is perfectly possible to derive even more money from the 'star' event than would have been achieved had it been marketed conventionally.

There must always be a reason

I have said that in Sales Promotion there should always be a reason for using any particular method. Seat Preference is an accelerator of purchase and as such increases sales; it is the one form of Sales Promotion that can be and should be used on every occasion – unless, of course, you are in a true Seller's Market and then you can do what you like.

The Seat Preference method also has the virtue not only of not costing money to implement but also, in a world controlled by committees and accountants, not seeming to cost money.

Price Reduction

A simple way of enhancing the perceived value of what one is intending to sell is to lower its price but if this is not managed expertly then the effect might be to lower perceived value as well. 'They've dropped the price. This means no-one is buying it. This means that it isn't any good'.

Price reductions must always be used alongside a clearly stated reason that does not reduce the value of what is being offered. So we may say, 'Buy your tickets before such-and-such a date and save £5.00' without damaging value. Or we may say, 'Take advantage of our special Monday pricing policy – all prices reduced by half'. The public is used to price reductions of this kind and understands the reasons why the organisation is making such special offers and does not think ill of the product because of them. These reasons may not always be exactly what they appear to be: it is always pleasing to see sales coming in early on in a campaign but in one sense it does not matter *when* purchases are made so long as they *are* made but the wise organisation wants people to book early because if they do not they may not book at all. Or they can be exactly what they appear to be – audience attendances are lower on Monday evenings and so we offer these inducements to persuade you to attend then – for a theatre running six days a week the performances on the days other than Monday maintain the value.

In the typical arts marketing scenario the potential customer reads the Product Publicity for a specific event and is brought to the point of purchase. It has probably cost the organisation quite a lot of money to attract and win this customer so it makes sense to try to make as good a customer as possible of him. Selling him more is a wise and achievable aim. Price reduction can assist here. The time of purchase is the time when the attractions of future events can be brought to his attention and a price reduction offered if he buys tickets. Obviously the best place in which to put the proposition is the box office and the best people to handle it are properly trained Sales staff but printed Product Publicity can do the job quite well.

So, Price Reduction can be used to help persuade people who have made the decision to buy tickets for one event to buy tickets for other events; it can also be used to encourage people to buy more expensive seats within a multiple price seating plan or, indeed, to encourage people to buy cheaper seats. Essentially this method of Sales Promotion can be used to direct audiences into patterns of purchase that your marketing objectives have defined. When presented to the Available Audience with imagination and a confident style Price Reduction can also produce the accelerating effect that is so vitally important to the Sales function and is fundamental to Sales Promotion.

Different forms of Price Reduction

Price Reduction may take several forms both in fact and in how it is described. Where unit pricing is in use then one simple price reduction may be all that is necessary: 'All tickets will go on sale at £12.00: tickets ordered and paid for within seven days benefit from a £3.00 Early Booking discount – send only £9.00 per ticket.' This could also be described as a 25% reduction. When multiple pricing is in use then a varying percentage discount approach would generally be appropriate so that the higher priced seats would attract a higher percentage discount than the lower priced ones – the higher percentage would tend to be the figure used to increase the interest of potential customers'. Product Publicity could then speak of 'Up to 25% off normal tickets prices'. Of course there is no fixed rule that says higher prices should always boast higher percentage discounts so if it is desired to improve sales figures in the lower price range it is there that the most generous reductions should apply.

Sales in Quantity

So far the concentration has been on the individual member of the available audience whose buying behaviour we seek to change by changing the way value is perceived. Usually the social circumstances of such individuals determine the number of tickets bought at each purchase and we know from box office statistics that a typical purchase involves on average between two and three tickets (the figure most commonly quoted is around 2.4). Some people will buy only one, most will buy two, some three, some fewer four and very few five tickets. Just as it is good to persuade customers to buy tickets for more than one event so it is equally good to persuade them to buy more tickets for the same events; Sales Promotion can help achieve this.

In *Guide to Arts Marketing* I said:

The attractions of being able to sell tickets in bulk are obvious and most arts bodies have a concession scheme offering price reductions to groups. Unfortunately the schemes are often rooted deep in the history of the organisations and are rarely taken out, dusted off and reconsidered. Somewhere at the back of a brochure there may be a line of very small type saying that a reduction of ten per cent is available to parties of ten or more. This is sometimes backed up by the organisation's PR person going out to give talks within the community and encouraging them to form parties. Although there are few exceptions, and we may include theatres offering Christmas shows among them, the group concessions are rarely taken up in quantity and are general unsuccessful. This is due, I believe, to a failure to see these schemes as being methods of Sales Promotion and a failure to look at what is being offered from a customer's viewpoint. Even the word 'concession' implies the wrong relationship with the customers (it suggests that something is being yielded).

The whole of the orientation of the 'concession' approach (the word is still repugnant to me suggesting as it does an entirely unsatisfactory relationship with one's Available Audience) is based on the notion of the 'party organiser', some worthy citizen who derives pleasure – and not much chance of profit – from persuading others to make a commitment to attending an event in what is probably a remote city or town so that group travel (and all the horrors that this implies) is also necessary to make the proposition economically attractive. There are such people as party organisers and they are usually to be found in community organisations whose purpose is nothing to do with the arts or entertainment; the theatre trip is probably an annual item in a varied programme of activities. Of course, a reduction in price for such parties will encourage them and will ultimately make a contribution to the organisation's sales achievements but such basic and modest use of Price Reduction should not mask the true potential of the method when applied to individual purchases.

It is an most valuable exercise for an arts marketer to calculate how much it has cost the organisation to bring one customer into fruitful contact with it and then to assess how much, on average, each customer has spent on each occasion of purchase. Imagine then how much better this ratio of expenditure to income would be if customers were persuaded to increase the number of tickets purchased from, say, two to three or four. There may well be potential amongst party organisers but I believe there to be far, far greater potential amongst ordinary customers who are encouraged to do no more than take a friend or relation along with them.

The arts marketer would do well to look at the cars entering the car park, each bearing the standard couple of customers and to wonder how the two empty seats at the back of the car may be filled for if they are then in all probability two more seats will be filled in the auditorium and the value of that particular sale will have been increased significantly. Sales Promotion, in particular Price Reduction, can help achieve this.

Suppose that if three tickets are bought for the same event the third ticket was significantly cheaper – say, half price – would this tend to achieve the desired result?

Suppose that the purchase of a fourth ticket would be even cheaper, say one third of the basic price. Would this help achieve the desired result?

The arts marketer can only discover the outcome by experiment. Such experiments, of course, have no chance of success if in the Product Publicity they are given only a 'line of very small type' .. 'Somewhere at the back of a brochure.' As with Seat Preference, methods like these can only succeed if they are wholly and generously integrated into the product message.

And while our concentration is upon the encouragement of people to buy more let us not forget those traditional offers of group discounts contained in those lines of very small type. It would indeed be splendid if one could attract bulk sales along such lines with such small effort but have we examined just what is involved in organising a party of, say, forty people – sufficient to fill comfortably and cost effectively a coach and are we confident that by offering one free ticket in twenty, which is a fairly typical 'concession', we are truly compensating for the work involved? In *Guide to Arts Marketing* I described the business of persuading school sixth-formers to:

.. give up an evening and pay out good money not only for the ticket but for the coach or train fare, distributing and collecting parental consent forms, making sure that parents are waiting to collect them on their return, ferrying home those who forgot to ask their parents to meet them and making good the financial difference when two of them decide not to come at the last minute.

And since I wrote those words may now be added the extra chore of collecting even more money in order to pay the school office which, in these days where infernal internal markets must operate, demands its tithe for receiving the various items of payment, banking it and writing out a cheque for the arts organisation.

Add to this the frustration that starts in the party organiser's breast when the box office, convinced as ever that it is in a Seller's Market and determined to behave as though it is, shows resentment in the face of such high demand and gives the worst possible value in terms of seating location.

If party booking is deemed to be of potential value to the arts organisation then the traditional way of looking at it must be re-assessed. Half price tickets for young people – of course and even larger reductions if it can be countenanced. Significant reductions in price or many more free tickets for party organisers so that there may be some slack in their financial arrangements to cover party members who do not show up. Careful and considerate treatment from a staff member, who is not necessarily a member of the box office staff but is, most definitely, a Sales person, whose job it is to know these important customers and to, as it were, negotiate on their behalf with the box office and to oversee ticket allocations. Rewards for party organisers need not consist only of courtesy, helpful treatment and free tickets – there are other ways both for them and for all customers whom you persuade to do what you want them to do.

Vouchers

The use of the voucher is a variant of Price Reduction which has the distinct advantage of making tangible the benefit, the enhancement of value, that Price Reduction can only promise at the time the potential customer is becoming a would be customer. Typically the voucher is no more than a piece of paper that promises something if the customers do what the arts marketer wants them to do. Just as with Seat Preference and Price Reduction the first intention the arts marketer has is to encourage buying action sooner rather than later; the voucher is an excellent way of conveying the reward for this action as well as specifying what action is needed to obtain it.

Thus a simple 'accelerator' voucher might accompany the Product Publicity and state that if purchase is made within a certain time and the voucher is sent with payment the payment may be reduced by the value of the voucher. This approach also mollifies the customer if purchase is made after the deadline and the reduction in cost is no longer available for it is the life of the voucher that has expired rather than the offer made by the arts organisation. This may strike one as splitting hairs somewhat but such is human psychology.

The voucher may be used in almost all cases where it is desired to offer a Price Reduction. If the arts marketer wants to 'make more' of customers by encouraging them to commit themselves to the purchase of tickets for several shows, or to lead them into thinking of the friends that might accompany them to one or several shows, then the voucher is the perfect device for it can be collected – 'Each time you buy a ticket from us we send you one of these special *regular customer* vouchers: when you have collected four your next ticket is absolutely free!'. Or, 'Thank you for your order, your tickets are enclosed: please accept two vouchers which if used towards the cost of your tickets for our next show will bring your cost down by £10!'. Or, 'Here are details of our next show and with them two special *Bring Your Friends* vouchers. If you order more than two tickets for this show your third and fourth tickets cost you 30% less than normal box office prices. Do you want to bring a fifth person? Just call us now and we'll send you a special half price voucher that you may use when making your booking'.

And so on. The possibilities are virtually endless. Vouchers are particularly suited to use in campaigns where the method of Product Publicity distribution and the method of purchase are both postal. If the arts organisation has built up a pattern of encouraging booking by telephone then clearly the voucher which requires the customer to use it as though it were cash is at a disadvantage but it is not beyond the wit of the arts marketer to make the voucher both a tangible means of obtaining a price reduction as well as a promissory note which can be referred to over the telephone.

The all-purpose, ready-for-anything Voucher

Sales Promotion is the arts marketing method which must be capable of responding to situations as they arise. All other decisions in the arts marketing arena are usually made well in advance and once committed to are hard to change. Product Advertising, for example, is almost impossible to change once the copy and the design have been chosen and implemented. All arts organisations need the capability of moving rapidly in response to unforeseen circumstances such as poor sales generally or poor sales in a certain seating area or on certain dates or at certain times. Sales Promotion is the tool for situations such as these and none is more useful than the voucher. Unless the organisation is capable of generating design and print in a very short time indeed it is wise to keep a supply of blank vouchers that have all the characteristics in terms of appearance but have a blank space into which may be printed specific details of Price Reductions intended to meet short term needs. The amount of the reduction, the conditions under which the reduction may be obtained including, most importantly, the date on which the offer closes, may all be added at the last minute by a street corner printer or even, in desperate times, by hand.

Such a voucher may be tested over a two or three day period at the box office so that the reaction of customers and their response to the offer may be assessed. Changes may be then be made if thought to be necessary.

Vouchers as an aid to targeting

If a particular section of the Available Audience is to be aimed at the voucher is the most effective way of targeting it and achieving the highest possible response from it. It could be that it is decided to see what sort of response may be obtained from a certain geographical area or from a mailing list of, say, solicitors or doctors, then a specific Sales Promotion using vouchers aimed at the area or group will not only maximise response but it will also aid the monitoring of the response which is a useful aid to market research.

The voucher is also probably the only way of offering significant price reductions to people with low incomes without harming their dignity. Returning once more to *Guide to Arts Marketing* I believe that what I said then applies equally today:

The special consideration of sections of the community that are hard up for one reason or another is a matter of duty for any arts organisation that receives financial support from the community. It is also a matter of duty to try always to achieve the best possible financial outcome from any activity. Thus, if it is your wish that no charge, or a reduced charge, should be made to a certain section of the community, then do so but not necessarily for the best seats on a Saturday night. One of the few (probably the only) advantage of being unemployed or retired is that there is more time available and as art does not vary much from Monday to Saturday, no harm is done if the reduction applies to weekdays and seating areas that are not in heavy demand.

Perhaps the biggest problem that arises from this situation is in openly identifying a customer as being hard up. The thought of having to join a box office queue and having to produce documents to prove that you are unemployed is sufficiently daunting to put off most people. The all-purpose, ready-for-anything, go-anywhere voucher could be useful here. If one can find a way of distributing appropriately validated vouchers that can be used instead of money, this will keep embarrassment to a minimum.

The essential point is that although one may be charging very little for tickets because of the special circumstances, one should still approach it from a Sales Promotion viewpoint using the techniques of discounting to guide people to where sales are less good.

As a way of saying Thank You

And for those saintly party organisers what better way of saying Thank You than a gift of a pair of vouchers that are valid for a performance other than that which the party attends, that reduce the cost to zero. In this way the people who help you can enjoy an evening free of the cares of party organising and it may give them the impetus to start all over again.

The appearance of Vouchers

However designed and printed vouchers should convey their value to the available audience for they really do have value to the person who intends to make use of them. To the cynical the £5 voucher may not be worth any more than the paper it is printed on but to the customer who intends to use it it is worth every penny of £5. Vouchers should be conceived and designed with every bit as much care as any other piece of Product Publicity. They will then be treated as though they are valuable by potential customers and are much more likely to be used.

Gifts and Special Offers

Gifts

We have examined Sales Promotion based on Seat Preference and Price Reduction; let us now examine a method of improving the price/value perception by means of enhancing the product we intend to sell. Here the price remains fixed and part of how the organisation presents itself to its public – always offering high quality product at a fair price. Such a presentation is worth striving for. If there is a negative side to Price Reduction it is that if it is practised for too long and across too many activities then the essential integrity of the organisation's pricing policy will be eroded.(I shall give my views on the negative aspects of Sales Promotion very shortly). A method of Sales Promotion that does not carry such risk is worth keeping in the arts marketing tool box. Such a method is the use of Gifts and Special Offers.

As with all Sales Promotion methods the technique is essentially simple. The implicit message to the customer is 'Do what I want you to do and I will reward you. Buy. Buy now. Buy more. Buy more, now. Do this and I will ensure you get the best possible value in terms of seating and on top of this I will ... '.

'I will send you a free copy of this excellent book or this excellent CD'. A gift, preferably one that has some relevance to the product you have on offer, can work as a powerful incentive to buy, to buy now, to buy more and to buy more, now. Of course, a reduction in price offered in the form of a voucher can take on the characteristics of a gift but here we are considering something possessing a different character altogether. Gifts, whether from an arts organisation to its customers or from friend to friend should always be carefully chosen and should reflect the personality of the giver and the receiver. If an arts organisation wants to use the Gift as a means of persuading would be customers to go through their metamorphosis then the item should be just as carefully chosen and should, if possible, be something that is not widely available in the High Street and ideally be something that would appear to be only available because of the unique contacts that the organisation has. Whatever it is, the item should not already be in use as a promotional gift by other organisations, commercial or otherwise.

The Gift is concerned with enhancement of value and this should never be forgotten. A badly chosen Gift could actually work in opposition to the arts marketer's intention. So the Gift must be seen to have value – irrespective of how much it has cost.

Gifts used in Sales Promotion almost always cost money and the arts organisation must be as commercially shrewd in acquiring such items as any other kind of organisation. One tries to buy in at the best price all kinds of services and products – design, print, distribution and so on – and Gifts used to promote Sales are no different. So the arts marketer must always keep an entrepreneurial eye on what is available and rule out virtually no source.

In the commercial sector what are known as 'sales incentives' constitute a large industry. Companies produce items ranging from ballpoint pens through to engraved glass mugs, from clocks to umbrellas, from desk sets of day-glo highlighters to paperweights and from key-rings to calenders – usually identified with the client's name and logo. Arts organisations would usually do well to steer clear of products like this. They are almost always intended to be used by large companies capable of ordering large quantities and thus able to obtain the items for quite low prices; arts organisations will almost always need small quantities and prices will be high. On top of this there is the matter of the style, originality and value of the Gift and such products as these, being widely available through commercial companies ranging from insurance companies to the local Ford outlet, exclude themselves automatically.

Creative thinking is what is supposed to characterise the good arts marketer and let this apply to the choice of Gifts used as customer incentives. My company, Rhinegold Publishing Ltd., has published *Opera Now* magazine since 1992 and has regularly used Gifts to encourage the enrolment of new subscribers so that almost every month a new proposition is put to those casual readers who have bought the magazine at the newsstands whom we wish to convert into subscribers. We have successfully established a value in back copies of the magazine, many of which we acquired when we took over the magazine (should they go to the waste merchant or could we do something profitable with them?), and now sell them through the pages of the magazine using the device of what is called the Back Copy Shop. Therefore, if we offer the choice of, say, six back copies as an incentive we are offering something of established value that could not be obtained anywhere else: both criteria are satisfied.

We regularly identify items such as book on opera and tapes and CDs of opera that are of particular interest to our readers. We contact the companies that are marketing them and negotiate a good price. We have offered *The Pocket Kobbés Opera Book* which was then only otherwise available at full retail price from bookshops and the two CD boxed set 1937 Beecham recording of *The Magic Flute* from Nimbus Records that was currently on sale at record shops at a price in excess of £20. In both cases the prices negotiated were sufficiently low to make possible the gift and – a very important factor – the products were available to us on demand, that is, we did not have to commit ourselves to large orders which might cause embarrassment if the take-up of the offers was low.

Marketing magazines is very similar to marketing the performing arts. One tries to attract customers, turn them into regular customers and then hold on to them. Of course, in the performing arts there is no equivalent of *Opera Now's* store of back copies but we have used the idea of putting value onto back copies not only to assist in attracting subscribers but also in holding onto them year after year. Underlying the back copy idea is the notion of the reader as a collector, the reader who does not throw away copies of such a valuable magazine (because it has value constantly reinforced by the advertisements for Back Copy Shop). But how to store these magazines? Binders for back copies are widely available from magazines; they are advertised within their pages and priced at anything between £6 and £8. We discovered that it costs in the order of £2 to buy a binder that is attractively identified as being an *Opera Now* binder if quantities of 1000 or 2000 are ordered at any time and this sum is very low in relation to the financial benefits of having and keeping an annual subscriber. So, the provision of a free binder became part of every campaign to win over subscribers and the provision of further free binders, one each year when renewal was completed, became part of the *Opera Now* subscriber deal over and above any other Gift offers that might be made.

It is for individual arts marketers to develop their ideas along these lines, remembering always that Gifts used in Sales Promotion should be relevant to the main product that is being sold, should have value, should be available on demand – and should be affordable within the arts marketing budget. My first choice would therefore always be the main product itself as this must satisfy all criteria: that is, the best Sales Promotion is more of the product you are there to sell. A pair of free tickets is a most acceptable gift. If one may enhance this by choosing a particular evening and adding to the gift by arranging pre-performance drinks with, perhaps, a brief talk from the artistic director, so much the better.

Some organisations have fully developed merchandising functions where items are sold which have explicit connections with the organisation and its art form. The shops at the British Museum, the Royal Academy and the Tate Gallery are excellent examples of high quality merchandising ventures that can make money in their own right while reinforcing the relationship with customers. The items sold have value and would thus make excellent Sales Promotion Gifts, provided the buying price could be tolerated by the arts marketing budgets.

In the early days of our Sales Promotion work on *Opera Now* I bought as a present for a friend a copy of the Royal Opera House's Address Book illustrated with copies of posters, playbills and programmes. It was a very attractive item. We enquired of the Royal Opera House as to availability in bulk and very soon the Address Book was being used most successfully as a subscriber incentive for our magazine.

Special Offers

When an organisation has become adept at choosing, buying in and using Gift items it will inevitably come across products that meet all criteria apart from that of affordability; it may then choose whether or not it wants to make the items available to potential and actual customers at a price whilst still employing the item as an incentive. Such items, usually priced at a low level so that the perceived value is high, are known as 'Special Offers'. In one sense moving into this territory takes the organisation outside its usual marketing field turning it into a marketer of ... whatever it happens to be. There are implications of cost and risk in making such a move but arts marketers should be capable of assessing these and of deciding whether or not their personnel resources are capable of taking on the role of a shop or a direct mailing company for a little while.

Considerations aside of how such an offer is to be physically handled the crucial decision to be made here is whether or not the item has a good chance of incentivising the potential and actual customers in spite of a price being charged. Apart from the usual criteria applied to the selection of a Gift, the key factors must always be that what is being offered is a genuine bargain, a remarkable bargain, and unique, not available anywhere else. If the Special Offer is truly *special* then it should succeed as a Sales Promotion method.

The first pressure an organisation is likely to feel to move into the Special Offer area is when existing customers, people who have already made the purchasing commitment, complain about Gifts being offered to newcomers. 'It's not fair,' they say, 'We'd like one of these. We are being penalised because we are your loyal customers'. Their response is entirely understandable. The first point to make is that in arts marketing today the majority of work is done by direct mail and so it is generally possible to keep separate offers made to different parts of the available audience but one can never keep each part of a campaign wholly watertight and such protests will be received. I receive them every time we make another outstanding Gift offer to readers of *Opera Now* but fortunately the numbers are small and when I explain the reasons behind what we do and ask to enlist their understanding most customers go along with our approach and see that it is in their interests as well as ours for the magazine to increase its readership.

So, with this in mind, it is sometimes a good idea to make available a Gift intended to incentivise new customers as a Special Offer for such customers who have already jumped over the Sales barriers for you. The pricing of such an offer is difficult for if it is to be a real Special Offer then its price should be extremely attractive, that is, low, but if one is offering the item as a gift to new customers then one wants it to have the highest possible perceived value. With magazine subscription where there are three categories of customer – the newsstand customer who is happy to be so and to stay so, the newsstand customer who is just teetering on the brink of paying an annual subscription and the person who has already subscribed; all could be interested in the gift item. We have approached the problem by giving the item three prices: zero for new subscribers, a Special Offer price for those already subscribing and a higher price for 'casual' customers. This seems to meet one's marketing needs in all three sectors.

The experience of running *Opera Now* has given rise to an extremely acceptable form of Special Offer that seems to me to have many advantages and few disadvantages. The magazine has teamed up with the champagne house Moët et Chandon and with a music organisation to offer an evening of musical entertainment combined with a champagne reception and tutored tasting. The cost of the evening is the price of the ticket for the music, the reception and champagne element being covered by Moët et Chandon. The supply of tickets is limited. Evenings like this are always over-subscribed and they do much for the magazine's relationship with its readers for not only do the participants enjoy their evenings of music and champagne (and probably feel quite good about the company that has supplied such excellent wine) they meet the editor and they meet each other. Furthermore, readers who have not attended can read about how things went in a subsequent edition and can see how the magazine provides for its readers. This kind of activity does not yield immediate dividends but the return comes when the renewal notice arrives and it is time to decide whether or not to go on as a regular reader.

In general it is probably better for most arts organisations to keep Special Offers strictly under control for it is all too easy to slip into a wholly different field of marketing and to find that one is actually running a different kind of company. There is no harm at all in the organisation entering the field once in a while when something very special is happened upon but the concentration must always be on the desired end result which is increased sales arising out from the use of the method as a Sales Promotion activity. If the organisation develops a knack for buying and even creating products that are of great interest to its customers then it would be better by far to consider opening a merchandising department or a special events department and going into that kind of business properly.

Competitions and Draws

In the large scale commercial sector the use of these Sales Promotion devices is very common but the situation where the marketer is trying to create a loyal buyer of butter is quite different from where one is trying to persuade a would be customer to jump over to our side and where the need for prompt action is paramount; they have their attractions to the arts marketer but they must be used with care.

A Competition involves the use of skill and knowledge whereas a draw does not, the winner being chosen by a wholly random method. The former has, incidentally, virtually no restrictions imposed by law whereas the latter, being a form of gambling, does. A Competition involves the participant in taking time, the Draw does not. If a Competition is to be used to help pull the would be customer over the final hurdle and if participation is required at the time of purchase it will delay rather than accelerate the purchase. The Draw, on the other hand, takes up no time and thus does no harm to the process of selling.

In neither case can the entrant be even remotely confident of winning and so, because the immediate benefit is no more than the opportunity or chance of winning, the effect of such an offer upon a nearly-customer is bound to be minimal. Few people would commit themselves to buying theatre tickets in order to obtain no more than the chance of winning something, no matter how exciting and glamorous it might appear to be.

How potent then, are these devices? For the normal, day-to-day business of selling tickets for individual events they are rarely worthwhile. They take up valuable time – and possibly money – in obtaining prizes, they need administration and they require the assistance of others to maintain their *bona fides* – judges of competitions and overseers of draws.

Perhaps the biggest risk of all with competitions is when the organisation takes them too seriously and unwittingly creates another Sales barrier by giving the customer far too difficult a task in order to obtain the chance of a prize. When I was consultant to a theatre in Essex and a major campaign was planned the idea of a competition was mooted and agreed. An extremely attractive travel prize was negotiated and the theatre's director and marketing officer set about creating the competition which consisted of six questions about the theatre's history. I calculated that it would have taken a trip to the local library and perhaps some scanning of local secondhand bookshops with possibly some grilling of older members of the community in order to have a chance of answering those questions. The prize was very attractive so how could one bear to send off the booking form and cheque without having completed competition entry form? Keep competitions very simple and use the rule 'First correct entry drawn out of the mail bag' to find the winner.

When an organisation has gathered to itself a substantial number of Attenders and wants to keep them in a close relationship with itself then there are times when these methods add a little zest to the proceedings. We have found the readers of *Opera Now* most of whom are regular readers, whether subscribing or not, adore competitions (where there are often quite modest prizes and only occasionally something extraordinary) and enter them in vast numbers. We are convinced that such activities, combined with a magazine they obviously like very much, some Gifts and Special Offers and a first rate subscription service, are responsible for maintaining a subscribers' renewal rate well in excess of 70% per annum. Competitions are never used by us to attract new subscribers, however.

Competitions and Draws may also be used to effect when the organisation is launching a major campaign rather than one of its more routine activities. Every organisation should consider making a serious bid for public attention every so often as the downward pull on attendances is ever present and one's Available Audience can easily begin to take the organisation for granted. The *big* campaign, with a large budget and large sales income targets, is a way of re-establishing one's position and here all the big guns of marketing must come trouping out not least of which will be Sales Promotion with either a major competition or draw to add glitter to the proceedings – but that is all it will do and for this reason should never form the main plank of a Sales Promotion strategy.

Sales Promotion as a bag-of-tricks rather than a component with a serious contribution to make.

Almost all arts bodies practise some form of Sales Promotion, the most common being the group or party discount and there are plenty of examples of half-price ticket offers, packages involving meals plus performances, special rates on local car-parking and so on, but such activities rarely form part of an coherent marketing approach with Sales Promotion seen as a vital component working in conjunction with Pricing, Product Publicity and Sales. Sales Promotion happens but it happens on the basis of 'Gosh, sales are looking grim, we'd better do something' and the hand goes into the bag-of-tricks to see what comes out: such last ditch attempts are often referred to, quite accurately, as 'gimmicks'. This points to a need for a widely accepted general understanding of what are the components of arts marketing and how they each contribute to its effectiveness.

The principal reason why Sales Promotion is still not fully integrated into the thinking and practice of many arts marketers and arts managers is probably due to the reasons I outlined in the first chapter of this book; when marketing began to be taken seriously in the corridors of government and arts bureaucracy it was in a form that did not include serious regard for the place of Sales and hence Sales Promotion. I still regard the absence of *any* reference to Sales Promotion in the now notorious video and workbook 'distance training package' produced by the Arts Council, financed by the then Office of Arts and Libraries, with direct consultative input from (of all bodies) The Institute of Marketing and overseen by the then Arts Council of Great Britain's marketing director, Dylan Hammond, as almost beyond belief.

Such is the seminal influence of restricted thinking, myopic vision, stunted knowledge and wilful cussedness that as recently as 1992, when the Arts and Entertainment Training Council published its *Draft Standards for Consultation. MARKETING AND FRONT OF HOUSE (National and Scottish Vocational Qualifications Key Function 5: Enable people to experience arts and entertainment)* there was but one scant reference to Sales and that in connection with a vague, 'Contribute to the selling effectiveness of public areas' which hardly addresses the nub of the matter. Of Sales Promotion it said absolutely nothing.

Yet this document was published by the Arts and Entertainment *Training Council*, with the involvement of two well known arts consultancy organisations following discussions with no fewer than twelve leading arts marketers.

Why arts organisations are often uncomfortable with Sales Promotion

Without the benefit of status, without the value of its contribution recognised and without the ground rules for its operation being known, Sales Promotion can all too easily be seen as nothing more than a series of gimmicks which cheapen and downgrade the arts experience that is offered. Arts organisations, often fearful of offending their Available Audience which they see, with considerable justification, as being made up of sensitive, discerning people who are easily affronted, do not want to take the risk of doing more harm than good. This is not a serious problem and only arises when the arts marketer uses the method crudely. One might say that any aspect of arts marketing can adversely influence the perception of the organisation and the products it offers if it is handled crudely. Look to the people behind the scenes: crude people handle arts marketing crudely. The first step for the arts marketer using the method for the first time is to take no step until Sales Promotion is fully understood and the possible effects of what is planned have been carefully weighed up – move slowly and carefully at first.

There is also the fear that when Sales Promotion involves spending money as it well might do where Gifts are to be used, or if Vouchers are to be printed, the extra financial return might be less than the outlay. Where extra product is to be offered, as in the 'You buy six tickets and we charge you for five' approach, there is then the lurking suspicion that one might be giving away something that might otherwise be sold.

If Price Reduction is used regularly, without variation, there is also the soundly based fear that the overall pricing structure will become eroded and people will always expect to buy their tickets for less money and will not take the step towards purchase unless there is some form of 'money off' offer. This may easily develop into an expectation applying to all forms of Sales Promotion so that previous customers on whom one relies for future audiences always expect some form of benefit other than that which the ticket promises. It is no bad thing to have one's regular customers so interested in what you are doing that they have such expectations and it is perfectly easy to vary the types of Sales Promotion so that the costs to the organisation vary from campaign to campaign, down to zero – with Seat Preference being the method constantly to the fore.

There can be little doubt that if approached negatively the only form of Sales Promotion that can be justified is Seat Preference – and even then I have met arts managers who have said, 'Yes, that's all very well, but what about our customers who like to book at the last minute; they won't be happy if all the best seats have gone.' To this, the ultimate form of negativism, all one can do is ask the pessimist to confirm that *all* seats are regularly and predictably taken and to point out that if they are not *some* form of action would appear to be called for even if it is possibly at the expense of those customers who think and behave as though they are in a Buyer's Market. It is sometimes worth running the risk of losing one group of customers if it can be replaced with a larger group that responds to one's marketing – and even then if the product is good and is supported by good arts marketing those customers can be recovered.

The biggest enemy of Sales Promotion is, beyond doubt, the fear that it simply will not work and that money spent will be wasted and tickets sold would have been sold anyway. This is a manifestation of the 'Audiences are made by God' theory that I referred to in Chapter One. Such arguments can be made with equal validity against Product Publicity. How does one prove that one's Product Publicity brought about sales of tickets and that the income therefrom is greater than that spent on designing and printing leaflets and posters? The best that can be said is that if one took no action at all, spent no money at all on Product Publicity, then probably there would be no audience at all.

The steps towards recognising and implementing Sales Promotion are not complex: first, understand the theory of arts marketing and the place in it occupied by Sales Promotion; secondly, believe that Sales Promotion can increase sales beyond those generated by the combination of Product Publicity and Sales alone; thirdly, give status to Sales Promotion in the arts marketing decision making process by putting it firmly in both formal and informal agendas and by allocating to it a specific budget.

Sales Promotion needs its own budget

Of the steps necessary to give Sales Promotion its rightful place in the organisation's work only the last is likely to cause problems because giving Sales Promotion its own budget will involve others and in particular the people whose responsibility is finance.

The 'accountant mentality' which is held to be responsible for so many of the world's troubles finds it hard to come to terms with risk, which is a fundamental part of this business. Accountants are good at examining and reporting on the past. When it comes to the future they often expect the same sort of relationship between cause and effect as they have observed in the past. All marketing has as its goal changing – improving – the relationship between cause (spending) and effect (earning) and to do this requires risk to be taken.

Every time a campaign of Product Publicity is undertaken there is risk that it will not succeed, that the messages it projects will fall on stony ground but the expenditures involved are enshrined in the spending traditions of the organisation and are, to an extent, protected. If £100,000 was spent on, say, Product Advertising, last year and box office income of a certain level was achieved then few accountants would object to £100,000 being spent this year in anticipation of achieving a similar result. If a little more income is sought then the accountant would probably accept a *pro-rata* (or smaller) increase in expenditure. It is when a substantial increase in income is aimed for, say to move attendance from an average 60% attendance to 80%, and when heavy increase in expenditure is suggested, that the accountant goes into trauma.

If a major impact is to be made on income which has perhaps settled down into a comfortable but unacceptably low level, then the tools of arts marketing must be used to the full and Sales Promotion methods of one sort or another are bound to be considered. Experienced arts marketers know that when major improvements in sales income are aimed for it is usually best not simply to pour more money into the same old channels. New thought is called for and this leads to Sales Promotion.

At such a stage it is better by far to work out and cost out a marketing plan that gives Sales Promotion its own budget and its own status. From that time on the activity will be recognised and the organisation will give as much attention to it as it has always given to Product Advertising and Product PR.

Whether or not this new budget will be accepted by the organisation's senior management cannot be foreseen but if it is not then the arts marketer would be well advised to take whatever is allocated under the Product Publicity heading and draw up a private division of the sum so that, behind closed doors at least, the newcomer's right to a separate existence is acknowledged.

But where is the budget to come from?

Where does any budget come from? All expenditures are ultimately paid for by the income the organisation makes from trading and, where it operates in deficit, from grants. A Sales Promotion budget is covered by the increased income that is planned for.

Does this mean that prices should be increased to pay for Sales Promotion?

Prices should always be increased to the point where price resistance is risked irrespective of one's planned expenditure ('Charge as much as you can get'). Box office income pays for Sales Promotion just as it pays for Product Publicity and for the wages of cleaners. Increases in expenditure *of any kind* must be covered by greater income.

****

The quintessential application of Sales Promotion

Over the past ten years the arts world has grown much quieter on the topic of Subscription, the marketing method that transformed the audience levels of so many performing arts bodies in North America, Australia, New Zealand, the UK and, I am sure, many other countries. In 1980 I was involved in a project to introduce to the UK the ideas and techniques of a marketing approach that its creator, Danny Newman, called 'Dynamic Subscription Promotion' and through a company I formed with my business partner, Tony Gamble, *Subscribe Now! (UK) Limited*, I worked for several years as a consultant, launching, advising on and managing Subscription schemes in the UK.

It is worthwhile taking up a few pages to examine the Dynamic Subscription Promotion idea and to relate it to the ideas of arts marketing expressed here and in particular the function of Sales Promotion upon which it leans heavily for its operation – for Danny Newman's inspired approach is in truth the very quintessence of Sales Promotion and merits a chapter in its own right.

SUMMARY OF SALES PROMOTION – GUIDE LINES

The techniques available to you may be categorised as *Seat Preference*, *Price Reduction*, *Free Gifts*, *Special Offers* and *Competitions and Draws*: these may be used in combination, one with another.

Seat Preference should run throughout all campaigns with greater emphasis given to those aimed at previous buyers. Customers should always be made to feel that buying sooner rather than later will gain them a significant advantage. Charging the same price for all seats is in itself a form of Sales Promotion and greatly assists the effectiveness of the Seat Preference method. Offering a 'star attraction' with all tickets at one price is an excellent way of promoting the sales of other events if they are linked together.

Price Reduction methods should not be used for every event and when they are used they should vary in detail campaign by campaign. If expressed as a percentage then vary the percentage according to the price of the ticket so that there is a range of reductions from, say 10% on cheaper seats up to, say, 25% on more expensive seats – then next time, consider reversing the percentages. Either way one may say 'Up to 25% off' but the former will cost you more than the latter.

Vouchers are tangible and capable of being put directly in the customer's hand; they are the most flexible Price Reduction method available to the arts marketer and also provide an easy way of making a Gift that is closely related to the product. They are less easy to redeem when purchase takes place by telephone but if the wording on the voucher is carefully planned it can take on the character of a promissory note so that the customer has only to refer to it, perhaps quoting a reference number from the voucher which is then matched against a mailing list, in order to benefit from it.

Never rely entirely on a Competition or Draw as the main Sales Promotion plank: use them only to add icing to the cake and only then if they offer little or no impedance to the process of buying. By all means use them independently of campaigns aimed at selling tickets – in a customers' newsletter, for example – here, of course, they are contributing to the organisation's public relations work rather than assisting as a Sales Promotion device.

Whatever Sales Promotion method is used make sure it complements the style of the organisation and does not conflict with its view of its customers.

Judge Sales Promotions in terms of their significance to the available audience. Price Reductions and Gifts must be 'worth having'. If you perceive your customers to be well-heeled, do not assume that Price Reductions may be smaller – quite the reverse is true.

Avoid Sales Promotions that will cause embarrassment to the customer when they are taken up. This links closely to the point about significance above. If the offer is that of a free glass of wine on arrival do not send a scrappy little piece of paper which has to be handed in very obviously before the customer has to join a queue labelled 'Free Glass of Wine' – have an attractive voucher which asks customers to go to a named part of the building, have them welcomed on arrival and directed there. And then do not display price lists of more expensive wines which locate the free wine firmly at the bottom!

Gifts should be related in some way to the organisation and the products for which it is known. The best Gifts consist of the product itself and the Voucher is a most convenient way of making them.

With the exception of Seat Preference, which should be a constant theme, albeit one which is expressed in varying ways, all Sales Promotions should be limited in duration. If they are not then they become generally available and there is no particular reason to respond to them – and so the reason for using them is lost

Vary the substance of Sales Promotions and vary the description of them, campaign by campaign. Never allow your organisation to be taken for granted.

Above all other matters; never use Sales Promotion in such a way that it makes the organisation appear to be desperate for business: use it with confidence, with the hint that you are in a Seller's Market, that what is offered is for *your* customers. Be particularly careful if a campaign appears not be be working and you need to give it a boost with some form of Sales Promotion for this is when you can most easily project desperation and this kills sales faster than anything.

Remember that Sales Promotion is intended to make people buy now, buy more and buy more now and each method used should have one or more of these objectives in mind.

Don't feel that you are failing if you do not use Sales Promotion; a Full House is a vindication of everything you are doing but if you do not have Full Houses on a regular basis consider how Sales Promotion may help you.

Dynamic Subscription Promotion is the very quintessence of Sales Promotion.

CHAPTER SEVEN

DYNAMIC SUBSCRIPTION PROMOTION

The invention of a dynamic man who has spent all his life promoting the performing arts

Danny Newman

It is fascinating to see how an industry such as ours and with the history that ours has had, reacts to the introduction of an approach to arts marketing which, although radically different in style and structure, embodies all the theoretical principles that you will find in this book and in my earlier books, whilst presenting it as a straightforward pragmatic package, easy to understand and with a proven track record of success.

Danny Newman's Dynamic Subscription Promotion is the invention of a dynamic man who has spent all his life promoting the performing arts. He is familiar with every technique, every traditional practice, every marketing blind alley, every old wives' tale, every old saw, that is used in our industry. He has met the gurus of the large scale commercial world and the academics and heard what they have to say. Now in his seventies his experience over a life time is vast. When he offered the performing arts world his 'miracle method' he was offering the distillation of all this experience in a form that almost anyone could follow. His is a very 'unintellectual' approach, and I do not say that in a pejorative sense for it has the exciting character of an evangelistic message and as such is far more likely to persuade and

125

energise the listener than something that merely plods the routine path in the manner of a school text book. When he speaks and writes he does so with *panache*, vigour, lucidity, passion and a confidence that comes from simply knowing that what he says makes sense and works.

Danny Newman in the UK

Having read his book *Subscribe Now!* in 1978, Tony Gamble and I went to Chicago where Danny was Director of Public Relations at the Lyric Opera, a title that did not do justice to his level of influence over audience development work for while he was carrying out all the usual tasks of media relations (including, I observed, rushing over to the newspapers after opening performances to lay out their reviews for them) he was running one of the most successful subscriptions schemes the world has ever seen. The Lyric Opera was regularly selling more than 100% of its tickets – that is, when subscribers could not attend their tickets were returned for resale and were sold very promptly. The Lyric Opera was by no means the only North American performing arts organisation to be enjoying high attendance from subscribers for by the time we met him Danny's influence was widespread through his consultancy work, his lectures and his book that had been published in 1976.

We invited Danny to come to the UK and he did so in the first few days of 1980. We arranged a series of seminars so that arts managers could meet Danny and we launched Dynamic Subscription Promotion in the UK. It became a major talking point in our industry, a very controversial talking point, and soon our company *Subscribe Now! (UK) Limited* became involved in providing consultancy services to a large number of UK arts bodies.

We knew that this was not Danny's first visit to the UK. He had already advised Scottish Opera, Scottish National Orchestra and the Birmingham Repertory Theatre. We were surprised to discover that Danny had also met a representative of the then Arts Council of Great Britain but who appeared not to have shown much interest in what he had to say.

The post-Newman period

After Danny's visit to work with us Dynamic Subscription Promotion enjoyed a period of great popularity with arts marketers that was sustained as long as we maintained the pressure and availability to provide consultancy services but eventually the wax turned to wane. There are today still subscription schemes in the UK but they have lost the 'Dynamic' and the 'Promotion'; in their visible aspects, the brochures that list forthcoming events, they seem to have been taken over by designers with a fine sense of elegance and there is little evidence of the hand of the energetic arts marketer who understands and believes in the DSP approach. Why this should have happened I cannot be sure but I believe it was that DSP assumed the character of a fashion and then went out of fashion, giving way ultimately to the influence of the large scale commercial invaders of the mid-eighties to whom I refer elsewhere in this book.

Time to take stock of DSP

Arts marketing is not an easy area in which to become confident and successful and we should not be surprised at the tendency there is to follow one fashion or another; this is what people do when they possess no true underlying knowledge; it is akin to what is called 'sentiment' in the stock market, investors putting their money where the current fashion says it should go without examining the fundamentals. New ideas should always be welcomed and examined carefully and used if they can make a real contribution but they should not become the overwhelming influence because then they will become a fashion and will pass together with those elements that were good. It seems that this has happened to Newman's DSP and it is surely now time to take stock of his ideas and absorb them, integrate them, into our thinking.

British reservations

Not that DSP was initially welcomed with open arms: there is always mistrust of 'American' ways in the UK where we are not happy about brashness and determination to succeed – they are not very dignified attributes are they? It was easy to dismiss the words and ideas of Danny Newman as being those of some commercial, hustling salesman – until you read them, that is. Many people do not take the trouble to read them, of course. When they are read they reveal the author as possessing impeccable arts management credentials (rather than commercial ones) and a witty, incisive style that always gets straight to the point.

I shared the mistrust in the early days before I read his book. I was working as a consultant and lecturer. I had just returned from a six week lecture tour of New Zealand, Australia and Hong Kong and hadn't mentioned subscription once, because I hadn't heard of it. When I learned that some damned Yank had been retained by Scottish Opera I was envious and resentful for it was the sort of job I thought I should have got and the money would have been more than just useful – but I should not have been anything like so successful as was Danny.

Danny Newman is 'one of us'

Danny is not a commercial person. He has never sold baked beans or motor cars. He is not an academic. He is an arts industry person. He is 'one of us'. If the energy, directness, clear thinking and determination to succeed that he has always shown embarrasses us then that is our fault, not his.

On top of this, what he has to say and what he has constantly advocated as being the best way to promote the performing arts, squares with theory – the theory you will find in this book anyway. That is why when I read his book the scales fell from my eyes for everything he said made perfect sense to me in spite of the fact that it approached the matter from a totally different direction and used a very different style.

I found it very stimulating to have discovered such a complement to my work. It seemed to me that the two approaches, when put side-by-side, influencing each other would work well; the evidence was that it did work very well indeed. I continue to be influenced by the Newman approach not the least part of which is the belief that subscription is very good system for our customers; once they have made the commitment they enjoy having this important part of their lives 'in the diary', so to speak, protected from the other, more mundane, aspects of life.

What is Dynamic Subscription Promotion?

DSP is about persuading people to buy tickets for several events in one go and thus appears to start by building into the situation a massive hurdle; what is to be offered for sale is not one or two experiences chosen from a shopping list but all of them or, at least, a large bundle of them. The product is not the experience of one show but a large number of shows – a season of them, or half a season of them. This immediately presents two major problems: the cost to the customer is obviously going to be much higher and the demand on the customer's time is going to be much higher too.

DSP says that both these problems can be overcome and are well worth the time and trouble of overcoming. It uses Sales Promotion to overcome them.

The contrast with marketing show-by-show

The traditional way of marketing shows is to approach each one with a different campaign. This has the one particular advantage of enabling the Product Publicity to focus on each event and can thus communicate persuasive information about each most effectively. It is the experience of the show that is being marketed and people are to be persuaded to want to buy tickets for the show beyond anything else. The method is a very appealing one and yet, wherever one sees this approach in use, there is the strong likelihood that the rather depressing characteristics of what we might call 'stretched' marketing will be discernible. The more events there are the more 'stretched' will be the visible evidence of marketing.

There will be a standard type of campaign, using more or less the same media, posters, leaflets, newspaper advertisements. There will be little or no Sales Promotion beyond the usual Party Booking Rates. The design of media may well have become standardised too because there is not sufficient time – nor does it appear to be worth the extra money – to brief a designer for each event although the ability to do this is the principle advantage of the approach. Press and media work have degenerated into the routine sending out of one release per show. The staff often complain of being equally stretched. This gloomy description cannot fairly be applied to all busy arts organisations promoting many shows but we have all seen the effects I have described.

The traditional way of marketing commercial theatre

(The traditional way of marketing commercial theatre on tour comes to terms with the problem of there being too many shows for the visited venue to market and too little time. The show comes complete with a Product Advertising package of so many posters, so many leaflets etc. A few weeks before the visit the touring company sends its PR person down to talk to the local media. The venue places newspaper advertisements and puts the information in its brochure for the season. And that's it. This is every bit as much of a standardised approach but the difference is that the touring show will have within it at least one 'star', so the show completes complete with a powerful magnet. This method has worked for a long time, it still works and it will go on working. Many performing arts organisations have to work without the powerful magnets and that is why this book – and DSP – exists).

Packaging events into marketable groups

DSP says that if you package together the events the advantage you have is more time to devote to that which is to be offered for sale because you have only one campaign to mount each time and you have long periods between each campaign. Given that each event probably had devoted to it one (relatively small) sum of money there is now a much larger pot to spend. So there is more money and more time. The product is now something different, of course.

The product is not *all* that different. A collection of concerts of one kind of music is not substantially different in its appeal from one concert – apart from being, to the Attender and Intender, more attractive. A repertory of six plays should appeal to the theatre goer – more so than just one play. One must constantly remind oneself that people who like an artform really *like it* and that if they are presented with an easy way of getting more of what they like then they will take it provided they are persuaded so to do. Moreover, once they have 'bought wholesale' they will so value having had so much of what they like that they will willingly come back for more of what they like. If true, this reduces part of the perceived hurdle which DSP appears to introduce so that the major barrier is one of price rather than the time commitment required of the customer which arts marketers have always worried about. Seen this way the 'packaging' of events into marketable groups is not a negative factor at all and once theatre goers have enjoyed the way in which a whole season of pleasure is laid out for them, written into their personal schedules, so ensuring that their lives are not taken over by less pleasant activities, they will seek to repeat the experience, season after season.

Does DSP restrict customers' choice?

And what of choice? Should not people be allowed choice? DSP says that if you offer people a list of events with the implicit request that they should choose from the list they will do precisely that and pick just one or two. Danny Newman says that 'the fickle single ticket buyer' will just 'pick the cherries from your cake.' The pressure on the people who make and choose the events is thus to concentrate upon the tried and true, keeping the breadth of choice fairly narrow and focused upon that which is known to attract a good following in the hope that people will choose more. If this path is not acceptable to the artistic policy of the organisation then the implication of appealing to a wider spread of tastes is to attempt to find a different audience for each event – which brings us back to the traditional marketing approach that stretches marketing resources to the point where they became ineffective.

The DSP argument says that if people are offered instead a broader range of experiences generically collectified under an implicit banner saying 'Excellent theatre' or 'Exquisite dance' or 'Great jazz' and this is backed up with a strong projection of the presenting organisation's *bona fides* as a creative, inspired, well-connected impresario – and if choice is not offered to them – they will buy the package. Not all will buy the package but the end result obtained by multiplying the number of purchasers by the number of tickets they each buy will be higher than had the marketing effort been focused upon selling show by show.

DSP brings freedom to the artistic director

If this can be achieved then think of the freedom this gives the artistic director! Think of the flexibility within the product budget where there is now no longer the need always to obtain well known, and hence more expensive, artists and shows. DSP says that by placing the emphasis upon a range of experiences the strong, the immediately attractive, will attract audiences for the less well known. This is much more in harmony with the philosophy that underlies our work.

Choice still remains for those who must have it. It is unlikely that in the UK DSP will ever lead to seasons being wholly sold out to subscribers and so, once the DSP campaign is over, normal service is resumed with box offices selling tickets just as they always have.

Let us take this new product – the experience of attending six, or seven, or eight or even more events over a period of anything from six or seven weeks up to several months – as our starting point and examine DSP in the light of the approach to arts marketing outlined so far in this book.

The Audience

The audience is seen in exactly the same way. One retains the notion of an Available Audience made up of Attenders and Intenders but the DSP approach sees an important distinction between the first subscription campaign of an organisation and subsequent campaigns. The aim of the first campaign is to attract every single last Intender from the catchment area; one may not in the end persuade them to make the commitment but one must try, one must put the subscription proposition before them and one must make it as appealing as possible. This is where the 'D' for Dynamic starts to be brought into the process.

For a first campaign it is not uncommon for the organisation to say 'We know who are our Attenders, we have their names and addresses, and we can communicate with them directly but we do not have enough of them to ensure success. We need to know who are our Intenders. They could be anywhere. We shall therefore aim to tell *everyone* in our catchment area about our new subscription series. If we can communicate with everyone then we must, therefore, reach those who are favourably inclined towards the experiences our shows offer them.'

As we shall see, the first visible evidence of DSP is a very eye-catching and persuasive brochure that is both Product Advertising and Sales instrument combined which carries all kinds of inducements intended to make the would be customer jump the final hurdle. In a first campaign this document is put into the hands of *every household in the catchment area* and if this is not possible, it goes to as many as humanly possible; the choice clearly depends on the size of the catchment area. The aim is to make a huge simultaneous impact on the community and so, the bigger the better.

Of course it may be possible to be selective and distribute according to the socio-economic character of different neighbourhoods (that is, don't waste the paper on poorer people) but often even this apparently rational approach is not always the best course. To cover a complete area, without any selection, costs money in distribution and for printing. To be selective costs money in finding out how to be selective and costs more in tailoring the distribution to follow the selection; the print bill will be lower but the real costs of selection and distribution may be higher than that saved in printing. The costings must be done with care.

Time is involved as well. DSP has to be *dynamic* and this means moving the campaign forward rapidly with a high output of energy. Any process of scientific evaluation of neighbourhoods is likely to take up time and the time between *now* and the end of the campaign is getting shorter and shorter.

However approached the first campaign is on a very large scale indeed and this alone gives it impetus and impact. The organisation is reaching out to the Intenders saying 'We don't know who you are or where you are. Step up and show your faces'.

And then the organisation can start doing business.

The Product – The Subscription Series

The people with Arts Marketing on their doors frequently have no say at all in the selection of the product to be offered; that is, they do not choose the plays to be performed, nor the music to be played, nor the performers. When it comes to planning a Subscription Series, however, they almost always have considerable influence; they are allowed to make up series from the building blocks that others have selected and this can be quite a creative, even challenging, process.

Here the different traditions of presenting music, theatre, dance and opera, make it impossible to speak of applying DSP to 'the performing arts'. Music is presented event by event, often with periods of several days, or weeks, between them: a Subscription Series is often so defined; it is the musical events that have been arranged and there is nothing that can be added or taken away. In the theatre there may well be a tradition of running plays each for three or four weeks with, say, five or six plays before Christmas, a Christmas show that aims for a very broad audience, and then another run of different plays going through to a break for Summer. How does one approach the planning of a Subscription Series within these different traditions?

It is one of the first jobs arts marketers have where they have to think like an impresario, where they have to imagine what their typical audience member would find acceptable, would find pleasing, would find (hope upon hope!) exciting – choosing a series that:

Begins and ends within the foreseeable future – say, starts three months ahead and spans three months.

Contains sufficient events to make up a satisfying, artistically representative (of the organisation, company or artform) collection of experiences for the customer – say six, seven or eight and includes work that is not necessarily immediately recognised by the available audience if such work forms part of the organisation's artistic programming and includes work that is immediately recognisable.

These criteria would probably be sufficient for a series of musical performances presented by a typical club but for a major orchestra, performing in its regular venue, such a series would probably need to be combined with other series in order to cover the season so that the presenting organisation would be trying to attract subscribers to several series which could easily be running concurrently. Within, say, a London series by a symphony orchestra, there might be offered three or four series at the same time, selected according to period, theme, composer or even simply the day of the week. For example there might be a Beethoven series over a three month period with, perhaps, six concerts on different evenings of the week: there might also be a Tuesday evening series or a Sunday afternoon series.

With the typical theatre running in repertory the choice of play is far more restricted than with a music series but there are many more performances for which to find audiences. Each play might easily be given eighteen performances so there would be only one series in terms of content, consisting of five or six plays, but there would be eighteen different series according to the evening of the week and which week of each run was chosen.

Beyond this one cannot go at this stage. Suffice it to say that the arts marketer must build up one series or several series running concurrently or consecutively that are appealing and convenient – and are, in the arts marketer's opinion and in the words of Danny Newman, 'a horse to ride.'

Choice is given to the available audience but it is choice between series, choice based on seating area, choice based on price.

The Price

The price that the would be customer will be faced with is obviously going to be higher than it would be for a single event. If the organisation adheres to a policy of multi-pricing then there will be a range of higher prices to face. It is clearly important that the *value* of what is being offered must be given great emphasis. The 'eye catching and persuasive brochure' must do its job by making the series of events and all the advantages of subscribing irresistible and well worth the price that must be paid or the price that must be chosen. On top of this Sales Promotion will make its own contribution to the perception of value and the methods chosen will feature largely in the brochure.

Price is clearly a negative factor acting upon the potential customer that the arts marketer must contend with but it is much more likely that it will act negatively upon arts marketers, damaging self confidence and making them too generous in their use of Sales Promotion. Motto: Don't be frightened of the price: it's a hurdle that is overcome by the projection of value.

Sales Promotion

In a first subscription campaign Sales Promotion must be used to add value to what is being sold and to make people eager to buy and eager to buy soon: this is the 'P' of DSP.

Seat Preference: A subscription campaign run along DSP lines always opens long before the box office starts to make single tickets available and so the first and best kind of Sales Promotion – Seat Preference – is there to be used – and it must be used vigorously. The use of the seating plan in the booking form where customers mark their preferred seating areas is highly recommended (see Chapter Six) as a way of giving emphasis to the advantage being offered to subscribers.

If the campaign is launched on a grand scale (which is how a first campaign should be launched) then there will be projected the first hints of there being a Seller's Market in operation (although, of course, there almost certainly is not), so the customer has yet another reason for buying quickly.

A purpose of Sales Promotion is to offer enhanced value; it is also to encourage rapid purchase ('A sale delayed is a sale lost'). Giving emphasis to the Seat Preference benefits of booking *now* combines the two effects perfectly. 'If you subscribe you have the best choice of seats (Remember? The best seat in the house is the one the customer wants) so you get best value. Buy now to ensure you get that best value'.

Price Reduction/Vouchers/Free Gifts: If we are expecting customers to buy 'wholesale' then it does not downgrade the quality of what we are presenting if we offer a price reduction or if we offer something extra and we need to do this to overcome resistance to the higher payment we are trying to extract. With a truly dynamic campaign we should probably do both. The intention is to make the Available Audience sit up and take notice – and take action.

So, if five events make up the season then they are offered at a lower – a significantly lower – price – perhaps 20% off. This may be also be expressed in the form of a cash amount or as a free event, 'Buy Five and Pay For Four' or 'Subscribe and Be Our Guest at the Start of the Season' or 'Save £15.00 When You Subscribe'.

Such methods are used principally to make the higher price charged more palatable, to enhance value; they are not in themselves useful for accelerating purchase in the manner of Seat Preference because they are available to whoever subscribes whenever they subscribe. – but they can be made so if they are made conditional upon purchase before a certain date. The brochure may carry the details of a price reduction but an accompanying letter might say that for customers buying before a given date something extra is available: it might be a set of five free car parking vouchers, a voucher for two free bottles of house wine in the venue's own restaurant, an item from the organisation's range of merchandise, and so on.

The 'star event' referred to in Chapter Six also has a part to play in such a campaign and so can almost all methods of Sales Promotion (provided that the basic guidelines given at the end of Chapter Six are followed).

When launching a subscription scheme one must create impact at every level so that old perceptions of the organisation are swept away by a new, dynamic presentation of the organisation, the products it offers and the way they are put together into series, the value for money that the subscription prices offer, the choice of seating offered and all the extra benefits that the arts marketer can put into the package. Sales Promotion adds the glitter – the sizzle of the message – and so this is the time to build in the special, easy-to-enter, subscribers' competition with a wonderful prize that has been negotiated by the arts marketer with a supplier in exchange for advertising space either in the brochure or, later, in programmes. There is also considerable potential for sponsorship of entire subscription campaigns; there are many precedents for this extremely useful form of financial input.

The role of the arts marketer as impresario continues. Not only in deciding the make-up of the series but in building in a variety of Sales Promotions that create a totality that the arts marketer believes to be the best that can be offered. There is no science here: just like impresarios arts marketers use their noses, their gut feeling for what is a 'Horse to ride.'

Product Publicity and Sales

A piece of Product Advertising has to be produced that carries all the essential product information, the details of the series and the events that make them up, conveyed in a way every bit as persuasive and convincing as would be the case if the events were to be offered singly. It is essential that this product information makes an immediate and dramatic impact on the person who reads it. At the first stage of reading *product is all*. People do not buy price reductions, nor do they buy free entry to competitions.

The only people who will respond favourably to this piece of paper are people who are already attending similar events and those who are already favourably inclined towards similar events. These are the people to keep in mind when creating the brochure. In a first campaign most of the people who receive the brochure will discard it – if they ever bother to pick it up; one has to use the shotgun to hit each sparrow. The brochure must be capable of creating an immediate response of interest from the Available Audience. So *product is all* and so is the description of it in the brochure.

I cannot believe that the discreet and elegant little booklets that I see today masquerading as subscription brochures can possibly have the impact that this first contact with the Available Audience demands; these are directed at the most committed of Attenders and offer not so much Subscription as a modest financial inducement to buy more than one or two tickets. They strike me as being impotent and I doubt if they are effective in maintaining levels of subscribers. As campaign follows campaign there is always steady attrition acting on the numbers of 'signed up' Attenders, due to what Danny Newman terms 'transiency and mortality', and so there must always be secondary campaigns going on at least to make good the lost subscribers. DSP demands more, of course, seeking always to keep the dynamic moving in the direction of expansion.

There is a reason why the classic Newman style campaign uses large sheets of paper which open out from carefully planned folding. The DSP brochure tells an exciting story from its front cover, through the exposures carrying summaries of what is about to be revealed made as the brochure (and the story) unfolds, to the final revelation as the full glories of the subscription series are revealed, all together with exciting accounts of the events, photographs of performers, each series laid out giving dates and times, prices – and, given a high level of emphasis, the savings, the bonuses, the free tickets, the vouchers, the wonderful free-entry competition – and the booking form right there where it will do most good alongside information on how to secure the seats *you* want *now*. This final spread seems to me to be a vital part of DSP, and its design is a challenge to any arts marketer and designer.

Perhaps the reason why arts marketers in this country have never wholeheartedly embraced this energetic and ebullient approach is that we allow our personal tastes to intrude into our business responsibilities. We are, it cannot be denied, a wonderfully sophisticated group of people, very knowledgeable about the arts; we know what we like and no-one can con us into going to see something on the basis of pretty pictures and some hyperbolic language. We are also very conscious of what others, our colleagues in particular, might think of us if we try too hard to attract audiences. In the great British tradition we are laid-back, preferring under-statement and the assumption that the real arts lovers will know what we are talking about.

I would also observe that Mr Newman himself is knowledgeable about the performing arts. In his brochures he often has to give synopses of operas and plays, for example, and in these he reveals not only a gift for entertaining abridgement but a very broad knowledge of the subject matter. His obvious love for the works does not inhibit him from describing them in such a way that others are tempted to try them too.

The DSP brochure is aimed at the Available Audience and recognises that at a certain level energy moves into vulgarity and crassness and so does not go that far. The Available Audience is an educated audience that should not be spoken down to; that is why *product is all*. But the Available Audience has also all the usual human characteristics: it worries about spending money that it cannot afford, it procrastinates, if it is offered a free choice it will take it, and so on. The DSP brochure contains within it the perfect package of attractions, products and incentives, displayed so that they may all be seen together, so that they are irresistible.

The brochure is more than a piece of Product Advertising, it is also a potent device for Sales. Long before the brochure was planned all the barriers to purchase were examined and steps taken to ensure that little or nothing would stand in the way of a would be customer going through the metamorphosis. Once the Advertising element had done its job and created a desire to buy and the Sales Promotion had got to work on this to make immediate purchase an imperative then the system for buying would be clear and easy and carefully explained alongside the booking form. Telephone booking? If so, then what will be the hours when a telephone service would be available? 9.00am to 5.00pm or 8.30am to 10.30pm? Will someone booking by telephone be able to describe the favoured seat location? (Perhaps the seating plan should be divided into clearly labelled areas). How will payment be made? Over the telephone? (There are now many charge and credit cards in circulation – which will be acceptable?) How can a telephone buyer pay by cheque? (Will such a booking be held until receipt of the cheque? What happens if the cheque does not materialise?).

The brochure carries the reader through a series steps that follow the classic A.I.D.A. formula. The brochure:

Is strikingly designed, with a very eye-catching cover, to make the Available Audience Aware of it.

The performances are attractively and excitingly described and illustrated, the Sales Promotion incentives are clearly stated in a lively manner, the brochure is folded in a manner that helps the 'story' to be told as it is unfolded, so that when it is taken up and perused it immediately creates Interest.

When the final revelation is made, when the brochure is fully unfolded and all the attractions can be seen together and the prospect of being there, having these experiences, enjoying the satisfaction of a good seat in the venue, all at an affordable price, becomes a distinct possibility, then the Desire to make the purchase is created.

And there on the brochure, in full sight, are the means to satisfy the desire; clear information on how to book and pay and a booking form combined with seating plan – not tucked away out of sight and not denied adequate space by a designer who resents business intruding into art. The now motivated reader is moved to take Action.

Styles change and people weary of visual and verbal approaches that are maintained year after year. There are fashions and bandwagons in many walks of life and they eventually become clichés. And people receive considerably more through their letter boxes than subscription brochures for performing arts organisations. The ever-increasing amount of direct mail marketing creates a serious challenge for arts marketers who do not always have access to the best and brightest designers and yet must compete on the doormat with the commercial sector. Subscription brochures must maintain the competitive edge by changing campaign by campaign, by being more original, eye-catching and interesting whilst maintaining the vital qualities that turn a piece of advertising material into a Sales instrument.

There is more to it than a brochure. Product PR has its part to play in generating an atmosphere in which the campaign can flourish. People should read about the organisation's new season and about all the wonderful benefits that are being offered to them in their local papers and hear about them on the radio. A first subscription campaign can be presented as fresh news even if the organisation has been in business in the same place for years.

The organisation's Attenders should receive special attention in the Product PR aspect of the campaign. They are the people who are most likely to respond favourably but they are also the people who may feel proprietorial about the organisation and resent, albeit very slightly and probably articulated not at all, the very visible attempts being made to attract newcomers. This problem was identified by a wise theatre director whom I was advising and he suggested that before a single brochure was distributed there be held in the theatre a launch party, a modest reception with snacks and wine, at which he would speak to announce the campaign. Brochures would be distributed there and then and subscriptions bookings taken there and then. This was, of course, a very well directed use of Seat Preference as an incentive to speedy purchase as well as a well considered piece of PR, not only for the product but also for the theatre.

The campaign gets underway.

The campaign begins with Product PR blowing fanfares wherever it can and the large-scale distribution of the brochure. There may be some assistance provided for the campaign by press advertising but this should not really be necessary. With DSP as practised by Danny Newman every form of social contact the organisation and its committee has is exploited to create more situations like the theatre director's party, coffee mornings, meetings of Friends, trips out to visit community groups – and certainly sessions with the saintly folk who organise party visits – where the idea of subscription may be put across and brochures distributed.

The distribution of brochures should also be centred on the performing arts venue itself for it is there that Attenders and Intenders will be from time to time, attending shows that are not part of the new season and perhaps calling in for a drink or meal. The centre of the Sales drive should reflect the excitement and energy of the brochure itself, with large illustrations, posters giving details of Sales Promotions and emphasising the high value of what is on offer, exhortations to secure the 'best' seats in the house by buying now, large diagrams of the seating areas, competition or draw entry forms and boxes where completed entries may be left (the entry procedure not being tied then and there to purchase but being something to be done afterwards, at leisure) and so on.

As time goes by the probable success of the campaign will be capable of being gauged and areas of weakness detected. It may be a particular series, or a seating area, or a price range but there will almost always be some category where sales are disappointing. This is where small, focused campaigns using leaflets and newspaper advertisements can be used to mop up the stragglers. Such campaigns do not refer to the season as a whole but concentrate exclusively on what it is that needs to be sold and may have special Sales Promotions devised for them: it is possible to create new packages and new incentives without conflicting with the original campaign or appearing to be unfair to those who booked at the start.

As the end of the campaign draws near an assessment of results is made and decisions made on the next phase when tickets go on sale in the usual way.

Single ticket sales

In a perfect situation the subscription campaign is overwhelmingly successful and 90% of all seats, or more, are committed long before the performances start. If this were to be the case then almost no more money need be laid out on marketing what remains. Most people agree that a good subscription campaign does more than sell subscriptions to series, it also builds up considerable demand for single ticket sales. No-one to my knowledge has put a figure on it but most would agree that pre-selling of 80% or 90% on subscription would almost guarantee sell out when single tickets go on sale. Even a 50% pre-sold season would have a powerful effect. The reason for this is hard to tell but it is as though the appeal of subscription has nearly worked with some individuals but not sufficient to generate a commitment so that when single tickets go on sale they respond in a more selective way: these are perhaps the people to whom choice is a overwhelmingly important. I have also heard it said that the classic DSP campaign is so much bigger in every way that it simply makes more people aware of the organisation and its programme of events and so greater sales are almost inevitable.

It is for the organisation to decide when to close subscription sales and start selling tickets in the traditional way. Once the subscription campaign has run its course (sales figures will reveal this unmistakably) there is no reason why the two should not run together until the season opens. What should be said is that the subscription campaign must be given a clear run without competition from people wanting to steal 'the cherries from your cake.' In theatres I have seen subscription sales running in parallel with single ticket sales right through to the final performance of the first play in the series which may be three weeks after the official end of the campaign, which is perfectly sound practice provided that the subscription campaign was allowed its clear run many weeks before.

Assessing the results

The organisation must, as soon as possible, draw its conclusions as to the results of what it has done; examining the rate at which purchase took place following distribution; the extent to which systems for selling and processing tickets were stretched during peak times; series, days of the week and seating areas that were most in demand and least in demand and so on. An assessment of the effectiveness of the different Sales Promotion methods is most important. It is in this post-mortem period that an organisation that believes in research would do well to put a questionnaire to a representative sample of subscribers right at the beginning of the season, to assess what were the most powerful elements in the campaign and then to return to the same group at the end of the series to assess their level of satisfaction with the performances they have seen and how the regular commitment of subscription has fitted into their lives. This might be used as an opportunity to obtain favourable quotations from subscribers to be used in the next campaign.

The next campaign

The range of the next campaign will be very influenced by the success of the first which, if it has achieved very good results, will have yielded up a goodly supply of what Danny Newman calls 'Saintly Subscribers'. If this is the case then there are now on file the names and addresses of people who are not only Attenders they are people who have made a longer term commitment on the basis of the first campaign. They responded to DSP; for them the combination of all the attractions moved them into purchase. These people will form the core of future audiences.

In Chapter Six I spoke of the advantage of producing a special edition of a brochure for known Attenders and in such a situation as this the technique is highly recommended. The next campaign will first of all be focused on the 'Saintly Subscribers' with a brochure that contains the basic elements planned for the season, the series, the prices, the Sales Promotions and so on, but is a special edition with certain extras built in that encourage the current subscribers to respond very quickly to take advantage of their privileged position. The extras may be lower prices through superior discounts, or vouchers for a star event, or a special free draw but, as always, the really important incentive is the Seat Preference offered by a brochure that states that it is distributed only to existing subscribers and for a certain period of time they and only they will have the pick of the seats.

How much wider the campaign must go will depend on local conditions. It can almost be guaranteed that not all subscribers will respond the second time so an element of 'broadcasting' must be done to replace lost subscribers and to improve the figures. It could well be necessary to make the second campaign as wide-reaching as the first, and even the third.

What must never be done is to assume that failure to respond to the second or third or even fourth campaign does not mean that the person has lost interest in subscribing. As Richard Thomas, once subscription manager of the Philharmonia and involved with ten or more consecutive subscription campaigns (and now marketing manager of Rhinegold Publishing Limited) says, 'Never strike a subscriber from the file – you never know when they might come back.' Richard Thomas based his view on regular monitoring of buying patterns of those on the subscriber register which revealed subscribers often taking two or three year breaks before coming back into the fold.

The basic guidelines for Sales Promotion (see the summary at the end of Chapter Six) apply very much to the planning of campaigns after the first and, in particular, the need to keep changing the incentives. The organisation must never allow itself to be predictable; changes must be made in the series, the prices, the sales promotions, the design of the brochure – everything apart from the two things that must be consistent: the quality of the performances (no matter how unfamiliar they may be) and the service that deals with the first enquiry of would be customers through to their attendance at the performances.

Time to look again at Dynamic Subscription Promotion

The reasons for DSP ceasing to be regarded as the major force for achieving high audience levels and high incomes (that is, achieving the objective of arts marketing) was not because the approach was found to be intrinsically faulty. It was because it required creative talent to create good campaigns, because the campaigns required a much larger financial commitment well ahead of the season's start (the 'all your eggs in one basket' syndrome); committees and managements often found the perceived risk as being more than they could bear particularly if they did not have complete confidence in their marketing staff and, of course, they did not always understand the method themselves. DSP really needs the organisation's total commitment to the idea and does not work to best effect if resources are restricted or held back to provide for the belt of single ticket marketing to back up the braces of subscription.

For these reasons many organisations did not get involved with DSP but during its heyday many did and some notable results were notched up. Commercial sponsorship proved to be a major influence in carrying the idea forward. Sponsors were attracted by the idea of the large scale campaigns and even expanded on the plans of the arts marketers making possible things that were beyond their dreams. I introduced the idea of using full page advertisements in national Sunday newspaper magazines to 'mop up' series and seating areas that had not been sold by the Philharmonia's subscription brochure and these costs were covered by the orchestra's then sponsor, Du Maurier, which backed the scheme over several years. Imperial Group Limited backed the first scheme of the Old Vic and later John Player & Sons supported subscription campaigns for English National Opera, Welsh National Opera, Opera North, Scottish Opera and the National Theatre on tour.

But slowly the enthusiasm which later brought into the DSP camp major orchestras like the London Symphony Orchestra at the Barbican and London Philharmonic Orchestra at the Royal Festival Hall, as well as a large number of regional organisations, ebbed away. There was no central spine to what had assumed the character of a 'movement', no agency that would inform arts organisations of how DSP had succeeded or failed with other arts organisations, no forum for discussion, no systems for training. Our tiny *Subscribe Now! (UK) Limited* could not even begin to tackle the problem even if it was then aware of these needs – which I very much doubt. In *Guide To Arts Marketing* in 1984 I said that we needed there to be an 'Institute or Academy or Association' for arts marketing and I suggested that out of a conviction that the then Arts Council of Great Britain, having turned its face away from the exciting prospect of DSP, would never occupy this pivotal role. There is now, as I write, the Arts Marketing Association, formed towards the end of 1993 – just a little too late to pick up the strands of the DSP boom of the eighties but not too late to start another one in this decade.

The crucial ingredient in DSP is its simple, direct, energetic, naked ambition to locate, attract, commit and hold on to audiences. It is wholly pragmatic. It does not need science to back it up or to justify its actions – or to impede them. For an industry that has always relied upon the talents of the impresario it offers a sort of synthesis of how impresarios think and behave: 'Think big. Act big. Get big results'.

The dynamism vital to arts marketing that is so evident in DSP has been eroded and downgraded by the phoney 'scientists' who appear to believe that the process can be reduced to a series of research projects. It is research, they say, that can tell us where our customers live, how much they will pay, what language will appeal to them most, what colours will please them and so on. Consultants and bureaucrats make money and justify their salaries by advocating these ideas. There may well be something in what they say but, whatever that is, *they slow down the process*, they sap the drive of the organisation. The performing arts are in a constant state of flux, they do not stay still, they are not comparable with a consumer product which may have a life of ten years in the marketplace and so justifies extreme care being taken in analysing the market and developing the product for that market. With such a product time must be taken but with the performing arts quick response is vital.

While DSP has been ebbing away, while arts marketing fashions have come and gone, the real impresarios have been to work. They have just got on with it in the old fashioned way and they have revolutionised the art of making money out of pulling in vast audiences for events that were once thought of as being only suitable for traditional performing arts venues. The Three Tenors phenomenon. Turandot in Wembley Arena. Recitals in stately homes with tickets prices to make your eyes water. In 1976 I wrote in my first book *Marketing the Arts*:

A serious limiting factor on the marketing of the art experience is the numerical restriction on the number of experiences that can be marketed which is imposed by both the buildings housing them and by the intrinsic demands of the art forms themselves ... It may make good economic sense to build an opera house with a capacity of 15,000 seats but artistically it could and probably would be a disaster because very few people in that large gathering could actually see or hear what was going on.

In 1994, as I write, there is evidence that not every big-thinking impresario has got it right. The willingness of people to pay very large amounts of money to run the risk of getting drenched in a British summer or not to be able to see the Bolshoi Ballet from a very long distance has been pushed to the limit in some cases but what is significant is the drive forward to see what the limit is. The successful impresario is like the successful gambler who never wagers what cannot be paid and having reached the limit, withdraws a little and plans the next move. Those who fail and welsh on their debts, claiming the protection of limited liability for their companies and themselves, are not impresarios at all; they are just people who take risks with other people's money.

Arts organisations must think of themselves as impresarios too and start to behave like them. They do not have to restrict the art they make and select to that which is immediately popular as does the commercial impresario – that is why, after all, they receive subsidy from public funds – but they have to go for their audiences with the same levels of focused energy. Of course the traditional way of marketing show by show will benefit from the same quality but, as we have seen in this chapter, DSP still carries the day in its ability to make the fullest use of resources to the greatest and longest lasting effect.

It is time arts marketers looked again at Dynamic Subscription Promotion.

SUMMARY

The product is not the experience of one show but a large number of shows – a season of them, or half a season of them.

DSP says that if you package together the events the advantage you have is more time to devote to that which is to be offered for sale because you have only one campaign to mount each time and you have long periods between each campaign.

One must constantly remind oneself that people who like an artform really *like it* and that if they are presented with an easy way of getting more of what they like then they will take it provided they are persuaded so to do. Moreover, once they have 'bought wholesale' they will so value having had so much of what they like that they will willingly come back for more of what they like.

DSP says that if you offer people a list of events with the implicit request that they should choose from the list they will do precisely that and pick just one or two.

DSP says that by placing the emphasis upon a range of experiences the strong, the immediately attractive, will attract audiences for the less well known.

The first visible evidence of DSP is a very eye-catching and persuasive brochure that is both Product Advertising and Sales instrument combined which carries all kinds of inducements intended to make the would be customer jump the final hurdle.

The DSP brochure contains within it the perfect package of attractions, products and incentives, displayed so that they may all be seen together, so that they are irresistible.

DSP has to be *dynamic* and this means moving the campaign forward rapidly with a high output of energy.

A good subscription series: Begins and ends within the foreseeable future – say, starts three months ahead and spans three months: Contains sufficient events to make up a satisfying, artistically representative (of the organisation, company or artform) collection of experiences for the customer – say six, seven or eight and includes work that is not necessarily immediately recognised by the available audience if such work forms part of the organisation's artistic programming and includes work that is immediately recognisable.

Don't be frightened of the price that must be charged for a subscription series: it's a hurdle that is overcome by the projection of value.

When launching a subscription scheme one must create impact at every level so that old perceptions of the organisation are swept away by a new, dynamic presentation of the organisation, the products it offers and the way they are put together into series, the value for money that the subscription prices offer, the choice of seating offered and all the extra benefits that the arts marketer can put into the package.

With DSP as practised by Danny Newman every form of social contact the organisation and its committee has is exploited to create more situations like the theatre director's party, coffee mornings, meetings of Friends, trips out to visit community groups – and certainly sessions with the saintly folk who organise party visits – where the idea of subscription may be put across and brochures distributed.

Most people agree that a good subscription campaign does more than sell subscriptions to series, it also builds up considerable demand for single ticket sales.

The organisation must never allow itself to be predictable;

changes must be made in the series, the prices, the Sales Promotions, the design of the brochure – everything apart from the two things that must be consistent: the quality of the performances (no matter how unfamiliar they may be) and the service that deals with the first enquiry of would be customers through to their attendance at the performances.

* * *

Author's note:

While writing this chapter a letter arrived from Danny Newman (whose ears had obviously been burning) after a break in correspondence of two years or so. Amongst other things he announced that at the age of 75 he had just remarried and that the Lyric Opera of Chicago's subscription scheme was still going strong. He also included a subscription brochure to gladden one's heart, written by his colleague Susan Mathieson, Lyric's marketing chief for the past five years, and a brilliant practitioner of DSP. I replied and told him that this book was soon to be published and that I would be saying the DSP was long overdue for re-appraisal, He wrote back immediately as follows:

Yes, it's time that we shake 'em up – not only in the UK, but here too! It's fourteen years since we had our sessions in the UK and that's hard to believe. We now have a number of entities here which went from 0 to, let's say 30,000 subscriptions, fifteen, twenty or thirty years ago, and have been living 'high on the hog' for a long time. Recently, mostly because the people who did it (the ones I taught) have retired or died, they have fallen off several thousand subscriptions. Now they run around saying that Subscription is finished! And remember they may still have 25,000. Instead of retraining the new generation of promotional practitioners they're looking for ways to sell more single tickets, and if they go in that direction, they'll all go out of business. Remember there is no subsidy in the USA for the arts. My opera company, from all three governmental levels, federal, state and municipal, gets a total of 2.5% of our budget! However, with our 37,500 subscribers with which to open our new season (more than ever) and with the many millions of dollars those subscribers will give us via contributions, we're solidly 'in the black'.

CHAPTER EIGHT

FINANCIAL PLANNING

Estimates – discipline or bondage?

With any business you plan the year ahead (many plan several years ahead), drawing up estimates of how much income you think you might take and how much money you will have to spend in order to achieve it; arts businesses are no different. According to the type of business the estimates will show an anticipated profit or an anticipated loss. It is good and satisfying if the real results match up with the estimates and even better if they show an improvement.

Estimates are both a vital discipline and debilitating bondage for the arts marketer. It is good to start the year knowing what you have to achieve in sales income and good to know what is your financial resource for achieving it but if success is to be measured only in terms of bringing those estimates into reality then this will not ultimately be in the interests of the organisation which needs growth. In Financial Planning for the arts it is hard to strike a balance between prudence and progress but we must because in any trading situation it is dangerous to stand still and never more so than in the arts where the objective is always:

To bring an appropriate number of people, drawn from the widest possible range of social background, economic condition and age, *into an appropriate form of contact with the artist and, in so doing, to arrive at the best financial outcome that is compatible with the achievement of that aim*

Who is to say what is the *best* financial outcome? The best – the best possible – must surely mean that one must take advantage of opportunities as they arise. That is what the impresario does. A rigid set of estimates and a rule that says they must never be departed from, will make it hard to be entrepreneurial. The tradition of worship of estimates still obtains in national and local government circles and makes it very difficult for people working in those environments and under those influences to operate in an entrepreneurial way.

So, the first principle of Financial Planning and hence the first requirement of the organisation's estimates is that growth should be encouraged not stifled. Estimates should define the minimum acceptable net outcome (that is, income set against expenditure) of the year's work and should be capable of being interpreted flexibly. Year by year they should, if at all possible, set higher targets of income and provide greater financial resources with which to achieve them – and, in an ideal world, the increases in the former should be greater than those in the latter.

The model is always the spiral, underlined by the knowledge that spirals go both ways, they may expand or they may contract and if they are not made to expand they will almost certainly contract: setting higher targets, year by year, is the only way to avoid contraction.

The Gap Principle

When it comes to putting the estimates into practice what matters is not that planned expenditure is adhered to or that planned income is achieved, but that the difference between them ultimately proves to be no worse than that forecast: if the organisation operates in deficit then the deficit at the year's end should be no greater than that planned and if at all possible, smaller. The spiral effect works day by day as well as year by year. But it is not just a matter of money; arts are judged by more than financial criteria, they exist to provide public benefit and as much of it as possible for the money that society is putting their way. So achieving, or improving on, a planned deficit is fine just so long as the organisation's resources are used to the full and the results are experienced to the full.

So arts marketers must operate within a management structure that recognises the importance of taking opportunities to increase expenditure (not only on the specific costs of marketing, of course, but also on the product itself) as much as is humanly possible whilst achieving better results in terms of attendance and income from sales. The 'Gap' between expenditure and income may stay the same, or be smaller, but the turnover should be pushed to the limit: generally, turnover is a fair measure of activity level.

(The world of arts bureaucracy and funding has yet to find a way of measuring the level of achievement of arts bodies when comparing one year's performance against another's. Should we not consider a system of measurement that is comparable with the commercial notion of *profit margin ratio*, which is defined as 'a company's profit expressed as a percentage of its turnover'? Would not a *deficit margin ratio* provide us with a useful measure? A successfully expanding organisation would show an increasing turnover and a decreasing deficit margin ratio.)

Committees must be helped to understand

The work of arts marketers is often at the mercy of an upper tier of management, a lay committee, made up of people who may have no experience nor understanding of how vital it is for the trading spiral to grow rather than contract – and such committees may well include people whose credentials are derived from the business world; no-one has ever explained how people, otherwise highly successful in their own businesses, appear to lose the knack when they accept voluntary responsibilities. Senior professional arts managers must convince these people that just because one end product of the organisation's work is a deficit it does not mean that it should not behave like an impresario – or a successful small business in the commercial sector.

Having the correct arts marketing budgets

The typical arts organisation will have one budget heading under which all expenditures concerned with marketing will be grouped; it may be called 'Publicity' or, out of lip-service to modern trends, it might be called 'Marketing'. It *may* do no serious harm if the organisation so enshrines the view that arts marketing consists of just one activity but it is ultimately healthier if it recognises that there are three basic areas of expenditure and four if one sees Publicity as being made up of Advertising and Public Relations (when considering the operation of the arts marketing function with the Available Audience it is convenient to lump the two together as Product Publicity when speaking of their combined relationship with Sales and Sales Promotion but, in terms of how, where and why money is spent, they are very different activities with, as we shall see later on, Public Relations having work to do with the Unavailable Audience). The four expenditure areas are:

Product Advertising
Public Relations
Sales
Sales Promotion

It is better by far if the organisation can create these four allocations but if it cannot or will not there is nothing to stop arts marketers from creating their own working budgets from the overall, single figure allocated to them.

Why these budgets are important

At the most basic level, the presence of the four allocations will remind the organisation that there are four ways of spending money in order to achieve income so that no matter what changes there are in personnel and management structure the building blocks of arts marketing will not be overlooked. It will mean that at the beginning of the year someone will ask, 'How much should we allocate to Sales Promotion?' and this will prompt not only the question, 'How much have we spent this year?' but also, 'How much did it achieve?'. Simply having these budgets in the estimates will draw the attention of all management to the way that arts marketing works.

Avoid 'netting down'

Expenditures like Advertising and Public Relations are easy to account for; invoices come in and are settled and the figures entered into the appropriate column, whether it be of the cash book or the computer spreadsheet. Where Price Reduction methods are used it is more difficult to account for them. Tickets priced at £15.00 are sold for, say, £12.00 and so £12.00 goes in as income when, in fact, it is net income. It would be far wiser to show each ticket sold as yielding £15.00 and to enter an item of expenditure of £3.00 under the Sales Promotion column so that one has a record of how much it has cost to achieve the income. Of course, this will cause problems in accounting when the figures are matched up with actual sums of money banked but it requires no great change to have two columns so that the £15.00 receipt is recorded as £12.00 cash and £3.00 discount: the price reduction is thus shown on both sides of the cash book and thus cancels itself out. In this way a record is kept of all price reductions and this can be extremely valuable to the arts marketer in future planning when assessing the effectiveness of different Sales Promotion schemes.

(If this seems a difficult idea for people in charge of finance to accept I suggest that they consider the implications of following the argument to the point where all expenditure on Advertising and Public Relations is similarly lost in the netting down process. If £100,000 is taken at the box office and £20,000 has been spent on Publicity, then why not just show £80,000 as net income; why bother to show one expenditure and not another? Taking the idea further, why not lose the cost of the Product as well for it too surely played a major part in achieving the income? Indeed, then, why bother to keep records at all?)

Don't 'lose' expenditure

When a discount is applied to a ticket price or a voucher is used the value of the reduction is lost into thin air by the process of netting down. Traditional practices also lose expenditures by putting them under other headings. An incentive for Sales staff, to encourage a more active approach? Is this better added to the wages column or to a column where those who examine the figures subsequently will see evidence that the Sales function is being operated actively? A training session for ushers: under which allocation should this be placed? Sales, surely. Commission paid to credit and charge card companies? Sales, surely. I would go further and suggest that the salaries of Sales staff be made an item under the Sales allocation so that the relationship between these vital staff members, their level of ability, their motivation and the hours they work may be seen in direct juxtaposition to the results they achieve.

Monitoring

As the year progresses the organisation keeps a constant watch on its income and expenditure, constantly comparing reality with estimates. This is a vital part of routine financial management; it is passive and reactive, only moving to change things when detrimental deviations are observed. Routine financial management stops the train running off the rails but doesn't make it go faster during the run of the year.

Arts marketers monitor their spending across the four categories and must receive box office feedback on a daily basis, not only in global sums but broken down into types of response (telephone, postal, personal caller and so on) if this is at all possible. Wherever possible the particular strand of a campaign that has provided the means of purchase for a customer is identified and recorded. The most common example of this is a directly mailed leaflet that is aimed at several different categories: say, people on the organisation's general mailing list, people who have subscribed to a particular series, doctors and lawyers living within a twenty mile radius. The order forms on these leaflets would be coded so that the source of postal bookings could be recorded. This would be of special value where Sales Promotion methods were being tried out with certain groups and not with others.

Arts marketers are constantly monitoring the effects of what they do in order to find ways of increasing audience sizes and income at the lowest cost. It is an imprecise business. How can one measure the effectiveness of Product PR, for example? Measuring column inches in the press gives quantity but certainly not quality of coverage. Seen campaign by campaign, however, where all activities intended to generate audiences for specific events or series are planned and costed and where there is a target income, it is possible to obtain a 'feel' for the aspects of the campaign that have been particularly effective and to develop future campaigns on this. The more one monitors the better one gets at developing the 'feel'.

Remuneration of arts marketers

If estimates are flexible, if the four arts marketing budgets are incorporated into the organisation's work, if campaigns are monitored, arts marketers who are creative and well motivated may well be able to improve on forecasts during the run of the year. An enlightened arts organisation that is able to provide the proper working environment should recognise this and build reward for such achievement into the remuneration package of those directly concerned with building audiences and achieving income from them. Motivation based on one's own personal standards and ambitions is fine but a little pot of gold at the end of the annual rainbow does so excite the spirit!

SUMMARY

The model is always the spiral, underlined by the knowledge that spirals go both ways, they may expand or they may contract and if they are not made to expand they will almost certainly contract: setting higher targets, year by year, is the only way to avoid contraction.

A rigid set of estimates and a rule that says they must never be departed from, will make it hard to be entrepreneurial.

Arts marketers must operate within a management structure that recognises the importance of taking opportunities to increase expenditure (not only on the specific costs of marketing but also on the product itself) as much as is humanly possible whilst achieving better results in terms of attendance and income from sales.

The four expenditure areas are: Product Advertising; Public Relations; Sales; Sales Promotion. The presence of the four allocations will remind the organisation that there are four ways of spending money in order to achieve income so that no matter what changes there are in personnel and management structure the building blocks of arts marketing will not be overlooked.

Routine financial management stops the train running off the rails but doesn't make it go faster during the run of the year.

Senior professional arts managers must convince their committees that just because one end product of the organisation's work is a deficit it does not mean that it should not behave like an impresario – or a successful small business in the commercial sector.

CHAPTER NINE

LEARNING TO JUGGLE

Keep the ideas of arts marketing in motion, like a juggler, relating each one to all the others, weighing up the effect each one has upon the others. It's not a scientific process. It's a matter of judgement as well as the product of your own creativity and the more you do the better you should become at it.

Here, at the end of Part One, is the natural time to stop and take stock of what I have said so far.

I have tried to give a simple break-down of the parts that make up arts marketing, to explain what they do and how they relate one to another. Inevitably this has caused me to repeat myself on many occasions but this, I have concluded, is inevitable when one tries to describe thought processes which are, in a sense, three-dimensional and dynamic, in a form of communication that is two-dimensional and static. In conversation one tries to avoid repetition — it seems such bad manners to go on and on saying the same things – but in a book like this where the intention is to influence and to teach, then repetition is no bad thing. In Product Advertising, for example, and in particular when substantial advertising brochures are being written for large 'bundles' of events, the sense that it is bad manners to repeat oneself can have a very negative effect upon the work. Repetition is part of how one teaches and how one learns and it is also part of how one communicates all the information that Product Advertising must carry. I would have no compunction at all in telling my Available Audience the title of a performance, or the name of a performer, or the date, or the price, or the special offers, several times.

Remember that the way of thinking is dynamic and requires each thought to be related to the other parts of the process. Perhaps the way of thinking could be described by means of a diagram with arrows running here and there, with labels attached but I have not been able to come up with such a diagram. In my last two books I have given a simple diagram to show how an advertising campaign is planned, with four circles labelled *USP, Potential Audience, Selection of Media* and *Use of Media*, and the necessary arrows. This diagram became known as 'Diggle's Balls'. I am pleased that I no longer feel the need to employ this diagram although it did, from time to time, provoke some interesting conversations.

But balls come into it all right and not just the reprehensible and sexist use of the term to mean energy and determination (as if I ever would). The most apt metaphor for arts marketing is the juggler keeping the balls of Product, Pricing and Planning, Sales Promotion, Sales, Product Publicity, and Corporate PR all in the air at the same time – and, simultaneously, casting an eye towards the future, into the zone of Unavailability, without dropping them.

The cover of this book (which took some clever photography, I can tell you) sums up how I feel about the process. I am aware that in using this picture I am leaving myself open to a more ribald comparison but in the arts one must be prepared for the occasional catcall. And the balls are new, as you can see.

PART TWO

A CLOSER LOOK AT PUBLIC RELATIONS AND ADVERTISING

CHAPTER TEN

CORPORATE AND PRODUCT PUBLIC RELATIONS

Make them know you, make them understand you, make them like you, make them respect you, make them admire you, make them forgive you, make them defend you – and make them feel the same way about the things you choose to present

In Chapter Three I outlined the rôle of what I termed 'Product Publicity', the combination of Product Advertising and Product PR (Public Relations) the job of which is to bring members of the Available Audience to the point where they are ready to make an irrevocable commitment, ready to purchase, the experiences we have to sell. I also said that later on I would cover the techniques that must be used in order to bring about changes in attitude within the Unavailable Audience. I must delay for just a few more pages before I can deal with this fascinating topic so that I may first complete my coverage of marketing to the Available Audience: this will make up Part Two of this book.

CORPORATE PUBLIC RELATIONS

Building a relationship with the Available Audience

The heading to this chapter sums up the benefits that flow from any relationship and is as important to an arts organisation as it is to individuals. It is a mutual matter. Not only does the arts organisation care about its audiences, its audiences care about it and the results extend far beyond the short term target of filling seats over the next few weeks. Arts organisations are subject to all kinds of pressures including financial and political ones as well as the inevitable variations in quality of artistic product and so, expressed at its simplest level, they need friends.

Building credibility

As well as building support for the future the practice of Corporate PR does for the organisation what Product PR does for the product: it creates favourable awareness and trust. By presenting the organisation in the best light it builds its credibility in the minds of the Available Audience so that Product Publicity may achieve maximum effect.

Arts organisations appear rarely to say to themselves: 'We say these things, we make these claims, we promise that the experiences we offer will be good according to the lights of 'our' audience, but *do they believe us – why should they believe us*?' Arts marketers, being simple and honest souls, seem frequently to believe that all one has to do is say that something is good and worthwhile and people will take their word for it. Not so. Would that it were.

If I offer you, the reader, the Rolex watch (it's a gold one) from my wrist for £200 is that not a bargain? It goes to the first person to 'phone me at my office at Rhinegold Publishing.

Let us look at the proposition in arts marketing terms. Are you in the market for a good watch at a very good price? Yes, you probably are given that most people need to tell the time and most people are suckers for glitzy watches so even if you have a Swatch watch you may well still be interested in getting a really good one, particularly if it is very cheap in relation to its value. So you are a member of my Available Audience.

Have I described it persuasively? There is scarcely a need to do this for Rolex's Product PR is so good that the job has been done for me: all I needed to do was give the name and say that it was made of gold. So the Product Publicity is perfectly adequate for someone who is in the Available Audience. Just a minute. Is it working? Yes, it is in perfect working order.

How does the price strike you? Is it affordable? Certainly it is. But isn't it rather cheap for what it is? That is true but there it is on his wrist so ... Mr Diggle, it isn't a fake is it? No it isn't, it's the real McCoy. It's a very good price then, for a watch that costs several thousand pounds.

Sales Promotion? The best kind. First come, first served. I am certainly not going to offer a price reduction on top of this astounding offer.

Sales aspects? Here and now. Just pick up the 'phone and call me. I'll take your word about payment. Just put your cheque in the mail and I'll send the watch to you by Securicor.

So, why no calls?

No matter what I say, you don't believe me. The offer is too good to be true. I have given you no explanation as to why I am selling the watch at such a low price. Come to think of it, you haven't actually seen my watch at all, have you? Yes, you have. Look at the cover of this book.

Although in basic marketing terms I have done nothing wrong in how I set about trying to make you want to buy the watch, you don't feel inclined to bite, do you? Because you don't believe me.

But supposing I were a close friend and I told you that a relative had died and left me a gold Rolex watch and – would you believe it? – I already have one. And suppose I then said that if you gave me the price of two bottles of Chateau d'Y Quem 1983 (pure gold, in itself) I'd let you have the watch.

I'm a close friend – which means that you have known me for a long time and know that I would never lie to you – so you believe me. And you get for yourself a very nice watch for the price of a couple of bottles of very nice wine (going rate, at the time of writing, is around £100 plus a bottle).

And so it is, in a less dramatic way, when anything is offered to the public. When a Rolex watch is offered to you through conventional channels at a conventional price you have no problem at all in believing the proposition because Rolex has devoted a lot of time and money to projecting an image of the product and the organisation that makes and markets it. Rolex enjoys high credibility because it has consciously set out to achieve this. If you do not buy a Rolex it is not because you don't believe what is said about it, it's because it is too expensive or you really are very happy with that Swatch. If a new company sets up to offer a similar product at a similar price it is going to have to work very hard to bring the public to the point where its Product Advertising messages are believed. The decision to buy is strongly influenced by one's belief in what is said and that is largely determined by one's belief in who is saying it.

The 'aura' effect

When buying such an elevated kind of product as a Rolex watch there is, of course, more to the effect of good Corporate PR than supporting the credibility of the advertising message. At the Rolex level one is also being offered all the associations that go along with a glamorous product that is advertised as being worn by the rich and famous. The same 'aura' effect is used to motivate purchasers of fashion garments, jewellery, perfume, cars – and even, these days, once in a while, the performing arts, particularly opera and ballet. For ordinary folk such as we, however, such appeals to people's vanity or personal inadequacy, will never seriously enter into our professional lives because of the kind of arts organisations with which we are associated and perhaps, even, because we believe such an approach fights the philosophy of the business in which we work. However, there is nothing wrong at all with projecting an impression of creativity, originality, high quality and all the other characteristics of a successful arts body: this is the kind of aura we should all strive for.

Using the 'me too' factor

Corporate PR can also be used to portray an image of the arts organisation's typical audience ('our' audience) and this can do much to make it seem more approachable, more accessible, to newcomers who have similar characteristics to that audience. So, in printed material, whether it is intended for Corporate PR or Product Advertising, photographs of audiences and quotations from members of audiences, help to give the impression that the organisation is not obsessed with itself and its products and that people, *real* people are enjoying the experiences it offers. Making use of the 'me too' factor is part of Corporate PR. Here the projected image is a true one and using it in this way should not conflict with any arts marketer's personal or professional philosophy.

Achieving credibility takes time

It is hard to work out just how an organisation achieves credibility; it is something that develops once there is compatibility between the artistic policy, the notion of 'our' audience and the ability to deliver the manifestation of the artistic policy at a level which is acceptable to the audience. This takes time and if steps are not taken to accelerate the process it can take a lot of time and meanwhile audience revenues are lower than they need to be, the abilities of artistic director, general manager, person in charge of arts marketing and other key staff members are challenged by a fearful committee, and the evidence of there developing a contracting economic spiral becomes clearer day by day.

Do not be surprised, therefore, if when an arts organisation sets itself up it experiences frustration when it is convinced that it has the artistic side right and is aiming in the right direction for its audience and it is still not achieving the audience levels it believes it deserves: it may be doing everything right but the wider potential audience does not yet know about it.

Many, many years ago, when I was director of Merseyside Arts Association an artistic director, Alan Dossor, was appointed to the Everyman Theatre in Liverpool. He worked away diligently and rapidly showed that he knew his craft; the theatre was producing good work but not attracting audiences. He discussed the problem with me and he said that what made the situation even more frustrating for him was the certainty he had that his next production, a strange musical piece set in the Second World War called *Soft Or a Girl*, was going to be absolutely wonderful – and if something wasn't done there would be a half empty theatre for, at least, the first week of the three week run. He had hopes that after the first week the show's quality and entertainment value would 'get about' and the old magic of 'word of mouth' would come to his assistance.

It struck me that Alan Dossor and his theatre had a classic credibility problem; what they did was good but not enough people knew that it was good. I suggested that he went away and wrote for the theatre going public of Merseyside a letter which told them exactly what he thought. He had expressed himself to me very eloquently so 'Put it in writing,' I said, 'Tell them – your audience – what they are going to be missing.'

He wrote an extremely convincing letter, direct, graphic and very amusing. I had suggested to him that we used the Merseyside underground railway system (very similar to the London tube system with hundreds of poster sites located very close to waiting passengers so that posters have time to do more than simply shout a brief message) as the means of communication. The letter was turned into a 20 inch by 30 inch poster. The typeface suggested was that of an ordinary 'steam' typewriter. The print was black on white. The letter filled the poster area from top to bottom and from side to side. At the bottom was Alan Dossor's signature. It was densely packed with script and looked unlike any other poster being used at the time by any other advertiser.

The usual campaign to promote the show was already planned and ready to get underway and the poster for the play was scheduled to appear on a number of the underground railway sites. I suggested that the number of posters for the play itself and sites be substantially increased because I thought that whatever else might be the reason for low attendance I wanted to rule out any suggestion that for this important occasion the theatre was under-promoting itself.

The 'letter' poster was then posted alongside the play poster and it also appeared by itself on sites chosen at random. For the four or five week period leading up to this crucial show there was heavy exposure of the play and equally heavy exposure of Alan Dossor's dramatic message: in a city where a very high proportion of workers are commuters using the train it would have been hard to escape Dossor's words.

The show was full on its first night and played to such good audiences that another three week run had to be arranged for it.

I have always believed this to be an excellent example of how credibility can be accelerated by positive intervention.

Credibility can only develop if the ingredients are right

Of course, the Everyman Theatre would not have gone – as it most definitely did – into an upswing of popularity that lasted right up to and beyond Alan Dossor's departure, had the three essential ingredients not been present: the right artistic policy, the right idea of what kind of audience was appropriate to this policy and the ability to deliver the goods. When these three factors are present, this aspect of arts marketing can step in and move things along.

Credibility is almost always low at the beginning and lack of credibility can develop later on

Arts marketers must keenly observe the results of the day to day marketing activities looking for evidence that lack of credibility is restricting the effects that might otherwise be expected. The 'credibility factor' will almost always apply to new organisations no matter how brilliantly well they start. The same is true of any small business. Restaurants probably offer the best example, but any new shop or service is liable to suffer from the same problem. Seen from a customer's viewpoint it makes perfect sense to wait until a new organisation has shaken down, sorted out its staffing problems and until a few people, whose judgement is respected, describe favourable experiences to one. Lack of credibility will almost certainly remain until someone steps in to do something about it.

Matured arts organisations can find the problem develop quite quickly if there is a change of policy or personnel. A shift in artistic direction is obviously the change most likely to cause uncertainty to develop in the minds of the audience that is currently 'ours'. It will happen because there really is a change in artistic policy because, in these matters, a change in artistic director will inevitably change both policy and the manner of its implementation; such is the nature of the arts business. The extent of the change must vary but change there will be – there is no factory turning out artistic clones, thank the Lord. And even if the change is minimal there will be some members of the audience who will object to change for its own sake – it may simply be that they don't like the style of the new person.

Change in arts marketing personnel can also affect audiences. The three ingredients necessary for credibility may all be present and the arts marketing staff may have been doing all that should be done both to market the experiences offered and to keep the audience reminded of the organisation's qualities, but one new person can change all that. A change in the 'language' used in Product Advertising – a new design approach, a different copy-writing style, it can be anything. A change in Sales Promotion methods. A change in the approach to Sales, perhaps new personnel being put on the job without adequate training and preparation, or changes to the facilities for payment that are offered. Unlike the change in artistic personnel, where concomitant change is inevitable, change caused by change in arts marketing personnel can and must be kept to a minimum. Unless the arts organisation is already experiencing a downturn in its fortunes no arts marketer should initiate change in the first months of an appointment; it takes time to assess the situation. The temptation to show off one's brilliance must be resisted until the organisation is convinced that any change will result in improvement.

Influencing a wider world

In commercial Public Relations work reference is often made to the 'image' an organisation has. It is a useful word because it reminds the organisation that it must constantly be aware of how it appears in the eyes of its audience. In the arts our audience – our Available Audience – consists of those who may very well be regular Attenders, either of the organisation or of others offering very similar experiences, or those who are capable of being tempted or nudged into one day becoming Attenders. Whichever end of the spectrum one considers, from the hottest of hot Attenders to the coolest of cool Intenders, all will be influenced by much more than what happens in the auditorium when the curtains go up. If Corporate Public Relations worked only upon the credibility factor using the trio of artistic policy, target audience and effectiveness of policy implementation as the criterion of success, how would it ever work with those who have so far not attended? It must, therefore, move beyond influencing people who are in direct contact with the organisation and its products to the use of the media of communication that can put it in touch with the wider world.

Corporate PR involves every point of contact with the public, direct and indirect – this has a bearing on staffing

Arts organisations usually manage to avoid the charge of modesty and so the idea of active Corporate PR activity comes easily to them but unless the crucial part it plays is fully appreciated it may be more difficult to enshrine it within the arts marketing management structure as an activity that should be practised continually with, for organisations of even quite modest size, at least one person handling it on a day to day basis, whether dividing time between this and other activities or not. On examination of the needs of this activity it quickly becomes clear that the employment only of someone bearing the title 'Press' or 'Media Officer' is inadequate.

Points of contact

Examine the ways in which an organisation comes into contact with its public. There is the direct contact on the home base, as it were, when people come to attend performances and, if the organisation has its own building, for other reasons such as buying tickets, stopping off for a cup of coffee, visiting an exhibition. It all depends on the type of arts organisation. Every point of contact is an opportunity to present the organisation in a favourable light. The appearance and behaviour of personnel is very important so every member of staff who comes into contact with the public should be made aware of their responsibility, their rôle as ambassador for the organisation. Training of sales staff in the box office and ushers is always necessary. When new staff join they should go through an induction course in which their wider responsibilities are clearly established as part of their jobs. In these days where employers are required to provide employees with written statements of employment particulars this may well provide an opportunity of writing such duties into job descriptions and job titles so that any departure from these high standards can be made a serious issue.

For building based organisations the building itself is another point of contact where members of the public may – or may not – be favourably impressed. Cleanliness and order are vital. Imaginative, interesting decor and design will reflect the 'personality' of the building and the organisation that runs it. Clarity in the way different parts of the building are sign posted is equally important. Displays of material that illustrate the organisation's current work and its audiences and its history provide another reason for walking around the place, soaking up its atmosphere and hence slowly becoming part of the organisation's 'family'. For an organisation that values people as much as it does money there should be no difficulty in appreciating the importance of these things.

People approach the organisation from their own home base, communicating by letter and telephone. Impressions are made through these contacts. The letter not answered or unhelpfully answered or – worse still – sent with inadequate postage stamps so that the receiver must pay a surcharge; a telephone that is allowed to ring unanswered for several minutes; the person who answers the call and cannot deal with an enquiry and cannot quickly refer the caller to someone who can; the enquiry that is dealt with brusquely without an attempt being made to find more out about what the caller really wants to know: these are all experiences we have had and we know how our view of an organisation is damaged by them.

(Bad reception of people, in whatever circumstances, is often the direct outcome of the organisation believing itself to be in a Seller's Market and that, as we have learned, is rarely the case and even if it is, such behaviour will quickly turn it into a Buyer's Market.)

There are so many points of contact with members of the public, so many opportunities to influence them favourably, to make them aware of what the organisation does and why it does it; to establish in their minds an impression of a successful business that regularly satisfies its customers; to show that other people, perhaps critics and other arts journalists, have a good opinion of what the organisation has done; perhaps to set the organisation in its national context so they may see their local purveyor of good experiences as part of something much larger and more significant. Such work surely calls for a staff member with specific duties in this area, with a title that accurately reflects the job.

The Press/Media Officer plays a major rôle

People come into contact with arts organisations far more by indirect means, via the media of communication, than they do directly. Their attitudes are very strongly influenced by what they read, hear and see. One has only to overhear conversations around one, in pubs, restaurants, on buses and trains, to learn the opinions people hold, and hold emphatically, on politicians, actors, musicians, personalities of all kinds – that they have never met. Organisations enjoy similar 'third party' reputations; people do hold quite strong opinions on the qualities, or lack of them, of major national companies as well as those organisations in their immediate vicinity.

The rapid development of a good reputation does not happen by accident. If an arts organisation does its job of presenting the arts well, that is if the three ingredients necessary for credibility amongst 'our' audience are present, then the 'word of mouth' effect will undoubtedly contribute to the building of a reputation amongst an ever widening circle within the Available Audience – but the process will take its time. The appointment of a member of staff with responsibility for the development of corporate awareness through use of the media, a Press or Media Officer, will accelerate the building of the favourable reputation that is so important an ingredient in arts marketing.

What does the Press or Media Officer do?

A Press/Media Officer first sets out to bring the name of the organisation into prominence, to make it part of that group of organisations and activities that journalists regard as being relevant and hence important to their readers, viewers and listeners. Having established its status the job is then to spot every opportunity that occurs to bring the organisation before the general public via the media in the form of news reports, articles, profiles, previews *et al*. The importance of journalists in the process should not be under-estimated; they (and their editors, who are also journalists) have their own criteria as to what is important and what is not and very little can be done to change these. So the very first step must be to find out are the 'important' things in their working lives. Then the objective is to bring the organisation, its policy, its personnel and the artists and art it is presenting before the journalists with suggestions as to how they might make interesting subjects for the readers, viewers and listeners.

Developing a *working* relationship with journalists is the clue to success in this area for journalists, no matter how much they might enjoy free lunches and free drinks, are primarily interested in finding good, interesting topics to cover in their newspapers, magazines and TV and Radio programmes. Journalists are generally spoiled in the free food and drink area and it takes far more than the average arts organisation has in its Corporate PR budget to meet the standards set by the big spenders in the commercial area. Concentrate upon the story. Don't waste time trying to persuade a good professional journalist to cover something that just isn't of interest – and if you go on trying then eventually it will be the Press/Media Officer who develops the reputation and when the really good story turns up the journalist just won't bother to return the telephone call.

In developing a working relationship with journalists the best first step is to read what they write, to watch and listen to their programmes. There is no substitute for this as a way of forming opinions as to what is likely to strike a journalist as interesting and hence as a way of working out which journalist to approach with any particular idea. Move on from this to try out ideas with individual journalists. When you obtain a reaction of interest then the best way of keeping the journalist interested is to concentrate on providing the facilities needed to get the job done. The journalist wants you to provide a photograph? Then you provide a variety from which to choose. Wishes to send a photographer? Then make sure the photographer knows how to find you and have the people and things to be photographed ready and waiting at the appointed time – and don't get visibly irritated if the photographer is late. An interview with a famous person? Choose a quiet and comfortable location and don't hesitate to pay for a taxi or hired car with driver to bring interviewer and interviewee together there.

Opera provides an example of how very expensive facilities can be provided to journalists: it is an international art form and for a variety of reasons opera companies usually want to establish their reputations far beyond the countries in which they are based. Coverage of their productions and of the companies themselves in magazines from overseas is of great importance to them. Journalists working in this field are therefore regularly offered free flights, hotel accommodation and tickets by opera companies from other countries in order to encourage the kind of coverage they deem to be important in building their international reputations. Where costs are so high the provision of such facilities are often beyond the willingness of the media to pay and so must be provided by the opera companies.

Press Releases and Press Conferences

It is a matter of personal preference but I believe it is almost always better to try to place ideas with individuals whose interests you have assessed over a period of time. The Press Release, the large scale dissemination of the same information to many journalists and media, may well attract a paragraph here and a paragraph there and may occasionally prompt a response that leads to bigger things but, in my experience, it does so but rarely. The same is true of Press Conferences, where a large number of journalists are gathered together to be fed and watered prior to an announcement the importance of which is usually high in the eyes of the representatives of the arts body and of supreme indifference to those of the media who are present.

These fundamental PR techniques have their place in the routine business of keeping the organisation to the fore but if Corporate PR is about creating favorable awareness of the organisation then to be truly effective it must concentrate on developing ideas that will show off the organisation to the very best advantage and this will almost always call for the larger canvas of the interview or profile or, in the case of Product PR, which we shall soon examine, the preview and the review.

Never forget the objective

It is all too easy for Corporate PR and Press/Media relations in particular to become a routine, a series of activities that may from time to time yield a few column inches in a periodical or newspaper, or a 'mention' on a local radio programme, without there being any specific view of the organisation that is to be projected. Success in this field is not measured in column inches.

Corporate PR should start, and be regularly refreshed, with a session of introspection at which all key members of the management team, including artistic director, discuss and agree upon, as far as possible, what it is about the organisation that is both true and likely to contribute to the build-up of the atmosphere of favourable awareness and credibility. It is a good idea to start such a session with each participant being asked to supply, say, three adjectives or three short phrases, that can honestly be used to describe the organisation – and then to see to what extent the chosen words may be summarised and collected into one statement that can form the basis of the 'image' that is always to be projected, that is always to form the heart of any overt Corporate PR project whether it concerns direct or indirect contact with the Available Audience.

If sessions like this take place the person in charge of Corporate PR will always be sure that what the organisation is saying about itself is both true and likely to contribute to the development of the reputation that everyone concerned has agreed to be desirable.

Help your Available Audience to understand what you are about

As we have seen, developing contact with the Available Audience by indirect means via the media, is but part of Corporate PR; it is sometimes the most visible part and frequently the part that will attract most praise when it succeeds and most criticism when it doesn't, but it is not the whole ball game by any means.

Most arts organisations have artistic policies that are quite subtle when you examine them; they may appear to be simple from the outside (shows go on, tickets are sold, seats are occupied and the process is then repeated) but they are rarely so simple. The organisation has aspirations both in artistic terms and in terms of its audiences and, of course, almost automatically it has financial aspirations. It has strengths that give it the belief that it will achieve its aspirations and it has weaknesses that will hinder it. The organisation is almost never what it appears to be to the people who buy tickets occasionally; only the most devoted of regular Attenders will know what it is about.

Given that there are far more members of the Available Audience who have not (yet) bought tickets for your shows than those that have, there is much to be said for taking positive steps to develop in their minds the view of your organisation that you have decided is the correct one. Others, including the media, may well encourage another view to form, so strike the first blow. A brochure, or booklet, is probably the best way of doing this: it can be made available within the building, it can be distributed when a company is touring and it can be sent by post to people whom you wish to influence. An incidental benefit is that in the production of such a piece of printed matter very many questions as to the character of the organisation, its policy, its history and so on, will emerge and will have to be answered before any further step may be taken. Producing a brochure like this focuses your thoughts so that you have a much clearer – and hence more easily communicated – concept of your organisation. One is thus in a far better position to give talks on the organisation, whether they be on visits to local groups who have expressed an interest or when groups visit the organisation.

For larger organisations the booklet idea may easily be developed into a short video presentation that can be sent out to schools and colleges, local community groups and so on and will always be of use when the organisation is visited by potential sponsors, local politicians and community groups.

Once this clear and uncluttered concept of how best to project the organisation is in your mind it will then filter through to all kinds of people: people responsible for Product Publicity will almost automatically be influenced by it and evidence of it will be seen in the work they produce; senior managers and members of lay committees will be influenced by it when they make speeches and write reports. Even journalists will be influenced by it.

Corporate PR is too important to be allowed to happen by chance or to degenerate into a boring and unimaginative routine of Press Releases and Press Conferences. The arts marketer in charge of this aspect of the business must establish what is to be projected, how best to project it and then must make sure that it is projected using whatever means are appropriate.

Defensive Corporate PR

Arts bodies frequently come under attack of one sort or another. A bad run of performances may start to attract adverse comment amongst audiences and in the media. An application for money to the local authority or funding body may stimulate one of those irritating, intellectually challenged, philistine councillors into launching a diatribe against you and all your works. Perhaps a theatre production ventures into 'dangerous' territory and the self-appointed guardians of public morality go for you – from abusive letters in the newspapers to screaming and shouting placard waving horrors outside the building.

The best defense is to have done all your homework on establishing a sound Corporate PR base as I have just described. If all the arts managers have a common understanding of the organisation's policy and have discussed how the organisation is to be projected – in short, if they are able to speak with one voice – such attacks can easily be handled. The person in charge of Corporate PR should co-ordinate the defense and make sure that if anyone is to speak on behalf of the organisation (it will frequently have to be the artistic director or senior manager) that person is properly briefed and, if necessary, rehearsed.

People who work in PR are usually so addicted to the idea of getting media coverage that they forget that there are times when it is best to decline offers and when under attack it is not wise to agree to every invitation to appear for interview. Journalists are not always fair and they do not always tell you when they plan to attack. If such an invitation comes along it does no harm to involve the journalist in a casual conversation to establish the purpose of the interview. 'Why?' would be my first question, 'Why me? Why my organisation? Why now?' and, most important, 'Who else is going to be involved?'

I was once approached by a journalist who worked for *Time Out*, the London listings magazine. He had heard that I had written a book on arts marketing and wanted to chat about it. He came to my office, then in Floral Street, London, and we chatted away for an hour or so during which time he drank quite a lot of my whisky. We had a few things in common; he had a famous father who had worked in a city where I had worked and who was very much respected by my own father who had often spoken of him – that sort of thing. We seemed to get on quite well. When the piece eventually appeared he savaged the book and he savaged me. In order to make his attack the stronger he extracted from my background one eleven month period of my life when I stopped working in the arts and went to develop an arts sponsorship programme for a tobacco company. The author of the book thus became, not an ex general manager of a chamber orchestra, nor an ex director of a regional arts association, but no more than 'Ex tobacco company PR man'. What else would one expect from someone who had, as it turned out, used his inheritance to help finance the Militant Tendency?

When Danny Newman (of Dynamic Subscription Promotion) appeared in the UK at the invitation of my colleagues and myself, the media started to show considerable interest in arts marketing and one day I was telephoned by a female television journalist who wanted an interview with me. Overwhelmed by such an opportunity (does one never learn?) I agreed and I few days later my tiny office was filled with female interviewer, camera operator, sound engineer and another, much more famous male television interviewer who turned up because, I suspect, he had designs on the female interviewer. It was only when we had started the interview I realised that the woman interviewing me had no idea what arts marketing was and had confused it with arts sponsorship, a topic that I certainly knew about and could speak about but one that interested me not at all. I manufactured a terrible coughing fit to render the filming useless and then, with difficulty, extricated myself from the situation.

A preliminary conversation is to be recommended

Even when one is confident that the interview is going to be capable of being handled successfully, ensure that the canvas is going to be adequate to the needs of your situation. If there is to be a confrontation with an attacker, who is to chair the discussion? Will each side get the same amount of time? Where in the programme will the interview or discussion be slotted? Is it to be at the end so that it may be conveniently ended by running the credits over your side's face just at the critical moment? Is your piece to be used just to add a bit of minority interest balance to a general interest programme largely given over to sport and people who manage to grow carrots that look like Donald Duck?

Finally, remember that the best defence is not always attack; sometimes it pays to lie low and let the storm pass. People's memories are very short.

Public Relations Consultants

Most arts marketing activities are carried out by personnel employed by the organisation; Public Relations is one where it is possible to use either a freelance individual or a consultancy firm to provide the same or similar service. The advantage of retaining an outsider is that, with luck, one should then be in contact with someone of considerably greater experience and skill – and possessing superior media contacts – than one could afford to employ in-house. PR people tend to specialise in sectors and so, for any art form, a PR consultant would know the appropriate journalists and would know how best to interest them.

PR consultants can bring themselves to a point of considerable influence over journalists by assembling a good clutch of newsworthy clients. If the consultant controls access to the famous then, from time to time, journalists must be particularly co-operative if they want that access: the co-operation may very well involve showing interest in another, less famous, client – and that could be your organisation.

Notwithstanding the attractions of being able to buy in more 'PR muscle' (as I am sure it is called, in the industry) I would counsel against using outsiders for Corporate PR work in the arts. Independent PR consultants can rarely afford to spend the time studying the subtle details of an arts organisation's artistic policy and will rarely have the ability to communicate the right image in a way that reflects that subtlety. Corporate PR, involving direct contact with the public and indirect contact via the media of communication, is a day to day business and is better handled within the arts marketing department.

Product PR is a different matter, however, and it is this that we shall consider now.

PRODUCT PUBLIC RELATIONS
(Before reading on it would be helpful to the reader to return to Chapter Three and read again about Product Publicity)

We know that the function of Product PR is to work complementarily with Product Advertising to create effective Product Publicity that will be focused on the Available Audience with the intention of motivating people within that group to *want to buy*. Product Advertising (which will be covered in the next chapter) carries very specific information about the product, carefully chosen and expressed to have the maximum persuasive effect. Product PR sets out to provide the 'climate' in which Product Advertising can flourish. Both activities work on a campaign basis, that is, they have a beginning and they have an end, unlike Corporate PR which continues day after day.

As we have seen in Chapter Three Product Advertising making use, as it is usually forced to do, of media such as small pieces of printed paper and brief messages on television and radio, is extremely restricted in the amount of information it can carry. By concentrating upon the Available Audience as a target it can reduce substantially the amount of explanatory information it needs to convey – it may make some assumptions as to the general level of knowledge within the group about the art form or the performer – and this helps considerably but the highly targeted, brief advertising message, still needs back-up.

The purpose is to motivate; to make people want something so much that they will perform the unnatural act of going to the inconvenience of actually buying a ticket and parting with hard-earned and highly taxed money.

The traditional show business way of achieving this necessarily high level of motivation is to present only performances that have *already* achieved fame by the time they are presented. A 'star' is someone who is already famous and the old-style arts marketing relied upon the built-in fame of the star to attract audiences and did not need to concern itself with much more than putting up a few posters and standing back to allow the queue to form. The show business style of marketing was, and still is, firmly founded on the notion of presenting nothing unless it put one firmly into a Seller's Market – marketing by the presenting organisation was thus reduced to a very basic form of Product Advertising plus a little Product PR and an approach to Pricing that was most definitely based on 'charge as much as you can get.' The arts marketing of today takes as one of its fundamentals the fact that arts organisations are constantly presenting performers and performances that are not famous or are known to comparatively few – and it is harder, far harder.

Fame

To be famous means that you enjoy a high level of public awareness, that people know something about you when your name is mentioned. We generally assume that to be famous also means that you are 'popular', well regarded, highly thought of, admired and so on – in contrast to being infamous. So, when your name is mentioned the mental response is likely to be favorable. When the name of a famous artist is mentioned (alongside information which tells you where, when and how much) the memory recalls all kinds of other impressions about the artist: previous experiences of the artist's work both live and recorded, things one has read and seen on television, things people have told you and, most important of all, you will be prompted into some form of appraisal of how the artist's work affects you. This mental reaction to one name probably takes place in an instant but it will significantly affect your reaction to the proposition that you respond to the information about where, when and how, and to the implicit question, 'do you want some of this?'

Product PR sets out to create fame

If you know nothing about the event that is being advertised then your reaction to it will be ... nothing. How can you react to something about which you know nothing?

Fortunately there are few situations where the arts organisation is presenting something about which *nothing* is known. The human mind relies heavily on association of ideas so if the event itself is unknown then the arts marketer in charge of Product Publicity must look for associations with the forthcoming event that *are* known that will produce some kind of favorable response.

This is why we see completely unknown young musicians who are giving their first London performances digging deeply into their pasts to come up with something or someone with which they can claim an association that their Available Audience will recognise – their teachers, their college, their radio and television appearances (whether their performance of music was involved or not), the fact that their dog is called Chopin and a close relation once dated Liberace.

Arts marketers should be able to do better than this by creating a certain amount of temporary fame at least. The very fact that the performance is being widely advertised will itself generate awareness (and this suggests that the less known an artist or an event is the more Product Advertising is going to be needed – hardly surprisingly). The content and style of the Product Advertising can contribute. Most of all, Product PR can arrange the interviews and the newspaper and magazine pieces that can add flesh to the bare bones of an image that Product Advertising is able to project and the promise of a worthwhile experience it is making.

One should never forget that although this artist or the event may lack fame there is – there must be – a genuine reason, an artistic reason, why the engagement was offered in the first place. It is this that gives the clue as to how the Product PR should be approached. One would start the process, therefore, by asking the artistic director why this event has been included in the programme and then move from this to a conversation with the artist or those that represent the artist. The objective is to obtain the supplementary information that will provide interest for journalists. In my experience the most useful information is discovered through casual conversation and is often not regarded as being of particular relevance or interest by the person questioned.

If useful associations do not present themselves then the use of what may be termed 'endorsement' might be considered, that is having some other person, who is famous or is locally connected and preferably both, being seen to 'welcome' the artist, so that media coverage is focused on her or him and through this means some more information on the artist is given and some extra status given to the forthcoming event. Failing this, one might suggest that the artistic director (who created this problem for you!) might be used to endorse the artist.

Using independent PR consultants

Product PR is, as we shall see in the next chapter, like Product Advertising, forced to work on a campaign basis; that is, there is a beginning and an end to the process and usually the two come far too close together. There is little time for creative thinking and no time at all for reflection. It can be a fairly unsophisticated business. Decisions on Product Advertising are made using the best information that is available and Product PR usually chases along as best it can. Under such conditions it may be wise to seek out extra professional help from outside PR consultants. Specialist PR consultants will have their own direct contacts with journalists and may well do better in the limited time scale than the in-house Press/Media Relations Officer.

Avoid 'ritual' PR activities

I have already expressed my reservations about the widespread use of Press Releases and Press Conferences and it must be said that independent PR consultants are as eager to use them as any inexperienced in-house person. They provide, after all, visible evidence that work is being done and hence justification for the next invoice. Beware of such rituals. With Product PR what matters is results. In PR no-one can guarantee results; it is an extremely uncertain business where one's precious stories are at the mercy of journalists, sub-editors and editors. It is better to start with this assumption and try to pick a PR consultant who has a good track record of success in the particular field and to make it clear that you would rather the time be spent in one-to-one contact with journalists than in time-and-money-wasting exercises that benefit no-one but the instant printer around the corner, the Royal Mail and the caterers.

An example of how unreliable is PR came about when Rhinegold's magazine *Opera Now* organised its first *Operagoer of the Year* competition. The press – including photographers – were invited to meet the prize winners at the restaurant where the awards were to be made at a special lunch. The restaurant was *Terrazza Est* in Fleet Street, London, home of the famous 'Spaghetti Opera' where singers serenade the patrons. The PR consultant had worked hard telephoning the press and doing his utmost to whip up some interest and to secure promises of attendance (one should never rely on a Press Release alone). The interest was fairly limited but the PR man did secure a promise from a national newspaper that it would send a photographer. For the first year of the awards that would do nicely. The photographer turned up on time and took lots of pictures – including several of the extremely attractive young woman who was to sing at the awards lunch a little later on. The photographer's rapidly developing affection for the young woman (clearly not reciprocated) led him into a determined line of chat from which he could not easily be prised. He stayed on and with him stayed his cameras and within them the pictures which, by the time he was persuaded that his future lay not with this young woman, had missed the newspaper's deadline.

Our PR person did as good a job for us as circumstances made possible. We knew the man's background and, indeed, had approached him because we had seen evidence of a creative approach to obtaining media coverage. When choosing someone to help out with or handle Product PR beware of consultants who, in their pitch for the business, list such ritual activities as the production of tee shirts, sweat shirts and badge buttons and suggest that a party be organised – if it is suggested that the party be held on a boat on the Thames with a jazz band present then boot them out instantly for they are time and money wasters.

Corporate PR is the best kind of Product PR

We have seen how good Corporate PR can substantially enhance the reputation of the arts presenting organisation, helping the Available Audience to know you, understand you, like you, respect you, admire you, forgive you, and even defend you. At the beginning of the chapter where these claims were made the final words were

– and make them feel the same way about the things you choose to present

A successful arts organisation, that works in harmony with its audiences, whether they attend regularly or not, will, as time goes by, build up its credibility to the point where its choice of event will automatically define the importance, the status and the quality (the fame, if you will) of what it chooses to present. When it achieves this happy state it will rely far less upon Product PR and Product Advertising because it is trusted and it will be trusted because it has consistently kept the promises made by its Product Publicity.

I have seen this situation develop in many arts organisations, where regular audiences seem almost not to care what it is they are going to experience; they go confident that whatever it is, it will be worth experiencing. This has certainly been the case with my own local theatre where I learned to trust the judgement of the director so much that I would buy tickets for plays and visiting companies that I had never heard of and because of this had some rare and wonderful experiences – I also saw one or two real turkeys but I forgave the director and the theatre in the light of all the good things that had been brought to me.

(It would be useful for the reader now to return to Chapter Seven, 'Dynamic Subscription Promotion' to read again about a technique that relies heavily upon developing the relationship between organisation and audience and almost not at all upon Product PR)

CHAPTER ELEVEN

PRODUCT ADVERTISING

Tells them about it strikingly,
interestingly, persuasively,
briefly, memorably and,
ultimately compellingly

Preface to the chapter

I have written about and lectured on advertising in the arts many times
over the past twenty five years or so and I have only changed my mind
on one aspect of the subject and that is the extent of its potency. Once
I thought advertising, Product Advertising of the kind we shall
consider here, was the power core of marketing and once one had
learned how to use the power people could be persuaded to want what
they previously had not wanted. I realise now that this cannot be so.
When used with the simple intention of persuading people to want to
buy tickets Product Advertising is lost if it is not aimed at those who
are familiar with and are already well disposed towards what we have
to sell. The rôle of PR is a much stronger one in my current thinking
than it ever was before: as the sun of Product Advertising has moved
downwards towards the horizon so the moon of Public Relations has
risen in my world of arts marketing.

The techniques of advertising can, of course, also be directed
towards support of Corporate PR and, as we shall see in Part Three
(which will consist of but one chapter – such is the extent of my
confidence in approaching the subject) towards support of the third
arm of PR, which is focused on what I have chosen to call the

Unavailable Audience, and advertising may then make a substantial contribution.

Preamble to a lecture

Imagine a box. The box is your theatre, or concert hall or art gallery. Now it is empty. At some time in the future your box will contain a play, a concert, an exhibition. The box is in the middle of a community of people, thousands of people none of whom know what is going to happen in that box at some time in the future.

Only you know. You know quite a lot about what is to happen in the box. You know names, titles; you have descriptions, photographs. You may even have seen something very similar before. But you do not know *exactly* what is to happen; that will only be known when it happens. But you know more about it than anybody else.

The thousands of people living their lives around the box may also know something about what is to happen. They too may know names, titles, have read descriptions and seen photographs, but their knowledge is quite irrelevant if they do not know that the something is going to happen in the box.

In this community of people quite a few will have gone into this box and boxes just like this one before and may even be confirmed boxgoers. Others will think that boxes like this one are Good Things and the activities that go on in them are Good Things but may not have gone into a box even once in their lives. Others may only go into boxes for very special things likes pantomimes or Nights Out With Friends. Some may be devoted to only one kind of box activity and never go into them for any other purpose.

Others may be totally indifferent to boxes and what goes on in them. Live and let live is their motto. They don't mind other people going to boxes. They don't object to what goes on in them. They don't care much either way.

There are some people in the community who think that boxes and boxgoing are really a waste of time and money and disapprove. Fortunately there are few of these people.

Now, how are you going to fill this box? How are you going to tell this community of people about the marvellous event that is going to take place? And it is a marvellous event, make no mistake. If it weren't going to be, if you didn't really believe that it was going to be then you wouldn't be very convincing and you probably shouldn't be opening the box for this event anyway. There are a lot of people out there. How are you going to tell them? Equally important, what are you going to tell them?

First, the *how*. Do you stop them on the street? Knock on their front doors? Telephone them? Write to them? You can't. There are far too many of them. You are going to rely upon devices of communication that enable you to speak to a lot of people at once. This will cost you money.

Now you realise that it will be very costly if you try to tell everyone about the event. You may even be thinking that with such a limited capacity to your box there may be no need to tell everyone. Why not just tell those that you know who are regular boxgoers? A little twinge of conscience here because you know that you really ought to try to give everyone the chance of finding out.

So what do you do? You realise that life is one long compromise and you do the best you can. It occurs to you that some communication devices are more expensive than others in terms of how many people they can help you speak to at once and in their ability to convey the sort of things you want to say to them. It also occurs to you that you may need to spend less time and energy and persuasiveness speaking to the regular boxgoers than you would to the people who teeter on the brink of decision. As for the indifferent ones, it will take you longer and cost more money to talk even a small percentage of them into coming into your box. And as for those who are just plain hostile ... well, it depends on how much of a crusader you are.

You end up creating a communication mixture in which you blend together different communication devices (which by now you are calling 'media'), different ways of saying what you have to say, different groups of people to whom you wish to speak and different levels of cost according to which media you use and how you wish to use them.

Now, the *what*. You know a lot about this event. Are you going to try to tell everyone everything you know? Of course not. No-one ever tells anyone everything they know. All communication involves selection. You want to do more than merely *tell* people about the event. You know that amongst the in-crowd, the real boxgoers, there are quite a few to whom all you have to do is whisper the basic facts but most people are going to need more than this. There are other people clamouring for their attention so whatever you tell them has got to be selected so that it gives them the basic facts and it has got to **grab their attention and turn them on!**

Whatever you say to these people, and however you say it, you must be persuasive. You know it is going to be a marvellous event and you must communicate this to the people.

Some problems start to occur to you. You really would like to tell people more about the box itself; it is a very nice box and some very interesting people work there. Forget it. That is not your job. You have a close professional colleague who will do that for you while you are turning people on. What about money? How much money can you spend? You will be told how much by your boss who is in charge of marketing budgets. You will also be told how much the admission charges will be and all the other little details.

How long do you have? From now until when the box opens. You become aware of the time problem. Suppose you start your persuasion now, suppose you walk out now and turn on the first six people you meet – get them really excited by the idea of going into the box in so many weeks time. Isn't there the chance of a slip 'twixt cup and lip? What happens if tomorrow someone else comes along and talks them into going to the Caged Bird Exhibition held on the same day? You realise that there is more to it than just plain persuasion. Somehow you, or your organisation, has got to make it very easy for your turned-on people to buy the tickets for the marvellous event. That is another problem of course and you cannot be totally responsible for solving it but you will realise that it isn't enough to persuade just once. You must keep up a constant barrage of persuasive communication, some of it specifically directed, some of it sown broadcast, so that people start talking about the marvellous event that is going to happen in your box. At the same time you, or someone else, is providing every opportunity for those people to clinch the matter by parting with their hard-earned cash. When they have done that you can relax – until next time.

(Marketing The Arts: Keith Diggle pub. The City University 1976))

A matter of direction

The conflict of ideas about marketing the arts has at its heart the matter of direction. There is no real conflict over whether or not one should set out to motivate, through what I choose to call Product Publicity, the people who make what I choose to call the Unavailable Audience. Not even the most self-confident large scale commercial operator would try to sell candy to diabetics or sexual instruction manuals to celibates; the person with only profit in mind leaves it at that and concentrates on pushing products and services out to satisfy needs, wants, tastes, foibles, fancies and whathaveyou. In the short term the arts marketer basically does the same thing but always has in mind the Unavailable - the *presently* Unavailable Audience – with a view to finding ways of persuading them to try a little taste, which they might enjoy and who knows what might follow from that? Arts marketers have a scope that extends beyond their own organisation of the time; they are part of a wider industry that includes not only those who select, make and present art but those who fund it as well. This industry has, without any doubt at all, responsibility for proselytising amongst the Unavailable Audience – although the extent to which it is able to carry it out is extremely limited and likely to become even more so.

If serious conflict exists within our industry it is on the extent to which present resources should be devoted to our missionary duties. There is, of course, to be found here and there the naive wing of the industry that goes on presenting arts events with a notion of who should make up 'our' audience that is pitched deep inside the zone of unavailability.

It is when we consider how best to tackle the Available Audience that there is some disagreement. If we go along with my very simple way of dividing this group into Attenders and Intenders there is no disagreement over how we should address the Attenders who are known to us and are easily contactable; one should never take these people for granted but obviously they are going to be far less resistant to our honeyed words than people who are more distant. This leaves only the Intenders.

This concept of the Intenders is a loose one and is intended to be so. So is the division between them and the Attenders because people move between the categories as their personal circumstances, tastes, knowledge, aspirations, experience and so on, influence their behaviour. The whole idea of the Available Audience is based on behaviour as well as attitude.

However defined, how best to approach the Intenders? That is one question that comes up time and again when Product Publicity is being discussed. There is one school of thought that says, in essence, 'See where your Attenders live and you will find Intenders nearby' and then applies analysis to post codes and comes up with geographical areas, defined by post codes, that should be more productive than others. The same school of thought argues that if market research can tell us some of the lifestyle characteristics of the Attenders (what kind of cars, what level of education, what jobs, number of children and so on) this will guide us to our Intenders.

I have no problem with any approach that helps one to narrow down the field. The 'see where they live' approach may produce results that are sufficiently better (than an apparently more random method that I shall come to) to justify the costs of buying into the systems, paying for consultants, hiring mailing lists and so on. When I lived in the charming little town of Gravesend in Kent the mailing list of London's Philharmonia Orchestra showed two subscribers in the road where I lived: one was me (and I was the orchestra's marketing consultant but nevertheless a paying customer) and the other was a 'real' subscriber. Statistically this road offered high potential for anyone promoting classical music for there were no other subscribers living in the town. In fact, between my house and the other person's house on a very long road, there was a very, very high proportion of people whose cultural background did not (I suspect) include listening to classical music of any country. The lifestyle approach is appealing until one asks how one is to make use of the knowledge so gained. With the post code approach one can organise distribution of Product Advertising material quite simply and cheaply but if you find, for example, that many of your Attenders have incomes greater than, say £30,000 a year and have two children in their teens, then how does one isolate the other, non-attending, people within the catchment area with those characteristics? I'm sure a consultant could tell us – but so far, as far as I am concerned, one hasn't.

If research can tell us something as simple as what newspapers and magazines my Attenders read then this will be of genuine benefit. One of the components of Product Advertising is the selection of media which will efficiently (that is, with the minimum of wastage) carry the persuasive message to people who are most likely to respond; newspapers and magazines do seem to attract readers with similar interests and similar levels of interest and thus may well appeal to both Attenders and Intenders.

Common characteristics between Attenders and Intenders

In terms of everything that matters to us Attenders and Intenders have the same characteristics of attitude towards whatever it is that we are hoping to persuade them to want to buy; the only difference lies in the degree to which each individual feels interested, enthusiastic, passionate about the art form and the particular manifestation of it that we want them to see and hear. It may be convenient to see the Available Audience as a spectrum of enthusiasm with one end labelled

The Hot End
Love it; very knowledgeable about it; attend many times; collect programmes; read about it; ask for books on it at Christmas; talk about it; are members of the Friends; may very well always opt for best seats (but not necessarily); are on several mailing lists; are prepared to travel outside the catchment area to experience more; may be financially well-off but not necessarily (passion may put the art form high on the spending priority list); would list it as an interest in a CV or a Lonely Hearts advertisement; ... and so on.

and the other ...

The Cool End
Approve of it; know a little; used to attend similar events when younger but hasn't much since marriage and children (or has only recently moved to the area and has been busy with the garden); middle to high disposable income but spend little or nothing on buying tickets; tend to think of attendance in terms of special occasions; read newspaper reviews occasionally; might talk about it under certain circumstances but reticent in the company of Attenders; possibly more interested when star performers are involved but not necessarily; think of themselves as being (for the want of a better word) 'cultured'.

The idea of a spectrum of course implies a straight line, left and right, top and bottom, hot and cold – but we are only looking for a simple model that will help us in our thinking; you may well identify other groups of characteristics, so think of this exercise as 'staking out' the outer extremes of your Available Audience rather than merely the ends of a line. For example, there is a well known phenomenon in which, as they grow into late adolescence and young adulthood, the children of parents who are definitely within the Unavailable Audience group, develop favourable attitudes towards the arts in general or one art form in particular: it may start off by being a contrarian reaction to parental attitudes and behaviour but it often ends by being a genuine love for the subject. Such a group may be ...

Rebels With A Cause

Can come from any socio-economic background; places of residence give no clue as to attitude or behaviour in relation to the art form; disposable incomes completely unpredictable but as all overheads are paid by parents may well be spending large sums on recorded music (usually cult stars-of-the-moment) and clothes; will tend to favour avant-garde, multi-media, the more obscure the better, manifestations; social life based on pubs and clubs; probably well educated in spite of voice, dress and behaviour that suggest otherwise; hard to attract to events that appear to them to be 'straight', middle-class, conventional etc. but once they have found the way in may well stay; high potential for developing into Attenders later on.

Such a picture may well stimulate thoughts of other young people and if a group of characteristics come to mind then the arts marketer who is trying to develop an approach to Product Advertising will find it a very useful exercise to list the characteristics, to make a thumbnail sketch. Could there be other groups? A group of people who were once Attenders but are now older, retired, perhaps living alone, with limited income and difficulties with travel in the evenings? Do some readers of *The Oldie* magazine constitute such a group?

Such group definitions contribute to decision making in arts marketing but are, of course, not of much value unless there is some medium or system of distribution that will reach the groups.

Thinking of one's Available Audience in this way is not so very far from the kind of socio-economic analysis that is used to sell and buy advertising in the commercial sector and even there I understand that it is sometimes necessary to think beyond the As, Bs, C1s and so on. In the Republic of Ireland the advertising industry has the usual categories but has found it necessary to add two more: rich farmers and poor farmers. This is very close indeed to the approach I am suggesting.

A common language

If one has a clear idea of the people one is aiming for – and the notion of 'our' audience, the Available Audience, and its sub-groups helps one to develop this – then it becomes far easier to speak a common language that is acceptable to the extremes, the categories of people that you have defined. Language in the advertising context of course means words, written and spoken, and it also means style, illustration and design (including typography), and, where radio and television are involved, accent, music and the whole gallimaufry involved in presenting dynamic statements.

This does not mean that the language employed has to be narrow, highbrow or exclusive – that is, focused on the *cognoscenti* – it means that assumptions may be made about the level of knowledge and awareness of the target audience – that is, they have a basic knowledge of the art form to which they can relate the advertising message. These assumptions influence both content and style of the advertising message.

It is extremely helpful to be able to make such assumptions when deciding what to say and how to say it in an advertising campaign. Anyone who has ever sat down, pen in hand, trying to conceive a way of describing a forthcoming event that is brief and to the point and is persuasive, has come up against the inevitable barriers of understanding that may be anticipated in a target audience that is assumed to be 'the public at large'. Working, as we do, with artists and events that are usually not household words, the questions, 'Will they know who this is? If I compare the artist with another, more famous, artist, will they know who she is? Will they have heard of this international competition or award that the artist has won? Does it matter if they haven't? This is a first play, with a most unhelpful title, being performed by a newly formed theatre company; how do I make it sound attractive?' ... and so on.

At this point, when the advertising message is being created, the Unavailable Audience is ignored. It is as simple as that.

The language, as I have said, should not be narrowly focused. If one refers back to the group I termed 'The Cool End' of the Available Audience range, one can see that a fairly broad approach would be necessary to tap into the level of knowledge acquired from dipping into newspaper reviews and casual conversations with friends.

(As a way of becoming familiar with appropriate languages I would recommend first the study of Product Advertising material put out by other arts organisations, looking out for examples of good and bad in terms of direction. I would also strongly advise regular reading of a much wider range of newspapers than one's own taste would normally lead one to. Too many arts marketers in the UK read only *The Guardian* whilst their customers are reading not only *The Times*, *The Independent*, and *The Daily Telegraph* but also *The Daily Express* and *The Daily Mail* and perhaps even *The Daily Mirror*. The extent and quality of arts coverage in these papers will give an excellent impression of how the newspaper assesses the tastes of its readership – and newspapers are more often right than they are wrong in such matters.)

The brochures generated by the Dynamic Subscription Promotion approach illustrate how broadly one may aim if the whole Available Audience is the target. Colourful, well illustrated, exciting, laden with Sales Promotion ideas of all sorts, with information repeated several times with different levels of detail, with the merits of the events and the subscription scheme trumpeted loudly, they demonstrate perfectly how focused advertising with this target in mind needs not be boring. In inexperienced hands, of course, damage may be done; if one is thought to be aiming for the Unavailable Audience by the Available Audience then many of its members (fearful snobs that they are) will turn up their noses at what you have to offer.If one group of people that you are aiming for is addressed in a language it perceives to be inappropriate to itself and to the art form it has regard for, then it will probably reject what is being offered. This applies, naturally, also to the reaction of the Unavailable Audience (fearful philistines that they are), which has always rejected material aimed at the other sector.

(In the early days of DSP in the UK there were several instances when regular audiences for opera, music, theatre and dance were being targeted for subscription and were exhorted to DIAL THE HOTLINE NOW! This may very well have gone down well in other parts of the world where language is racier but in London, in the early eighties (and, indeed, today) such a slogan might well have done more harm than good.)

Creating the message

At the heart of the campaign is the view of the event that is to come that has been chosen as the one that will most likely persuade members of the Available Audience to want to be present, to want to buy tickets. Because this 'view' must be carried by media that can only convey a little, it must be capable of being expressed briefly. As I said at the beginning of this chapter it must be stated strikingly, interestingly, briefly, persuasively, memorably and, ultimately compellingly. When this brief message impacts upon people it must strike an instant chord, and if it does not then it will be disregarded.

The term used for this brief message in the commercial advertising sector, a term I have used in my earlier books and in my lectures, is 'Unique Selling Proposition'. It uses the word 'selling' rather loosely but as the end result is to be a *sale* (and never forget this) there is no harm in having this constant reminder of what we have to achieve from all this.

'Unique' because only one view is capable of being communicated effectively. This does not mean, as people sometimes interpret it to mean, that only one word may be used. It is the 'proposition' that is unique and this word is used in the same way as I use 'view' – a concept that has been created – selected – out of all the information that is available about the event that is to come.

Too much information is the problem. Not only information that is provided for you by others but also all the associations in your own mind that clamour for attention; some will help and some will not. Out of this mixture of knowledge and impressions and feelings something must come that can 'turn on' members of your Available Audience.

(The arts marketer, looking for the right message, should never forget that Product Advertising does not operate in a vacuum; it is not supposed to achieve its objective alone. There is always Product PR standing by to flesh out the bones, to convey the information that will create the climate of awareness in which Product Advertising will flourish.)

The process of creating the 'view', the Unique Selling Proposition, calls for the talents of a storyteller; someone who can set the scene for a whole novel in one opening sentence. Or a brilliant dinner party conversationalist who can summarise a view of a performance in a few well-chosen words.

When I wrote of Corporate PR I suggested asking members of the organisation to come up with adjectives that best described how they would want it to be regarded by 'our' audience. The same method can be used for coming up with the 'view' that you wish to project. In my lectures I often use a poster that advertises a performing artist of whom no-one present is likely to have heard and I ask them to suggest adjectives that describe how they see him, what they pick up of him, from the poster. Of course this is reversing the process but it illustrates well how one apparently simple 'view' of an artist can incorporate many shades, many closely connected but different impressions. If everyone present writes down one adjective after having looked at the poster for, say, thirty seconds it is remarkable how reading the chosen words aloud reveals a consistency in what 'comes out of' the poster.

(It is equally interesting for me then to ask for those people to write down 'Yes' or 'No', whether the advertising intention of the poster made them want to experience the event or not – because the poster contains my 'view' of the artist and I wrote the words and designed it.)

Reversing that process, choosing the adjectives first, helps form the 'view' as the arts marketer forms a sort of mental consensus, a coherent composite of what is to be conveyed to the Available Audience. Some of the words will inevitably form part of the advertising message, others may influence the overall language in terms of content and style.

Putting the message into a context that will persuade and sell

It is one of the problems faced when attempting to break down an activity like arts marketing into its component parts so that they may be examined individually; how to explain the way in which each part works with each other part. In order to give emphasis to the objective of Product Publicity one must concentrate upon its persuasive rôle. One then considers Sales. In practice, of course, they must work side-by-side. Product Advertising material must do more than bring people to the point of buying, it must provide alongside the means of buying. Essentially the analysis is about the ideas of arts marketing and the point of creating the distinctions between them is so that each idea is given proper emphasis. In the past I have made the mistake of calling the pieces of paper used in Product Advertising 'sales material' which is fine in that it gives good emphasis to the end of the process – but it omits the beginning of it.

Once the advertising concept has been chosen it must then be realised in the form of words and design and when this is done the final work must have certain vital characteristics: it must say what it has to say ... strikingly, interestingly, persuasively, briefly, memorably and compellingly. Your Product Advertising material has to fight for attention with everyone else's Product Advertising so it must be striking, it must make people aware of it at first sight. It must be interesting so that it draws them into a more intimate form of contact. That it must be persuasive goes without saying. It must stay in the mind for a while at least because the act of purchase is never as instant as we should like it to be; it must be memorable therefore. Brevity we have already covered as a demand made on us by the limitations of the media we use. Compellingly – so that people who have been brought to the point of wanting to buy feel that they must buy now if they are to secure their right to the experience and *the best seat*.

The old mnemonic is worth remembering: AIDA. Product Advertising sets out to create **A**wareness, generate **I**nterest, stimulate the buying **D**esire and motivate to take the **A**ction of buying.

Stimulating the buying desire

This part of the book would be a good place to stop and return to

Chapter Six, which covers Sales Promotion. The 'view' of the product, the USP, that has been selected must take the principle rôle in the persuasion process but it does not have to work alone (unless you perceive a Seller's Market to exist). Sales Promotion, as we have seen, is about adding value to this experience you are trying to persuade people to want so that they want it even more, so that they are eager to move faster to secure it. Whatever Sales Promotion ideas have been considered, the time when the Product Advertising campaign is being conceived is when they should be reconsidered, shaken out and held up alongside the 'view' to see if they are appropriate and to assess their chances of helping the process along.

Conveying the message

Do not forget that the advertising language consists of more than words. Typography can change a sweet APPLE into a sour APPLE and can move a situation back in time by decades and even move it forwards up to a point. Colour can change SUMMER into WINTER. An illustration, a simple line drawing, can say more than fifty words. Bring words together with typography, illustration and colour, through the design process and you have a potent instrument of persuasion.

The 'view' you wish to project is the brief you either use to guide yourself in the physical realisation of the Product Advertising material, should yours be the kind of arts organisation that expects you to do this kind of work, or others, whether working within or without the organisation. Our arts business has a strange way of approaching this use of specialist skills when compared with the commercial advertising sector which, at this stage, would call in the skills of a designer and a word-smith, a copywriter. The two skills go together with the copywriter taking the brief (expressed perhaps as I have suggested, with a short string of adjectives or descriptive phrases) and then, working closely with the designer, coming up with visual ideas that incorporate the words and enhance their meanings. In our world the arts marketer seems to be expected to produce the words with the designer then called in, often from outside, to do the *real* work and, because of the professional status the designer has, is given a remarkable amount of influence over how the finished item will look.

There is no harm in writing the words yourself; practice will improve your craft. There is no harm either in using these words to form a very distinct brief for the designer *which you will insist is followed.* Far too many designers are given a free hand, even to the extent that they will change words – the copy – in an advertisement, given half the chance. If yours is the kind of arts organisation where visual perfection is not expected of you then there is no harm at all in your doing the design work yourself as well. You are the one who has the USP in mind, you are probably the best one to realise it. Even if you have few practical skills you can compensate for this by learning how to use the extremely clever computer programmes that exist today to aid design and learning about the technical processes involved in printing.

Whoever is to handle this responsibility of translating concept into reality must also have full regard for the Sales responsibilities carried by the material being produced. So important is this that one could fairly argue that the entire exercise has been a waste of time if the Sales element is not given its rightful place. Chapter Four, *The Fundamental Ideas of Sales*, goes into some detail about this and could profitably be re-read at this stage.

Above all you must want to make this Product Advertising campaign succeed. You must be able to see what it is about this forthcoming event that is most likely to appeal and then bring energy and imagination to bear on it. One cannot deny that this part of the process calls for a high degree of creative talent which is why, in the large scale commercial advertising world, great store is set by people who can extract the persuasive nugget and then display it through words and design so that people want to have it.

Delivering the message to the Attenders

Is no distinction to be made between the Attenders and the Intenders? Are they to be addressed in exactly the same way? So far in this chapter my concentration has been upon the Available Audience as a whole because I wanted to establish beyond any doubt the essential points about the message to be delivered and the language to be used to deliver it. When it comes to the physical delivery of the message via the various means we have available to use we must start to think of the target not so much in terms of attitude and behaviour but in terms of how easy they are to make physical contact with.

In a well managed arts organisation that has been in business for more than a year or so the names and addresses of Attenders will have been recorded. Every time a purchase is made the Sales staff will have noted names and addresses, from credit and cash card purchases, from cheque purchases (would you mind writing your name and address on the back of the cheque, please?) and by directly asking purchasers paying with cash to complete a mailing list slip. Modern computerised ticketing systems record names and addresses along with details of the event for which the tickets were purchased, price paid, number of tickets purchased and so on. From the moment it opens up its shutters the arts organisation that wants to succeed sets out to 'capture' every hot one, every person that has responded to its Corporate PR and its Product Publicity.

For the Attenders there is only one really effective medium and that is the piece of Product Advertising, inside an envelope, delivered through the letter box. Very sensibly the arts industry has paid a lot of attention to what experts in Direct Mail have to say and we have all learned something of value from them. If there is a snag it is that nothing stands still in marketing and the techniques that worked a few years ago have by now become clichés. The Direct Mail industry, enthusiastically encouraged by Royal Mail, took a very high profile ten years or so ago, with seminars being held, guidance manuals being published and so on. It did seem that if one produced a 'sales letter' that ran to four pages of A4, that followed the formula WISCDA (get on the **W**avelength, generate **I**nterest, **S**ell benefits, add **C**onviction and so on), with sub-headings printed in a different colour, with a facsimile signature, and then put it into an envelope with at least three other pieces of paper, success would be assured. But everyone did it and the general public has become resistant even to the point of joyfully embracing the term 'junk mail' and consigning anything that might fall into this category to the bin, unopened.

However, arts marketers know that they must keep on the move, in their Sales Promotion methods (ever changing – keep them guessing) and in how they 'talk' to their customers. In terms of the medium of communication, the means of carrying the message, however, the envelope addressed to an Attender, with the real McCoy therein, is the bullet aimed precisely at the middle of the target and cannot be bettered.

Delivering the message to the Intenders

(I apologise to the reader for already having suggested in this chapter that the memory be refreshed by re-reading earlier chapters and for suggesting now that Chapter Seven, *Dynamic Subscription Promotion*, be looked through once more. The DSP method addresses the challenge of how to communicate with the Intenders in a most universal way.)

There will always be Intenders; one never knows how many, nor do we know very much about them. Intenders are, of course, an hypothesis. We have to assume they exist and we have to assume that there are plenty of them. We have to assume that they exist because if they didn't, where did the Attenders come from? (It's a bit like old time religion, isn't it?). People are not born Attenders after all; they become Attenders.

An arts organisation gathers to itself more Attenders as it develops and as it does its arts marketing problems change; the problems are more about how to keep Attenders attending, how to keep them interested, how to develop their tastes along the lines of the organisation's artistic policy, how to persuade them to stump up more money, how to wean them off Sales Promotions that are becoming relatively expensive in relation to the job they have to do, and so on. In theory, an arts organisation could bring itself to the point where it has a sufficiently large pool of Attenders to enable it to stop spending money on trying to convert Intenders. Our major theatre companies in the UK appear almost to have reached that point with considerable reliance upon direct mailing to known purchasers and then a basic 'broadcast' (in the sense of being aimed generally at the public at large) campaign that is used to top up the attendance figures by pulling in Attenders from other countries (who are, while they are holidaying in the UK, in relation to us, Intenders) and any other Intenders who happen to swim into the net.

References to 'pool' and 'net' make one think of fish and that is no bad mental model upon which to base one's marketing strategy. Every fish that is caught goes into the pond where it can be nurtured and where it can be encouraged to eat a more varied and interesting diet. Every so often one sets out to catch more fish – and then, into the pond they go. (The sensitive reader will appreciate that in writing of the captured fish being *fed* I have resisted the temptation to make use of the American expression 'Easy as shootin' fish in a barrel' which is actually a far more satisfying and accurate a metaphor.)

To put one's Product Advertising message before the Intenders requires the use of media that are, in physical terms, broadcast. Earlier I referred to the Attenders being reached by a bullet, a message that is most accurately targeted, both physically and in terms of content and style of the message. For the Intender the appropriate metaphor is the shotgun, the weapon that blasts out in more or less the right direction and might, with luck, hit a sparrow or two.

I have already written of methods which attempt to narrow down the field by examining the residential characteristics of one's Attenders and looking for Intenders in the same part of town, and other approaches based on other characteristics to do with disposable income, socio-economic profiles, lifestyles and so on. Try these methods if you wish but all they will do – may do – is to limit the width of the shotgun's blast and, in so doing, may easily pass over individuals of potential.

The physical methods of communication must be as broadcast as can possibly be, as can possibly be afforded. As in DSP, the ideal is to reach every person in one's catchment area, Available Audience and Unavailable Audience alike. For an organisation that is promoting many events during the year such a vast communications project could not possibly be attempted for every individual event so they must be 'bundled', packaged into seasons or series or festivals, and these must be marketed. With this strategy in mind one can easily appreciate the attractions of DSP which is the quintessence of 'bundling' combined with all the energetic Sales Promotions, lively Corporate PR, and so on that are most likely to excite and motivate an Intender.

Each organisation and each arts marketer must make their own decisions about what it is that is to be marketed but, whatever that is to be, if the Intenders are to be aimed for then the entire catchment area must be aimed for – as often as can be afforded.

This suggests that there is to be no targeting at all. This is far from being the case. The targeting lies not in the physical means of carrying the message but in the message itself, its content and its style. It is the message that finds the target, triggering responses in the minds of people who already have an inclination towards the subject, who have some knowledge of the subject, who have aspirations towards the subject, those who have just been waiting for a 'way in', those who discovered only yesterday that they no longer had need of a baby sitter and that life could begin again, those who read a magazine article about the subject only last week and, gosh, 'What a coincidence, here it is in my own town!'

So the media may be brochures and letters within envelopes put into every letter box within the catchment area, they may be the same brochures and letters left in public places like libraries and colleges of further education, they may be posters that shout their brief messages that give the brochures and letters a context, they may be large newspaper advertisements (and here, remember, you may, most effectively physically direct your message by virtue of the kind of readership the newspaper has). Radio and television too, to give a wider exposure of the poster's shout.

Add to this scattering of the seed (it is an area rich in metaphors, is it not?) the energetic Product PR that tells your Intenders, wherever they may be, in their magazines and newspapers and on radio and television, much more about the wonderful experiences that are within their grasp than any piece of Product Advertising can ever hope to do.

Add to this a price (or prices, if you must) that is eminently affordable because the value of what you are offering is so high!

Add to this the Sales Promotions that pull the Intenders closer to the moment of commitment by offering opportunities not only to secure the experience but to secure the best possible experience simply by acting immediately and, on top of that, to save lots of money by ... acting immediately or by opting for an even better seat or by bringing a couple of other people. And on top of all this the chance to win a wonderful holiday (just a bit of fun, does no harm) with every ticket purchased.

Add to this constant Corporate PR that has made the Intenders very aware of the organisation, what it is, what it believes in, what it does and what it aspires to do. Its artistic director is quoted in the local newspaper at least once a week. Members of the organisation regularly give talks to the young, the old, members of this group and that group. Local schools invite members of the organisation to give talks and hold workshops and even to present prizes at sports day. The organisation is regularly mentioned in the national press and the cuttings are there, much magnified, in the organisation's windows for all passers-by to see. This organisation is part of the community; it is known, liked and, above all, it is trusted.

Add to this an effortless system of purchase that requires almost no effort. A telephone call ... now, while you are in the mood. A completed slip of paper sent off to a Freepost address (or, better still in a First Class Business Reply envelope). Pop around to the arts centre, the theatre, the festival box office, straightaway – we are here waiting to help you secure what you want and, if you do not know what you want, to help you come to a decision about what you want.

You see, Product Advertising may be weak but if it is planned together with and takes place alongside all the other arts marketing activities as part of a co-ordained plan, it can be very powerful.

(It may also be of some consolation to arts marketers to be reminded that their richer advertising agency cousins and their clients in the commercial sector spend their lives looking for something new to say about products and services that are often quite old. Do motor cars really have to change every year? Are they substantially different after the change? Does the safety razor really need to be reinvented just before Christmas every year? They change because there will be nothing new to say about them if they do not change. In the arts every Product Advertising campaign is different and new because the product is always different and new. This is a powerful advantage.)

PART THREE

THE UNAVAILABLE AUDIENCE

CHAPTER TWELVE

EDUCATIONAL PUBLIC

RELATIONS AND THE

UNAVAILABLE AUDIENCE

*On 5 February 1988, a symposium called CHANGING THEIR MINDS –
TOWARDS A NEW AUDIENCE was held in Glasgow under the auspices
of the Scottish Arts Council in association with the Society of Arts Publicists
(which metamorphosed into the Arts Marketing Association towards the end
of 1993 – for a brief account of my early attempts to effect this change and of
my involvement in setting up the symposium see Appendix Two). The subject
was how attitudes of indifference and hostility towards the art forms might be
changed so that the everyday techniques of arts marketing might have a
chance of success. Nearly 160 people attended. I gave the keynote address and
my words then still sum up my views today.*

Sad to say, the symposium itself was very much a curate's egg. The
morning was given over to presentations from three lecturers from the
marketing department of the University of Strathclyde who appeared
not to have read their brief; they addressed the assembly of
experienced arts managers as though they were first year marketing
students and delivered a standard, orthodox view of marketing in the
commercial marketplace whilst totally avoiding the topic which those
arts managers had collectively travelled thousands of miles to consider.
Later in the day Jeremy Shaw of Smith Bundy and Partners who had
worked on campaigns for the GLC, Greenpeace and Friends of the
Earth, gave an excellent account of how he set about changing people's
attitudes to important matters and John Archer of BBC TV (Executive
Producer. Music and Arts) spoke of how his programmes opened
doors for people unfamiliar with the arts. Contributions from Kathryn
McDowell, John Matthews and Don Keller, experienced arts
marketers of considerable standing, were excellent and with those of

Shaw and Archer saved what could have been a disastrous day.

At the end of my opening speech I suggested a way in which the Arts Council of Great Britain could make a major contribution by organising the large scale campaigns to 'win hearts and minds' that ordinary arts bodies could not hope to do. The suggestion was not taken up: I do wish that the Arts Council had done so for if it had I do believe that it would by now be enjoying far greater esteem than it presently does and we might know far more than we do about how this special form of Public Relations work can help us build audiences.

This is what I said then:

Changing their minds - towards a new audience

There are two things that I want to come out of this symposium. The first is a widespread acknowledgement that the methods of product marketing with which we in the arts industry are now familiar are, for all practical purposes, impotent in the face of attitudes that are not favourable to what we are trying to market. I say this because I am tired of seeing us waste money, time and effort in trying to sell to people who won't buy because they don't want what we are selling.

I suppose that if I were to say that you can't sell a refrigerator to an eskimo there would be someone here who would cite a case where this has been done but even the most gullible of eskimos only buys one refrigerator in a lifetime. Trying to persuade someone who has *made up their mind* about classical music (that is, they don't like it) to buy not only one ticket but to go on buying tickets for years and years is harder – impossible unless you set about it in a very different way.

And you won't do it by putting leaflets in their hands or by sticking posters up by their 'bus stops or sending them wonderfully conceived mail shots with four page letters with facsimile signature in blue ink.

Our attitudes, our beliefs, our tastes, are the things that bind us to other people and the things that make us different. Without them, what are we? We cling passionately to our attitudes because they help to define who we are.

My point is a simple one; that however attitudes are formed they are often held strongly and this can be as true of attitudes towards those experiences we collectivity under 'the arts and entertainment' as they are towards, say, politics. And you don't make a Labour voter vote Tory by waving pictures of Margaret Thatcher at him.

We say we want 'new audiences' but we are imprecise as to what we mean. To most arts managers a new audience member is simply someone they haven't sold a ticket to before. If the objective is to fill the seats *now* then what is wrong with that? The odds are that this new audience member comes equipped with a set of attitudes that already make this particular art form quite acceptable, thank you. The kind of basic product marketing that we have become quite good at over the years is designed to winkle out new customers like this. People who have just moved into the area. People whose children have grown up just enough to be left with a baby-sitter. People who have started to earn more money. People who are bored with television. These people are reached via our media and they respond to the message and the language of our advertising. They are not new to the arts so much as just new to us.

If there are enough of these people and if you are skilled enough to attract them and hold on to them, why do more?

Well, we take a longer term view of things in the arts. We are product led. No sooner do we get our marketing act together than the people who make the stuff move the goalposts. And we are missionaries. We want converts.

So we look further afield. Beyond the attenders. Beyond the intenders, to those who don't care and those who can't bear it. We want to be able to make these people – some of these people – *change their minds*. We want to make them take a fresh look at what we have to offer, make them take another look at their prejudices (for most of the attitudes we are trying to combat are based on prejudice – but not all), make them feel inclined to give it a try. It is only when they are in a receptive frame of mind that our bag of marketing tricks can succeed.

The second thing I want to come out of this symposium is how we are to do this – how we, as an industry and organisation by organisation, are to bring about in the minds of people a change in the way they regard the arts – or the art forms in which *you* are professionally involved – so that they are not seen as always boring, or always impossibly highbrow, or always stupid; so that they become *desirable*.

211

I want these art forms to be desirable for the 'right' reasons. I don't want to appeal to snobbism, or make them fashionable, or to base it on any superficial approach. I know and you know that within the broad spectrum of the arts there is rich sustaining nourishment that is worth having for its own sake.

It is important to start with the belief that attitudes *can* be changed. Look at your own attitudes. Were you born with them? Were you born into this world alive either a little Liberal or else a little Conservative? The attitudes you hold now – are they the same as the ones you held five years ago? How do you feel about smoking now?

What made you change your mind? It was the presentation of new information in a convincing way. The information might have come to you through radio, TV and newspapers or from relatives and friends – the cumulative effect was to transform you.

Let's ask how you came to like the art form that is your particular favourite now. At one point early in your lives you probably had few feelings either way. If you had an attitude it was probably one of indifference. Then what? A teacher who read some poetry to you or encouraged you to read – or go to see – a play? A mother or father who took you to a well chosen ballet? A friend at college who had a spare ticket for the opera? You were probably lucky and your first experiences were happy ones. And then more of the same, probably with you showing rather more enthusiasm. New information presented in a convincing way.

Or you might have listened to a radio programme, read a book or watched a television programme. New information presented in a convincing way.

There is always a person. There is always someone either directly or indirectly via the media presenting new information in a convincing way. For me it was a teacher at school who suggested I read Merrimée's story *Carmen* in the French. Which encouraged me to see the film *Carmen Jones*. Which made me listen to a record of the opera *Carmen*. Which made it one of my favourite operas – even if I still really prefer *Carmen Jones*.

What did André Previn do for attitudes towards jazz in this country when, many years ago, he presented Oscar Peterson on television, told us how good Peterson was and then sat down beside him and played just as well? What did Previn do for the image of classical music conductors when he did this?

Watch a film called *The Right Stuff*. Spot the book in a shop. Read it and realise that this author Tom Wolfe is really very good indeed. Read his other books. Spot the connection between *The Electric Kool-Aid Acid Test* and Ken Kesey the author of the book that became a film, *One Flew Over The Cuckoo's Nest* that you enjoyed so much. Discover New Journalism and the strange writings of Hunter S Thompson. Become interested in a different kind of writing.

Years ago when the Arts Council was run by *old* fogies, it made possible regular tours of two companies called *Opera for All* and *Ballet for All*. To the sophisticates they were probably a bit of a joke and it was probably the sophisticates that killed off these companies. They travelled light and could set up in your average parish hall in a trice. Opera with one piano and no chorus. Ballet with one piano and no *corps de ballet*.

They were frequently superb. Their potted versions of opera did nothing but do honour to the full-scale opera. *Ballet for All* introduced thousands of people not only to classical ballet but also to contemporary dance. In the early days of London Contemporary Dance Theatre some of their dancers were regularly seconded to this little company that toured the highways and byways of Britain – and they were *changing attitudes* towards dance. They did what they did with enormous conviction and whoever axed them was crazy for this was an organised attempt to give a first taste – a pleasant, interesting taste – of opera and dance – to people. It was an organised attempt to change attitudes.

We have to do this sort of thing as individual arts organisations. Not conning people into our buildings with promises of experiences that we cannot keep, but thinking of ways of easing people into the art form through skilled intermediaries and inspired programmes. Thinking of ways to give the first *dégustation* outside the buildings we traditionally use. We need more than public relations officers whose job it is just to get stories into the papers. We need the equivalents of *Opera for All* and *Ballet for All* for all art forms.

We need a closer involvement with television and radio. There are people of great talent working in those industries – people who take their viewers and listeners by the hand and lead them into new and wonderful places. Their power to influence is enormous. They are already doing part of our job for us though programmes on film, opera, theatre, dance, books, poetry – they make a great contribution. So we should get closer to them.

I can think of no better function for the Arts Council's new marketing department (*Then the Marketing and Resources Department of the Arts Council of Great Britain which is now the Marketing and Market Research Unit within the Arts Council of England.*) than for it to concentrate almost entirely upon this challenge. In my book *Guide To Arts Marketing* (*Pub. Rhinegold 1984 now o/p*) I cited the example of the Egg Marketing Board. I said that if you have a few million chickens laying a few million eggs every day you couldn't afford to wait until people got interested in eating more eggs. I said that our arts organisations *are* producing the equivalent of a few million eggs every day – and the eggs are going bad. Only a national body can hope to tackle such a major task.

Do we not need marketing boards for each art form? Boards that are concerned with changing people's attitudes towards each art form, using television, radio, newspapers and magazines – organising this combination of education and public relations to stimulate interest and to take people by the hand and lead them into – yes, I'll say it – a better world. Mental Health has it. Ecology has it. Philanthropy has it – with red noses.

Do we not need *another* Campaign for the Arts, I wonder?

All the indications are that the Arts Council is getting interested in the nuts and bolts of basic marketing. It wants to help you market more effectively. With respect, the people who do the job already can face this challenge – that is why we have a Society of Arts Publicists and I hope in the not too distant future, an Institute of Arts Marketing. What we cannot do is organise the large scale campaigns to win hearts and minds. *This* is the challenge that the Arts Council should face up to.

Today is a very significant beginning. As far as I am aware it is the first symposium ever *in the world* to address itself to this vital subject and all credit to the Scottish Arts Council and the Society of Arts Publicists for having made it possible. I look forward to an illuminating day and hope that having started the hare our good friends in the Arts Council – and you all – will pursue it vigorously.

Educational Public Relations and the
Unavailable Audience

Where to begin?

Let us return to the beginning of this book and remind ourselves of the objective of *arts* marketing:

The aim of arts marketing is to bring an appropriate number of people, *drawn from the widest possible range of social background, economic condition and age*, into an appropriate form of contact with the artist and, in so doing, to arrive at the best financial outcome that is compatible with the achievement of that aim.

The italicised portion is our beginning.

No immediate financial benefit in pursuing the 'widest possible range'

The objective above does not direct our attention to the Unavailable Audience in order to encourage us to meet the financial and audience targets of the moment; it does so because consciously to try to exclude any sector of the public or *consciously not to try to include any sector of the public* is contrary to the philosophy of the business we are in. We have accepted that for the purposes of meeting the targets of the moment we should employ the day to day tools of arts marketing where they will have most effect, that is within the part of the community I have termed the Available Audience. This is the soft target (although experience and empty seats tell us that there is still much to be learned about how to make the most of the favorable attitudes and relevant past behaviour of this group – it is not as soft as all that).

There can be no immediate financial benefit to our organisations in pursuing 'the widest possible range' of people. Indeed, even when setting out to motivate members of the Available Audience who are very well inclined to what we are offering it can cost more in direct arts marketing outlay than comes back to the box office on the first and even second or third purchase. This is, of course, the strongest argument for the 'fish in the barrel' view of catching and nurturing one's Attenders for each one can cost a large amount of money to hook; it is also the strongest argument in favour of Subscription marketing where the hooked Attender can actually pay to the box office enough money to justify the cost of the pursuit and will, if carefully nurtured, go on paying in large sums.

To set out to create a new audience from people whose current taste lies well beyond what we have to sell will inevitably be a long and costly process and it cannot be justified economically even in the medium term. It can be justified, however, in social terms and that is why the arts industry has every right to look to national and local government for direct support of schemes that have this 'missionary' objective.

Whether or not to pursue the wider audience is a decision that marks most strongly the distinction between *arts* marketing and commercial marketing. The mid-eighties influences upon our industry of people who did not subscribe to our philosophy, to which I make several references in the book, led to an approach to marketing the arts that was focused only on the Available Audience; it was, either consciously or unconsciously, a commercial approach and it had to be opposed. What made it worse, of course, was that the influences did not come from the highest calibre people so the commercial approach that was foisted on our industry was not only philosophically unacceptable it was cack-handed.

The tools for the job exist in the commercial sector

We accept that if we are ever to include those who are presently Indifferent or Hostile to what we are offering (from whatever social, economic or age group they may come) we must first bring about in them a change of attitude. None of the arts marketing tools we have met in earlier chapters can bring about such changes in attitude. Changing the way in which people regard things is, ironically enough, very much part of the commercial world and there exists an entire industry dedicated to the business: it is part of Public Relations work.

We have seen how the commercial world, unlike the arts where an holistic view is taken, can have a narrow interpretation of the word 'marketing' and frequently means to exclude Sales when using it (as in 'Marketing and Sales'). So it is with Public Relations which is often seen to be an activity separate from marketing, run by different people either within different departments or by outside consultancy firms and, like Sales, it may very well have simply been left behind when commercial marketing 'moved in' on the arts. There, as here, Public Relations divides into Product PR and Corporate PR but there is another kind of PR activity that is involved in identifying attitudes and opinions held by the public and setting out to change them if they do not match up with how a government department, an industry or an organisation wishes itself and/or its policies and products to be regarded. The process may start with commissioned market research and, on the basis of its findings, a substantial campaign may be undertaken that sets out – to borrow some useful words from the address that starts this chapter – to 'present new information in a convincing way' with the aim of shifting the public perception of whatever the subject happens to be.

History shows us that such a process can be perverted into the kind of truth distorting propaganda employed by many totalitarian states but this does not mean that the technique is bad; rather, the conclusion to be drawn is that the technique can be very successful. It often will not shift hard, entrenched attitudes, but it can certainly move the waiverers in sufficient numbers to affect sales figures or the outcome of a political election. Those who are Indifferent are moved into the Intender category. Then the day to day tools of marketing can come into play.

Of course, not all changes in attitude and opinion are so managed; the normal course of human activity throws up information that is reported in the media or is passed by 'word of mouth' and people respond as what they previously knew and believed is worked upon by what they have just learned. A politician is a wonderful person and then is discovered to have had her hand in the till. Scandals about several politicians in one party will create an unfavorable climate of opinion about their party as people generalise from a particular that is large enough to be noticed.

We know that attitudes towards the art forms change as part of a natural process, unmanaged, unguided, and our industry benefits from this as do those whose attitudes have changed – and, since change can work both ways, it is worth observing that the changes are probably never reversed, for once hooked on an art form one probably stays hooked – that is, once there people tend to stay within the Available Audience, possibly moving between the Attender and Intender statuses. But this is not enough, we cannot rely on chance particularly if it favours certain sectors of the community with better educated and better off parents influencing children and beneficial environmental factors generally providing better opportunities for experiencing art forms. We need to be able to make change happen using techniques that are known to succeed in other areas.

My scepticism about the application of large scale commercial marketing techniques is evident in many of these pages but, oddly enough, in this area of interest I have considerably more confidence in the ability of commercial practitioners to succeed than in any other. It was noticeable at the *Changing Their Minds* symposium how successful were the two 'outside' contributors, Jeremy Shaw of Smith Bundy and Partners and John Archer of BBC TV, whose specialisms were, in the first case, the overt practice of attitude changing, and in the second, the opening of doors into art forms.

I have seen attitudes towards, for example, the effects of the sun's rays, the benefits of low fat/high fibre diets, whaling, the rain forests and the dangers of unprotected sexual intercourse, change within quite short periods of time. The changes have been made to happen by the provision of new information in convincing ways – by people who know how to conduct mass research and then by people who know what new information should be provided to bring about a change in attitude and how best to present that information. I should imagine that such people and such campaigns come very expensive but they may very well be worth the money if they help bring about the kind of social change we have in mind.

Educational PR

This kind of PR work needs a name and I have found myself calling it 'Educational PR'. The activity is about establishing a relationship of some kind between sectors of the public and an art form and since so many of changes in attitude that we ourselves have experienced have been through some aspect of education (whether formal or not) it seems sensible to think of the process of trying to change other people's attitudes as being an educational one as well. Also, those people who are already pioneering in the field, particularly with the larger arts organisations, are almost always called Education Officers. The title Educational PR seems to fit, therefore.

Educational Public Relations and the
Unavailable Audience

What lies at the heart of Educational PR?

At the heart of Educational PR there must be the belief that in all sections of the community, no matter how the dividing lines are drawn, whether they be divisions according to age, socio-economic status, educational level, cultural background, there are people who have the capacity to appreciate what we are providing and who would benefit from it if they could be introduced to it in a way that was appropriate for them. Educational PR sets out to find out what are the barriers that come between the art form and those people and then finds ways of reducing or eliminating them.

What are the barriers? Ignorance is one

For people who have the capacity to appreciate something but have done little or nothing about it, the main barrier must surely be ignorance. People of such potential will either have a false impression of the art form or will simply know not enough about it to able to form an impression. The reasons why they have the false impression or the lack of knowledge one could not possibly go into here beyond saying that their own background, their social and educational background in particular, must be the principal influence. This is not a polite way of referring to poor people; I have seen and continue to see almost every day, examples of people whose lives have been very well favoured but live in a state of almost complete ignorance of what are really very commonplace and easily accessible forms of art.

Cultural deprivation is to be found in all strata of society and across all age ranges; let us not discriminate against those who are not poor. Also, let us not discriminate against those who are poor. At this stage of Educational PR money does not really come into the problem.

The barrier may be simple ignorance, in which case enlightenment is possible; it may be that the attitude was once based on ignorance but is now elevated to a declaration of faith – 'nothing on earth will make me do this!' What *can* be dealt with by our industry is summed up in the old Guinness advertisement: 'I haven't tried it because I don't like it'.

It may also be that people have tried it and have genuinely

concluded that this is not for them; so ignorance cannot be blamed. They are almost certainly beyond our reach.

Another barrier is the time it takes

Another barrier is the time it takes for an art form to start working with a beginner. Popular culture is founded on the quick fix based on the assumption that most peoples' attention span is very short and this becomes a self-fulfilling prophesy; if you only demand a few minutes then this quickly becomes what you get. Newspapers with a vocabulary of 800 words and no article longer than 400 words. Films with an explosion of excitement every four or five minutes (you can hear the audience noise level increase once the four minute threshold is past). Music, no matter what its content, that lasts no longer than three minutes. Hardly any, if at all, manifestations of the performing art forms are so constructed. So, even if one can find a way in to offer people, if a way is found to fill in the hole of ignorance with information that tempts a person to take a taste, the first experience is likely to be ... simply too long.

In recent years there has been what is called an 'opera boom' that is generally attributed to the Three Tenors phenomenon, Pavarotti, Domingo and Carreras providing good entertainment through television and video that has reached millions of people. – yet audiences for opera have not increased. The launch of Classic FM radio station with its rapidly gathered audience running into millions – yet audiences for classical music have not increased.

What has happened is that intelligent business people have modified the normal manifestation of the art form – the opera that lasts for three or more hours, the classical music concert that lasts for nearly two hours and may include one symphony that lasts for nearly one hour – and turned it into something else, something that is more easily assimilated. It is the approach to literature of Readers Digest which has never done much for the cause of serious reading.

The problem for us with the quick fix is that we are not in the business of selling quick fixes. The quick fix is fine with us if we can use it as stepping stone to the real thing but if we cannot achieve this then it is not for us, it is for people whose business it is to sell quick fixes. The traditional way of opening doors for people is to offer them

small samples but we see that many people can exist most happily on a
diet of samples alone. It is only where the sample is the prelude to a
developing programme that takes the taster into a more challenging
relationship with the sampled art that can offer us any longer term
hope.

Targets for Educational PR

We can see the Unavailable Audience in two ways. We can see it as
being made up of people of different ages, the watershed age being the
time a young person leaves the influence of school (where educational
programmes are, by the nature of schools and the educational system,
largely, but not entirely, imposed upon pupils). And we can see the
Unavailable Audience not in terms of age but according to its
socio-economic groupings and this leads us immediately into the very
dangerous and, in my view, unproductive, business of making
assumptions of the attitudes towards different art forms held by those
different groupings. I believe that Educational PR should have no part
of this latter approach.

Educational PR should start by seeing its target as two distinct
groups within the community: those who may be communicated with
directly because they are at school and because there are teachers who
have almost exactly the same objectives as we do who will help us. If
such a thing as a soft target exists in Educational PR, then young
people at school are it. The second group is simply ... everyone else.

Just as we do when we set out to build up a group of Attenders
from scratch within a community, we have to address the community
as a whole. With Product Advertising we may not be able to do this on
every occasion that we have a product to sell but, as a general
principle, we try to use a broadcast approach once, twice, three or four
times a year. Our Intenders are out there somewhere and we must use
a universal approach to make sure that their potential is tapped if it is
there to be tapped. We use language (which we take to mean the
whole range of words, typography, illustration and design) to 'target'
the Intenders so that although the physical means of communication is
broadcast, universal, the message is aimed at the sort of people who
might well already have a favourable attitude towards what we have to
offer. So it must be with Educational PR that is aimed at ... everyone

else ... but the use of language as a way of giving a focus is very much more limited for here we cannot make the same assumptions about the previous experience, the tastes and attitudes, the knowledge and so on that we can with the Intender group. By definition the group we are hoping to communicate with falls beyond the Intender category in terms of everything that is useful to us in the motivational process.

We can and must, I believe, make one assumption about the people within the Unavailable Audience that we have a chance of persuading to give our art form a chance. In *Guide To Arts Marketing* I wrote, 'Appreciation of most of the traditional art forms requires intelligence and a certain amount of persistence; the majority of people are not very bright and not very persistent. (Low intelligence is fairly uniformly spread across the class boundaries although it is better disguised among the middle classes).' After publishing those words I waited for the hate mail but it didn't arrive – perhaps readers agreed with me.

The assumption we make, of course, is that only people of average and higher than average intelligence – and this implies, although not exclusively, a reasonable level of educational achievement – will respond to our Educational PR attempts. Where the line is to be drawn I cannot say. Research might well come up with suggestions but in the absence of such research all one can say is, 'Assume your target to be intelligent and hence literate. Assume your target to have aspirations towards a more interesting life'. And no more than that.

Educational PR thus has two targets: young people at school and ... everyone else who is not already in the Intender or Attender categories and who meets the simple criteria above.

Implications of Educational PR for arts organisations

The implications of this line of thought for individual arts organisations are substantial. If serious attempts are to be made to make more favourable the attitudes of that part of the community that is currently Unavailable, there must be established direct lines of communication with schools so that programmes of introduction and development may be developed within the curriculum alongside and, where possible, integrated with the normal educational programmes followed by the schools.

The importance of teachers

As far as the performing arts are concerned there is no lack of interest within the schools. The subjects of music and drama may have experienced serious setbacks at the hands of political fools but the teachers are as well motivated as they have ever been. Teachers of these subjects want to pass on their enthusiasms and passions to as many of their pupils as possible.

Only the larger arts organisations have been able to appoint staff whose job it is to work with these teachers so that contact is made and maintained and programmes put in place to introduce young people to art forms in a way that does not alienate them. It cannot be easy to do this in the face of reducing subsidies in a political climate that sees everything only in terms of immediate return. Many more such appointments will be necessary if progress is to be made on this front.

The job of the Education Officer

The greatest contribution that can be made by the Education Officer is in the very beginning of the introductory process when young people first meet the art form. At that time there will be ignorance and no small amount of prejudice. Of course, within any group there will be some who, favoured with the right kind of parents, will already be over the threshold, but most will come to the subject knowing very little and quite possibly caring less. Here the Education Officer has to do a good 'PR job' for the art form in much the same way as the relation or family friend referred to in the speech quoted at the start of the chapter. Teachers do this all the time, of course, but the Education Officer has the advantage of being a visitor from an unusual and interesting background who specialises in this form of introductory work and has prepared material to hand.

The Education Officer works with the specialist teachers to decide which performances are suitable for visits by school parties. For younger children it may be no more than a visit to the building, a look backstage, a brief entertaining talk by a performer and a short workshop session in which children participate. For others it may be a performance – a carefully chosen performance that will supplement the children's experience and be at an appropriate level for them. For examination students it might simply be a straight performance of a play that is an examination text.

Where presently available performances are not deemed appropriate for audiences of a certain age or ability it is for the Education Officer to suggest especially created performances that are tailor made for the young people's group. They need not be expensive productions. It is exciting enough for young people to come close to, talk to and even work with, professional performers who always have, in the eyes of the young, a charismatic quality. The closeness of the contact is important. I cannot believe that a group of, say, teenagers who have been able to sit close to and talk to a dancer and watch, even something as basic as routine exercises, would not be eager to go on to see that same dancer in a full scale performance.

One can see here how the Education Officer must be a kind of impresario, knowing what will work for these very special kind of audiences and what will not, knowing what are the prejudices and thinking of ways of dispelling them, finding interesting, exciting and dramatic, ways of supplying 'new information in a convincing way'.

Throughout, the aim is to arouse the interest of young people and show them, by dispelling ignorance and prejudice, that the art form can ultimately give them experiences they will get nowhere else. It will take them time to 'get into' the art form for very few things that are worthwhile happen quickly – does one become a good cricketer without practice?

Favourable attitudes towards the arts cannot be developed on the basis of just one or two contacts either from visitor to the school or school party to arts organisation; there must be programmes that build and build again upon each contact so that experience is broadened and deepened as young people pass through the education system whilst increasingly seeing the arts as being one of the good options open to them for enhancing their lives and one that does not require a major effort of will to take. The late British cartoonist, Mel Calman, sold from his shop in Museum Street, London, a series of mugs with humorous illustrations and captions: 'We could see a play,' says the little cartoon man to his little cartoon wife, 'Or shall we just enjoy ourselves?'

The status of Education Officers

The status of Education Officers must be such that they are accepted as being equal with senior management having direct arts marketing responsibilities for if they are not woven into the management fabric there will not be the holistic approach towards the practice of arts marketing that is absolutely vital. It is very easy for the Education Officer to be thought of as someone doing a separate job, with a separate crowd of people ... kids ... and nothing to do with the real business of selling tickets.

I am forced to wonder about the status of Education Officers when I hear about the way some organisations behave towards the teachers who are so vitally important to the process of 'changing their minds'. It is as though the marketing wing believes not only that it is in a Seller's Market today but that it will always be in one. Incredible as it may seem, one can have an Education Officer working hard to develop relationships with schools, teachers and children while the box office is pursuing a policy of always allocating the worst seats possible to parties drawn from the same schools because, presumably, they are benefiting from some form of price reduction being (a) young and (b)many in number, both facts of which would seem to encourage generous treatment rather than the contrary.)

What happens when they leave school?

Once the Educational PR is underway the relationship between it and the marketing wing must be ever closer for as young people grow to maturity they will want to experience the arts as individuals and not as members of school parties and arts organisations must be ready to welcome them as 'real' customers – as Attenders. For the young person for whom Educational PR has worked, who has passed through the changes in attitude, from hostility or indifference into the Available Audience, the major problem may well simply be one of money and it is here that the Education Officer talks to the person in charge of Sales and Sales Promotion to arrange ways of reducing this barrier to purchase.

Would it not be a wonderful thing if young people leaving school who had been in contact with an arts organisation through its

Educational PR programme were each to be given a card that gave them substantial reductions on admission prices for the next five years of their lives? Hedge them with a few conditions, perhaps, but make the reductions substantial – and applicable to attendance by two people, not just to the student. Young people do not like to go out by themselves so make the reductions for two.

Who knows but if arts organisations were to embrace the idea of *seriously* courting the attentions of young people, from early school age onwards, might they not even consider charging half price for all young people, all the time. Charge as much as you can get, is true, but the true costs of travelling to experience the arts, buying tickets, eating out perhaps, almost guarantee that most parents on average incomes cannot include their children in their visits on anything like a regular basis. Our approach to young people, which is wholly egalitarian, must take into account that some will have parents possessing exactly the attitudes that we are trying to foster and the more we can help those parents fulfil their responsibilities by integrating young people into their 'arts lives' the better it will be.

National campaigns

Arts organisations can only work within their catchment areas and can only really hope to succeed in Educational PR with the 'soft target' of young people at school. I do not suggest that arts organisations in general try to look beyond this geographical and age target in their Educational PR work. There have been one or two attempts to aim advertising at people, not young people in particular, who are in the Unavailable Audience category – one thinks of English National Opera's poster campaign in London in 1992 saying 'Everyone Needs Opera' which is patently incorrect – but they have never, to my knowledge, shown any sign of success. Attitudes may be changed by posters but only if the posters are part of a wider campaign that is based on a real understanding of why the unfavourable attitudes are held in the first place.

This is where I return to the end of my keynote speech given in Glasgow in 1988. It is perhaps no more than one of the pie-in-the-sky ideas that people who make speeches and write books like this have and then offer up without suggesting any possible way of bringing them to life, but I believe – I am certain – that the way forward for each art form is to create for itself a 'marketing board' that will set out to raise money to finance research into prevalent unfavourable attitudes, and to create campaigns – national campaigns – that will use the media of communication to change the way each art form is regarded by those who are currently indifferent or hostile to it. Of course they will fail with most people but they will succeed with some and that may well be enough to aim for.

And what better rôle for the Marketing and Market Research Unit of the Arts Council of England than to assist and advise in the setting up of such marketing boards and in the commissioning of the market research that must precede any direct action?

And meanwhile television goes on doing what it is doing

Television today is probably the greatest educational force for the arts in existence. Within the industry there are people who are knowledgeable about the arts, who are highly creative and very eager to use that creativity to bring their favourite art forms before a wider public and who have the special gift of the teacher, the ability to understand why people have difficulties in 'getting into' an art form and the ability to open doors for them by offering tastes that excite and explanations that do not bore. When television is used to open doors it can, to mix a couple of metaphors, move mountains.

Radio has its own educational job to do but of the two main sources of arts programmes, BBC Radio 3 and Classic FM, there is I feel, far less chance of their bringing about the change in attitude that is needed. BBC Radio 3 offers a superb service for the Available Audience. Classic FM offers a different, wider, range of music with a much broader Available Audience in mind (and a definite touch of the Readers' Digest influence) but does not appear to have as a goal the changing of attitudes in the way that television frequently appears to have. For the purposes of this work I exclude radio, therefore.

It would be delightful if closer co-operation could be brought about between television people, arts organisations and teachers but it will not happen. Television will always be independent and will do what it wants to do; provided the arts elements in the schedules are protected from the scoundrels this is no bad thing because television has always attracted the brightest and the best and, apart from a tendency to go highbrow and follow silly intellectual fashions, its people do an excellent job. If its independence were the issue I would happily accept that in exchange for more of the same.

Once the different arts marketing boards are created it would be inconceivable not to have sitting on them producers whose business and pleasure it is to produce arts programmes. This is probably the only form of contact that would succeed offering as it does a 'without strings' relationship for the producers and an opportunity to learn from market research what are the current attitudes towards the arts of the public at large together with the views of the prime movers in each art form.

Ten years ago I expressed a wish for there to be an Institute of Arts Marketing and nine years later such a body was formed. I do now most fervently express a wish for there to be formed arts marketing boards for Theatre, Music, Opera, Dance and any other arts category where its protagonists feel there is a job to be done in creating a larger Available Audience for it. I shall live in hope!

PART FOUR

THE
ARTS MANAGEMENT WEEKLY
ARTICLES

A series that appeared from 1992 to 1994

SALES AND SALES PROMOTION

The underlying principle of Sales is to identify and try to reduce the obstacles that come between a person motivated to buy and the physical act of purchase, the principal barriers being Geography, Procrastination and Cost, each a negative factor in its own right and working its own malign effect upon the others. The worst customers in the world (even if they like and want what you have to sell) are people who live a long way from your venue, who don't have a telephone, who don't keep stamps in the house, who leave things like ordering tickets to the weekend and are natural procrastinators and whose washing machine has just gone irreparably wrong.

The Sales function tries to minimise those obstacles. Sales Promotion tries to make the customer willingly jump over what is left of them – eagerly to pick up the 'phone, to fill in a form, to pay money to you in the face of other demands and to do it *now*. It also tries to capitalise on the fact that while you have a customer's attention, while they are in the right frame of mind, it is the best time to sell them *more*.

Sales Promotion makes people buy, makes them buy more, makes them buy more frequently, makes them buy more frequently *now*. It remains the most little known and misunderstood marketing technique in arts marketing. Paradoxically almost every arts marketer uses the technique in one form or another at some time – but may not always know the ground rules for its use and may, therefore, quite easily come a cropper with it.

Sales Promotion works by changing the would be customer's perception of the value of what is being offered. At its most basic level the discount offer which says 'The usual price for this is £20 but you can have it for £15 if you buy before next Friday' is a form of Sales Promotion. The voucher which says 'Buy a ticket for a Monday performance and this will reduce the price by £5' is another. The notion is essentially simple. You offer the customer a better deal if he does what you want him to do.

You want your customer to buy sooner rather than later because you know that a sale delayed is probably a sale lost – so a Sales Promotion method is used to encourage faster response. You want her to buy tickets for several performances rather than just one (as in a Subscription campaign); the price to be paid will be higher so some form of special offer involving a price reduction, in whatever form, will assist here. You may want to encourage the purchase of tickets for more expensive seats – again a Sales Promotion method may well be the answer.

If you want to persuade customers to bring more people than the national average of 2.3 tickets bought per box office purchase then Sales Promotion will be the best technique for pushing that figure up to, say, 4 tickets per purchase. Some form of price reduction may be the best approach but it could just as easily be free car parking, a free bottle of wine at the interval or access to better seats ahead of the rush.

Seat preference is probably the most effective form of Sales Promotion. Customers have their own views as to where they want to sit. Usually they want the 'best' seats. Within each price range of seats there is room for choice. Giving the customer the choice as the quid pro quo for booking early, bringing two friends or buying a subscription ticket will tend to encourage the purchase. The ultimate form of Sales Promotion through seat preference is where all seats have the same price and the customer you have targeted has first choice of them. The statement to make is **The Best Seat in the House is the Seat You Want – and you may have it if you Book Now**.

Whatever the offers you make it is vital to be sure exactly what obstacle you are trying to persuade the customer to overcome and, wherever possible, to aim the offer at a sector where improvement in Sales is desirable and most likely. If most of your customers attend in pairs then a 'two tickets for the price of one' offer may appear to be highly effective but you could just be giving away money where there is no need to. One way or another, most Sales Promotions cost money and you should only spend money when there is every chance of getting more back than you have spent.

THE 'ART SHOULD BE FREE' CONTROVERSY

In 1988 Keith Diggle wrote an article for The Independent *newspaper on why he thought art galleries should not only charge for admission but should also sell tickets in advance. His views were not entirely well received by the paper's readers – but times change.*

16 May 1988

Museums and art galleries are being forced to consider charging for admission because they do not have enough money. Apart from a certain distaste at the thought of mixing art and cash and the belief that it is morally wrong to expect people to pay, the main worry of our custodians is that if admission charges are imposed attendances will fall (so the objective of bringing art to the people is lost); and if attendances fall the income will then not bridge the gap between expenditure and subsidy (so why bother?).

In fact, there is no moral issue. Why shouldn't we pay something for our pleasures here as we do with the performing arts?

And there is no evidence that making art free increases attendances. On the contrary, I believe that if the right system for making charges were introduced, attendances would rise. Those who would then attend would be from more or less the same socio/economic groups that had previously attended. Such a system could allow free entrance to people who were badly off and would have the power to increase attendance from them as well. It is a matter of confidence and know-how, and a 'pay at the door if you feel inclined' system is not the way to do it.

Why do theatres sell tickets in advance? One answer is that theatres like to have their money in advance, but that is not the main reason. They sell tickets because they do not trust the fickle public to keep the promise it made to itself when it first decided that this was a show worth going to see. The theatres know that at the first sign of rain or fine weather, political unrest or stability, illness or wellness, the public will think of something else to do.

Great importance is attached to the marketing of tickets. Pick up the telephone, walk into a travel branch of W H Smith, pay by credit card - the path to purchase is smooth and easy. The philosophy is simple and wholly realistic: the moment that someone wants to attend a show, obtain a commitment from them.

A ticket system also implies, in a subtle but effective way, that the supply of experiences available to be bought is limited. If you don't buy it now, you may not get it at all. No one accuses the theatres of being inaccessible – their trick is to make themselves appear accessible now but possibly inaccessible later. In contrast, you can walk into most museums and art galleries at any time; they are so accessible you can go later, and so you probably do not go at all.

I am suggesting that our great museums and art galleries should not only charge for admission but also sell tickets in advance. In place of the ever-open doors we would have a series of events – Monday morning, Friday afternoon, Thursday late opening, Saturday matinée. The period covered by the ticket is not as important as the fact that it has a beginning and an end, just like a performance. Tickets are on sale at the door (subject to availability), or from the usual agents. Call this number for credit-card booking. 'We'd better book our tickets for the Tate now, or we won't get in.'

Prices need not be constant. One exhibition might be priced higher than another, but certain times of the week might be deemed less attractive than others, so a Monday-morning ticket for a blockbuster show could well be cheaper than a Saturday-afternoon ticket for something less exciting. As in the performing arts, varying prices are used to encourage a spread in attendance, to avoid queues and crushes on one hand and emptiness on another.

And what of the poor? What of the school parties? The arts organisations can be as generous as they choose to be: they can give the tickets away if they like. They will be giving away something of value and they can choose which part of the week it suits them best to be generous with. It would not be beyond the limits of imagination to devise ways of making these gifts without depriving people of their dignity. Such a system would surely increase attendance from old and young, the unemployed and the low paid, for they too would place more value on the gift of something that others had to pay for.

It could work. I think it probably would work. Can you imagine, ticket touts outside the Victoria and Albert Museum?

* * * * * * * * * * * * * * * * * * *

Keith Diggle writes today:

At the heart of it was the idea that the ticket is more than just a piece of paper with printing, more than just a receipt; at the time of purchase it *is* the product, it is something tangible, something to acquire in order to guarantee a future experience. The availability of the product – or proxy- product – is essential to the effective operation of marketing for if publicity sets out to make people *want* to to buy something the sales function must bring it close enough so that they may consummate their desire to purchase more-or-less immediately. The buying desire is volatile and so you have to catch customers while they are hot or you lose them. My feeling has always been that art galleries have a vast potential market of people who are regularly excited by what they see advertised and what they read, hear and see about exhibitions but who are stopped from attending by the barriers of distance, time and all the distractions of life. These people need to be sold tickets then and there. Catch a person with two tickets to a top musical not turning up on the night!

The notion of limited supply that the sale of tickets in advance implies is a hard one to get across to art galleries. My point is that selling tickets in advance *implies* limited supply and this has the effect of making people move a little faster towards purchase. Whether there is or there is not a heavy demand for tickets will only be known at the event itself. There are times when the press of people at an exhibition does create a limit – but the customer doesn't know it until it is too late and this experience does nothing for his relationship with the gallery. When the article was published one letter writer pointed out that advance ticket selling was particularly valuable as a system of crowd-control for very popular exhibitions. This is another advantage of the approach because customers may be guided towards times when the gallery is less busy and when the experience they are buying will be better.

Have the galleries made progress in the past five years? I think so. When you see Royal Academy exhibitions being sold via Ticketmaster and tickets for specified viewing periods being sold at the Tate Gallery (viz. the 1994 Picasso Exhibition) you are seeing progress all right. Well done!

WHAT IS THE OBJECTIVE OF PUBLICITY?

There are as many definitions of publicity as there are practitioners of arts marketing. Forget the definitions; what is publicity – however defined – meant to achieve? Ask a group of arts workers what publicity is meant to achieve and the odds are that most will say that publicity exists to sell tickets. (They will; I've put that question within the last six months and many, many times before). This is a dangerous misconception and is responsible for so many people failing to understand the place in marketing of sales and sales promotion. If publicity sells tickets then that's that, isn't it? That's marketing wrapped up. Product, Publicity and Price – end of story. There's more to it.

The role of publicity in the marketing function is to bring people to the point where *they want to buy* something. It's worth leaving that statement standing alone so it catches the eye. If you practise embroidery run it up into a sampler and hang it over your bed. Have it printed on the front of your tee shirt. Write it on a Post-It note and stick it on the loo wall. Remember it.

How does the process work? How do you make people want to buy something?

It is better not to get involved with considerations of people's 'needs' at this stage. One becomes tangled up in the distinctions between 'needs' and 'wants' and only a psychologist can guide you through that thorny thicket. What counts, from your viewpoint, you who have tickets to sell now, is the attitude your customer has *now* towards what you have to sell. It is basic to the idea that attitudes take some time in forming and they take some time to change: the publicist has to go to work on the material available at the time. Missionaries change attitudes, publicists exploit the attitudes that exist.

Seen in terms of their attitudes the people that live within your catchment area can be categorised very simply into those who are favourably inclined to what you have to sell and those who are not. Of those who are, some are already buying what you have to sell so they are easier to identify and communicate with; some are not already buying so you must communicate with them in a way that is less precisely targeted: these are the *Attenders* and *Intenders*. Those who are not favourably inclined – the *Indifferent* and *Hostile* – have to be left for a later day and perhaps left forever.

By aiming for those who are favourably inclined you are taking a realistic approach to the publicity task. You have to get the best results for the money you have to spend. Don't waste it. Don't throw the seeds upon the stony ground.

The phrase 'favorably inclined' is a description of attitude *towards what you have to sell* – it will generally be an attitude towards an art form; it may be focused upon a period or style or, as it is quite commonly, personalities. It may be a combination of all and that may be associated with a whole lot of other things which are favoured. All that matters to you is that they like it, whether they are currently buying the experience of it or not.

Once you accept this approach you will find that the process of making people want to buy becomes immediately easier because you can make certain key assumptions. You may assume a level of knowledge, a level of literacy, a level of interest – even a certain congruity on matters of taste and style. You may assume that you do not have to persuade them that what you have to sell is OK *per se*. This makes the process of communication easier and gives you a chance of succeeding in your attempts to persuade.

You now have to estimate how much these people who are favorably inclined to the art form know about the thing you are going to try to persuade them to want to buy. It is not easy. Market research might help you but you probably do not have enough time or enough money to get involved with this. You have to provide yourself with a rough answer to the question, 'How famous, how well known, is it?'

This is the first step in Public Relations which is the first part of Publicity. Public Relations, in this context, is about making an estimate of how much work needs to be done to create in the minds of those *Attenders* and *Intenders* an awareness, a 'favourable awareness', of what you want people to want to buy. If your event already enjoys a high level of favorable awareness then your PR work need not be great. If you have to sell an unknown then you have much work to do.

The theory is that the second part of Publicity, which is called Advertising, can only succeed if it occurs in an atmosphere of favorable awareness. Advertising, involving the expensive use of print and other media, is very limited in what it can achieve and it can achieve almost nothing if it operates in a vacuum. Advertising is the principal tool of persuasion but it needs its targets to be informed and softened up by Public Relations.

THE PLACE OF CORPORATE PUBLIC RELATIONS IN THE PUBLICITY FUNCTION

In a recent article I said that Advertising can only be effective if it takes place in an 'atmosphere of favourable awareness'. It is one of the old saws of show business that the best publicity is by word-of-mouth and this indeed plays a most important part in the development of an 'atmosphere' – but opinions and information passed on by friends and colleagues to possible customers can rarely be relied upon by the arts presenter; that is why the activity known as Product PR is necessary as a means of organising, 'as much as possible, the dissemination of information that helps form favorable attitudes.' The word that is passed along by mouth is not only a view based on direct personal experience but is, more often than not, a secondhand opinion derived from something seen on television, read in a newspaper or heard on radio. Word-of-mouth publicity is basically gossip and good Product PR can feed it and help it pass along the good news in preference to the bad.

If someone were to offer you a one week holiday in, say, Crete, in June, hotel accommodation and half-board, including flight, for only £100, how would you react? Do you like the sound of it? Does it seem like an attractive holiday? Why are you not reaching for your cheque-book?

The holiday sounds attractive enough. You know that Crete is a lovely island from what your friends have told you and from what you have read in the holiday supplements of newspapers. June is a very good time to visit. To have a flight and hotel accommodation arranged makes it quite trouble free. The price is remarkably low. Why then do you hesitate? You think there may be something not quite right about the deal, is that correct?

In fact your reaction to the offer would be governed not only by the description of the holiday (ie the advertising), not only by what you knew of the place already (ie You already had a favorable impression of it – partly the result of earlier Product PR) but also by your own estimation of the value of what is being offered. It seems too cheap and therefore you are unhappy with it.

What has happened here is that you have accepted everything up to the point where you have found yourself doubting the honesty of the proposition. You do not believe that any commercial organisation would sell you something so good so cheaply. A rat has been smelled.

Suppose that the offer is being made by a close friend who has booked the holiday, paid the full price of, say, £300 and now cannot go because a job application has yielded an interview in the middle of the holiday week and the chance of this job just cannot be missed. The friend cannot cancel and claim on the insurance. He'll settle for £100 and write off the loss against the chances of a bigger salary.

Now the honesty of the offer is not in question; it is now a *believable* good deal.

We see from this that an advertising message combined with Product PR is not enough. The person or organisation making the offer has to have credibility. This is why it is always more difficult for a new arts organisation to attract audiences; it has not, itself, yet established a reputation for high quality and good value. This is why, in the early stages of building a relationship with a community, the presenter will be wise to choose events that bring with them an aura of quality and value that the public will not question: it costs more money but the results will justify the outlay in the short term and in the long term as well because the success will help build the reputation of the organisation.

In the town where I live, Oundle in Northamptonshire, there is the Stahl Theatre, a 250 seater offering a mixed programme of visiting drama and dance companies plus interesting odds and ends and remarkably good plays from the independent school that owns and runs the theatre. The modest impresario behind the Stahl's programming is John Harrison who has managed the theatre for many years and has achieved the highest possible level of credibility for the theatre. Stahl shows almost always do very well indeed even if no-one has heard of the company or the play. Advertising and Product PR are minimal; no more than is needed. Many people, like me, simply buy tickets for a season, without even thinking very much about the company or the show. One is rarely disappointed.

The relationship that builds over the years seems to be no more than the by-product of good management and the activity of a talented impresario. Good *Corporate PR*, as it is known, is not something that can be applied as a cosmetic for if there are cracks in what is offered to the public they cannot be papered over. That is not to say that the relationship between organisation and public cannot be managed and encouraged.

An arts organisation should be careful not to let all of the public attention fall on the performers; it should always make sure that its own role as presenter is made known to the public. When remarkable things happen the public should know who has made them happen.

The normal activities of Corporate PR would include encouraging the media to take a look at the people behind the scenes – especially the people who choose or create the events, the impresarios – and to convey information on future plans, future events, to their readers and viewers. The concept of Corporate PR would be behind the production of printed matter telling people not just about shows but about the organisation. The same would apply to visits backstage, the visits of organisation personnel to local bodies to give talks and so on.

If the vital role of Corporate PR is appreciated by the arts organisation it will show in every way in which the organisation meets the people, directly and indirectly. The appearance of buildings; the design, location and adequacy of signs within the building; the accessibility of the box-office; the helpfulness and professionalism of the staff; and so on and so on. Contact by telephone counts for much; how are people helped when they seek information? How long do they have to wait before their call is answered? The list is almost endless.

It is because good Corporate PR is the result of good management that its importance is sometimes overlooked or taken for granted. It is true that if an organisation does its presenting job well people will think well of it and will trust it when it offers the holiday in Crete for £100 – but it will be held in even higher regard if it brings its light out from behind the bushel. Then, should trouble threaten – shows not quite so attractive or a threat to the funding – it will have goodwill to sustain it.

THE NEED FOR A UNIVERSALLY ACCEPTED ANALYSIS OF ARTS MARKETING

(Prompted by the publication of Draft Standards for Consultation - MARKETING & FRONT OF HOUSE *(Key Function 5: Enable people to experience arts and entertainment)* published by Arts and Entertainment Training Council in 1993)

At the heart of the movement to develop National and Scottish Vocational Qualifications there is the implicit need to analyse functions. Whatever the subject, if it is to be communicated effectively it must be subjected to some form of analysis. If you watch the efforts of a practitioner – of almost anything, making clogs, writing, cutting grass, riding a bicycle – to communicate the *how* of the matter you will see an attempt to analyse the activity in order to explain it. The really effective communicator is one who hits on exactly the right analysis, the one that lays bare the essentials, so you have the all key elements laid out before you, labelled, with explanations of how they work together. Without this all one has is 'Watch me, see how I do it' and this is rarely a successful method of teaching.

Arts marketing professionals have yet to agree on what is the most useful analysis of the marketing function. The most common and, in my view, the least helpful, is that most frequently found in books written by commercial marketers. Professor Leslie W Rodger, of Heriot Watt University, wrote a book called *Marketing the Visual Arts*, published by the Scottish Arts Council in 1987, and in it he referred to the 'four main headings popularised in marketing literature – the four Ps of Marketing: Product, Price, Promotion and Place' which I find to be at best an oversimplification and at worst an encouragement to sloppy thinking. These damned Four Ps still form the basis of many people's thinking and working and certainly form the basis of the marketing element in the *Draft Standards for Consultation* referred to at the head of this article.

These four Ps can easily become a mental check-list. Their alliteration is appealing and memorable and it is so deceptively simple to tick them off, *Product* – there, I've got a Product: *Price* – there, I've got a Price. We'll leave *Promotion* for a bit because I've got another P to tick off: I know where it's taking *Place*. Now for *Promotion*; let's put up some *Posters*.

There's no law that says writers on marketing have to be modest. My analysis is better. It recognises the key decision areas. It contains within it an understanding of how marketing works. If you use it as a checklist you will not miss out vital steps. Let's look at the analysis:-

Product - products, services, public benefits, are invented, discovered, developed, selected or created and are then offered to the ...

Public - which will use, enjoy and otherwise benefit from the Product and will be defined in several important ways to do with geography, numerical size, income, needs and wants, intellectual level, social class etc. etc. The process of bringing Product and Public together will involve ...

Financial Planning - provides the economic mini-environment in which the contact takes places and ensures that the organisation achieves its financial objective and is able to sustain itself year by year. An important part of this decision making area is that of ...

Pricing - the price tag put on the Product which has a major impact on the Public's decision to buy or not to buy and carries with it important implications of value in the message that is projected to the Public by ...

Publicity - a combination of Advertising and Public Relations, charged with the responsibility of making the Public want to buy the Product, which desire is brought to fruition by ...

Sales - which brings the psychologically committed potential customer to the point of physical commitment to the Product by reducing or eliminating 'barriers to purchase', by providing a place or system in or by which the sale may take place and by making use of ...

Sales Promotion, the technique used to improve the potential customer's perception of the value (see Pricing above) of what is being offered which uses promises of improved value to enhance the publicised message and to assist the effectiveness of Sales.

You will note that apart from seeing *Public* as being important to the marketing of what is, after all, a public service industry, and making *Financial Planning* a key part of the analysis (because it is), this analysis replaces the Promotion of the Four Ps with: *Publicity, Sales* and *Sales Promotion*.

The *Draft Standards for Consultation* publication does acknowledge that marketing has to take account of the *Public* (see Unit 523) and it does make reference to *Pricing* (Element 5222) – although the impact of pricing upon the target public is given scant attention. It is where it gets on to Promotion that it loses track completely and this is because of the inadequacy of the analysis upon which it is based.

I acknowledge that these are but draft standards and I hope that they are significantly improved before they become final standards and are imposed upon an unsuspecting world, but it is not encouraging to see, at this stage, standards for Marketing that are so inadequate. The omission of any reference to *Sales* beyond a vague, 'Contribute to the selling effectiveness of public areas' and to *Sales Promotion* says little for the professional competence of the authors. The failure to distinguish between different types of Public Relations activities is equally serious.

An analysis has to be complete if it is to be useful. Why is it that the simple, workable, well-tested – and complete – analysis given above, which has been widely available since 1984 has been ignored? One can only look to Rick Welton (project director of Arts and Entertainment Training Council), standards development consultants from Positive Solutions and Boyden Southwood and the people who participated in workshops held between Autumn 1991 and Summer 1992 for an answer.

COPING WITH RISK - THE
CONFIDENCE FACTOR

The art of analysis is to omit nothing that is relevant and to include nothing that is irrelevant. The analysis of marketing that I proposed in my last article is no more than a list of areas where decisions must be made and such a list is useless unless it is comprehensive. My list of *Product*, *Public*, *Financial Planning*, *Pricing*, *Publicity*, *Sales*, *Sales Promotion* has worked for me and for others for a long time. It is a good working analysis. It probably fits the bill. But, paradoxically in the light of my claim for its comprehensiveness, there is something missing.

It concerns the confidence and energy of the organisation making the decisions; it is about the belief the organisation has in its ability to succeed, its wish to succeed and its ability to sustain itself if it fails. This 'missing factor' is to do with the skills, experience, motivation and creativity of the personnel and is significantly influenced by the financial resources of the organisation. If the factor *is* missing then marketing will only work if a Seller's Market obtains. There is rarely a Seller's Market in the arts.

All businesses need to operate in an atmosphere of confidence. If risks are reduced then fear of failure is reduced. Hence the importance (very much overvalued) placed on market research. Market research is essentially an attempt to reduce the risks that are inevitable in any speculative venture. The danger is that it is very easy to convince oneself that once the research is done the risk is gone. All businesses face risk of some order. The arts organisation faces a higher level of risk than almost any other; indeed, when it is operating as it should, risk is woven into the fabric of its life. In the arts, market research never eliminates risk.

How does an arts body cope with risk? How does it develop the belief that the organisation and its people, have the ability to face up to and overcome the risk of marketing failure? This is where the missing marketing factor comes onto the scene.

Before there were arts organisations there were *impresarios*. Theatre managers, concert promoters, producers of various kinds: people whose principal characteristic was their overwhelming belief in their ability to pick winners and, on occasion, to make winners out of also-rans. They frequently went bust and either went to run a pub, jumped off a tall building or conned some money out of an elderly aunt and started again. The successful ones combined three vital factors: knowledge (of marketing – not formalised but knowledge just the same), confidence (deriving from earlier successes) – and prudence; the possible financial loss was containable, there was money in the bank to cover it. So one flop did not make a disaster. In such one-man businesses there was a significant measure of ego, as well.

The arts presenting body of today finds it hard to act like an impresario bound as it is by the need to be accountable, controlled by committees the members of which are themselves liable in law for losses sustained. It is even harder when the funding body, whose job it is to meet the difference between income and expenditure, has no concept of how marketing success is achieved and would laugh at the idea of keeping money in reserve against a rainy day. Successes are achieved although many opt for the cautious path.

The ultimate in caution I found in Malvern in the sixties when I went to look for places where the English Sinfonia might play. There I met a man who, if he were around, would fit in very well with the arts bureaucrats of today. He was in charge of a very nice little theatre and he had observed that every time he put on an event it lost money – so he kept it closed and spent the money he had on keeping the place very clean.

Business activities tend to work in a spiral form; they either spiral upwards and outwards, growing and feeding their growth from their growth, or they contract. The contracting spiral is the destroying disease. You take less money so you spend less money. You spend less money so you take less money. You either end up running a clean little theatre in Malvern or you vanish up your own deficit.

Which brings me to the horror – the sheer, unmitigated, undiluted and stark horror – of the Arts Council's decision to axe the grant to two of London's orchestras. Not only is the decision itself appalling as far as the orchestras are concerned but what it has to say about the mental processes of those who made it tells us that it is time for them to *go. Go to Malvern. Take early retirement in the land of Onan. But *GO*.

The justification offered by these jacks-in-office is that audiences are getting smaller so it makes perfectly good sense to reduce the supply of concerts. Which way is this spiral going?

The Arts Council has dabbled a bit in marketing over the years, most notably during the time of a Secretary-General who thought that a double-breasted suit turned you into a businessman. Under him there was an undistinguished team who practised 'marketing by clipboard' (you present a list of marketing projects to the council, get approval and proceed, ticking off each project as it is completed irrespective of its relevance or its success – and then you jump swiftly to the next job with a better salary). The Arts Council never learned – and still does not know – how marketing works. It has had countless examples of successful marketing stuck under its nose but it could not, it would not learn. After nearly fifty years it has learned not one damned thing about marketing nor how to use its money to stimulate better marketing within its client organisations.

The Arts Council *has* learned that if you lose money you need money if you are to keep going. Until recently it has been quite good at supplying money but when the money supply was reduced all it could say was, 'Less money means less music– and look, fewer people want it anyway so it's only right.'

Arts businesses are organic. They are born, they grow, they fade but they rarely die. People move on, people are kicked out. New people come in. New goals are created. New strategies. New energies. Confidence blooms. And then the trough is passed and you are riding on the crest again. Does anyone seriously believe that audience levels cannot be brought back to where they were ten years ago? Obviously, some do.

To knock down the factory that makes the goods, because of a temporary decline in manifested demand is blindly stupid. To the perpetrators I put one question: if demand for orchestral music continues to fall, will you then destroy another orchestra? And if the decline continues will you then wipe out them all?

*1994 note. They went. The orchestras stayed

ONE STEP BEYOND THE

MIDDLE AGES?

It was the reference to 'devising and implementing marketing and publicity', provisional wording for an element in the proposed Level 3 NSVQ, Arts and Entertainment Marketing, carried in *Training Matters* that caught my eye. Having seen so many job advertisements over the years for Marketing and Press Officer, Public Relations and Press Manager, Publicity and Marketing Officer and all the others that reveal an underlying confusion as to what marketing is and what are its component parts, it struck me that perhaps it was time to see if there was now a consensus – and, if there was, to publish it for the enlightenment of all.

I drew up a list of people prominent in arts marketing, told them an article on arts marketing was in the offing and asked if they would answer three questions.

My first question referred to the published provisional NSVQ wording and said that it 'suggests that *marketing* is seen as something separate from *publicity*; it then went on to ask, 'In your view, are they separate activities – that is, are they mutually exclusive activities albeit activities that are operated in harmony? Or, as is sometimes thought, is *marketing* an all-embracing word for an activity that encompasses *publicity* as it does other marketing activities such as market research, sales and so on?'.

The encouraging news is that amongst those who replied (not all did reply) there is a most positive agreement that marketing is an activity that is the sum of many parts, of which publicity is one.

Peter Verwey, senior marketing officer of the Arts Council, simply agreed with the second proposition, 'Yes', he said, 'marketing is an all-embracing word encompassing publicity along with other activities such as market research, sales promotion etc.' Before going on to elaborate on what he saw as the role of publicity he expressed the interesting view that the term publicity was not much used outside the arts, entertainment, publishing, charity or voluntary sector.

I found myself agreeing with Peter as far as the working world is concerned; amongst the general public the word publicity is used widely and loosely to collectify advertising in the media, PR use of press, radio and television, opening garden fetes, swimming the channel, getting punched in a restaurant – anything that attracts attention. Within the world of commercial marketing, where roles are clearly defined, the word publicity would have virtually no place because it is ill-defined, too loose, not specific. In the arts we are more comfortable with it because our profession largely grew from people who were not trained, who came into it as members of the general public with a leaning towards the arts and the word was part of our day-to-day vocabulary. Nowadays, we have a much more precise understanding of what we mean when we use the word 'publicity' – although, as we shall see from a later article, we are by no means completely at one.

Now is not time for it but it would be interesting, would it not, to examine the backgrounds of the people who came into the work from, say, the sixties and seventies, when the Arts Council was well into its stride and the Regional Arts Associations were up and running, when the regional theatre movement was expanding and so on – when hundreds of new jobs were created? That was a time when the industry we know now was substantially created from people with different backgrounds, members of the general public who brought with them the ideas and language of the untrained, general public.

And with such a background perhaps it is no wonder that we still have confusion over our terminology.

Back to the original topic. John Matthews of McCann Matthews Millman said, 'There can be no question that publicity is one of many activities that fall within the marketing function. If the concept of the Marketing mix (the 4 Ps of Product, Price, Place and Promotion) is applicable to the arts, publicity is part of Promotion.'

Roger Tomlinson of A.R.T.S. said that if one takes the holistic approach, and believes that everything an organisation does involves marketing 'then it seems preposterous to separate publicity from marketing. Publicity is clearly an activity … which is part of marketing as a whole.'

Guy Chapman of the Royal Court Theatre and one of the prime

movers behind the newly formed Arts Marketing Association extended his reply to include practitioners (as well as revealing a small amount of terminological uncertainty). 'I wouldn't see that marketing and publicity were mutually exclusive activities but would subscribe to the view that the term marketing would include such specific tasks as publicity and press. The skill in one specialised area doesn't necessarily mean that the person is *per se* a marketing person but certainly one that takes part in the overall marketing function of the organisation.'

David Fishel, a partner in Positive Solutions, offered ' ... my perception is that publicity is a communications activity which follows decisions about the product, timing and pricing amongst others; whereas marketing is an activity which embraces those decisions.'

I had included Geoffrey Brown of Euclid and Rick Welton of Arts and Entertainment Training Council (AETC) in my list of those from whom responses were sought, because they are working together on the development of the National and Scottish Vocational Qualifications. They opted to reply as one and their letter completed the picture of unanimity that had emerged. It is good to see them saying that 'AETC standards no longer describe marketing as "devising and implementing marketing and publicity". Their view is that 'marketing should be seen as a generic or all-embracing term, covering publicity as one of many activities.'

In other respects what they had to say was as confusing as I find all their printed words for they clearly live in a world they have built for themselves out of analyses, structures, definitions, terminology, and numerology – and it is a world that I fear I may never inhabit. Others may feel the same. Whenever I read their meticulous breakdowns of activities with which I am very familiar I find myself saying 'But what about ...?' and I become aware of what I can only describe as *holes* and *warps* in their analyses.

Perhaps my failure to make sense of what they say is but an illustration of what happens when a profession expands rapidly without the benefit of the slow and painstaking development of ideas, rules, language and practice that underpins, for example, surveying, law, dentistry and engineering. Are we all, when it comes to marketing, still in the middle ages?

But we have agreement that marketing is an all-embracing activity and that publicity, however we define it, is part of it. That is a step forward.

My other questions to 'our panel' asked for a definition of the marketing function and their views on what is its objective. Their answers will form the basis of my next arts marketing article.

I should like to thank Geoffrey Brown, Guy Chapman, David Fishel, John Matthews, Roger Tomlinson, Rick Welton and Peter Verwey for their generous and prompt response to my request and thus their contributions to this article.

THE NEED FOR A UNIFIED
MARKETING THEORY

A month ago I reported that I had found a substantial degree of agreement on the simple issue of whether or not publicity should be seen as part of marketing. In spite of hints to the contrary – particularly emanating from the direction of the Arts and Entertainment Training Council – when faced with the direct question, the experts I approached, who included the AETC people, were unanimous in the view that marketing must be seen as the all-embracing function that incorporates ... well, certainly publicity.

The mini-questionnaire that I sent out prior to writing that article also asked if a *definition* of the marketing function and also a view of what is its *objective* could be offered. I did qualify my reference to marketing by saying 'as it relates to the arts' and, through a slip of the finger, referred to *arts marketing* – as though I thought it was something different, which, of course, I do.

I do think it is important to make this distinction between marketing, that is commercial marketing, and arts marketing. In July 1988 so concerned was I about the 'outside' influences that were being brought to bear upon arts marketing that I wrote and published a booklet called *Who is to market the arts?*. It makes quaint reading now that 'the suits' have moved on from the Arts Council but I think that I would today stand by much of what I said then. For example:

In 1970 I developed the combination of ideas I termed arts marketing. The essence of arts marketing is to accept the philosophical basis of the work we do (that is, it isn't done for profit and we don't always set out to give the public what it says it wants) whilst using an analysis and methodology – even terminology on occasions – that is derived from arts rather than commercial work. It aims to bring about optimum audience sizes and to yield the possible financial outcome. I summed it up in a statement made many years ago:

* See Appendix Two

The primary aim of arts marketing is to bring an appropriate number of people into an appropriate form of contact with the artist and in so doing to arrive at the best financial outcome that is compatible with the achievement of that aim.

It was this definition of purpose and function that eventually won for the arts marketing idea the support of the doubters and waiverers in the arts industry; for some years now arts marketing as defined above has not been a controversial topic amongst them.

This approach, the stating of primary and secondary objectives, and the confidence I expressed then in its general acceptance by those who work in the arts is in some way vindicated by the replies I received, but these are replies from just a few people, albeit experts; I am now not so sure about how the majority of younger arts marketers would have responded – in the light of the influences to which they have been subjected.

And not all the experts toe my line. John Matthews, with what I take to be approval, quotes from the recent Welsh Arts Council's Marketing Strategy (author unknown, I am afraid – can anyone help?):

Marketing is a management discipline which helps an organisation to achieve its financial, social and educational objectives. It does so through promoting and making readily available an appropriate product to chosen markets and gaining the optimum financial result from the process. In the arts, effective marketing helps to create the conditions within which artistic experiment may be encouraged and wider and more appreciative audiences developed. Because marketing takes the customer as its focus, everyone within an organisation who has contact with the public shares responsibility for the outcome of the process and for monitoring its success.

Note the absence of an arts connection; the first and second sentences do not mention the arts at all. The third sentence, grafted on rather awkwardly, happens, I believe, to be true but it does strike me as being something of a sop to help make meaningful the inadequacy and inappropriateness of the opening. The final sentence is a pious *non sequitur*. It looks like a definition borrowed from a commercial marketing textbook and then tarted up to make it 'arts relevant.'

And I'm not too happy about David Fishel's offering, taken from

Peter Drucker's *Management of Non-Profit Organisations*, it being an adaptation of a definition from Philip Kotler:

Marketing is a way to harmonise the needs and wants of the outside world with the purposes and the resources and objectives of the institution.

So is running a fish and chip shop. It is true enough, I suppose, but it is so general that it is almost meaningless. It is certainly valueless for any practical purpose.

Geoffrey Brown and Rick Welton, in their combined report, state in their Daleklike way (sorry chaps but that is the way it comes out) that

the key purpose agreed by AETC is: 'to create, present and promote arts and entertainment.' Within this key purpose, 6 key functions were identified. Key function 5 is:

'enable people to experience arts and entertainment.'
With this key function, a number of key roles were then developed. Key Role 52 is:
'ensure awareness and optimise consumption of arts and entertainment.'

This final statement, Key Role 52, they say *'reflects the view of the sector, as consulted by the AETC, and seems to us to encapsulate both the objective and function of marketing.'*

You may well see this as an explanation of why they overlook matters of, for example, Sales and Sales Promotion and if you find their approach inadequate then mark those words ' ... the view of the sector, as consulted by the AETC'. So, what is said here is just a reflection of what people working in the field told the authors. Do you see what I mean about the importance of getting the basics sorted out?

As a 'sector', we need to discuss these matters urgently; not only do we need an agreed objective/definition for arts marketing but also agreement on what are the parts that make up the whole. We need a unified theory to which we all subscribe.

COMMERCIAL INFLUENCES

When I read the American book *Waiting in the Wings* by Morison and Dalgeish (pub. American Council for the Arts 1987) I was very struck by their philosophical basis; they said we must keep searching:

for the perfect middle ground that will allow the arts to draw upon the rich resources of business acumen without allowing differences in values to distort the primary goals, the definitive purpose of art. They went on to say: *When the goal is creating a love affair between people and a certain vision of art then changing the product does not help to accomplish that end; it betrays it.*

These words were very much a defense thrown up against the newcomer – the board member, the sponsor, the ad agency superstar offering help 'in kind' – who just couldn't see that there was a problem. You just asked people what they wanted and then gave it to them; what could be easier?

At the time it did seem that the influence of commercial marketing ideas might well put the artistic 'product' in its place, so to speak, making it subordinate to the need, if not actually to make a profit, to make the marketing process as risk-free as possible by choosing 'product' that was safe, for which there was a predictable demand, which was 'popular'.

The disagreement is between those who do not believe that marketing can operate successfully in a risky business like the arts and those who do. Commercial marketing cannot tolerate the notion of having product that is out of control. Arts marketing accepts this situation as being part of the territory; by bringing those who choose or make the art close to the results of their decisions it hopes to keep feet mainly on the ground but ultimately the only real control lies in the right of the arts organisation to fire artistic directors. This is the first difference between commercial marketing and arts marketing and it is here that the philosophical basis of our work stands clearly revealed. In *Guide to Arts Marketing* I said:

> *We know that in practice most arts organisations do their best to strike a balance between what is artistically adventurous and worthwhile (and probably more of a box-office risk), and what is likely to receive a more predictably good response. Others follow an even safer course, sticking to known favourites ... Each approach is an attempt to respond to some kind of public demand as seen through the eyes of the organisation. It is guesswork, of course ... The whole art of programming for an arts organisation is based on a sensitive appreciation of who the market is, what it wants now* and what it may be persuaded to want in the future *and the relation of those perceptions to what the organisation is capable of delivering.*

I am saying that in arts marketing we know and accept ours to be a harder field to plough. We need and accept public subsidy because the income and expenditure equation, no matter how we try, no matter how good our 'product', no matter how large our audiences, no matter how economical we are in what we pay ourselves and what we spend on our 'product' and in our attempts to persuade people to experience it, mainly ends up with a loss. If we took the commercial marketing road then we are pretty sure that we would end up with something that ... wasn't right; we might be cheaper to run but we probably wouldn't be worth running.

When I first examined the business I was in the thoughts that came to me were uninfluenced by commercial thinking. I had no marketing experience. Most important, I had read no books on marketing. Indeed, when I published my first book in 1976 I had still read no books on marketing. I do not normally glorify ignorance but there is something to be said for an *a priori* approach to problem solving. I looked at the resources possessed by arts organisations, at the traditional attitudes and practices I came across, at what I was doing and why I thought I was doing it and, just about then, I was asked to give some talks on publicity. Standing in front of a group of people focuses the mind and out of respect for them I tried to come up with some useful analysis. And then there was (for me at least) a memorable meeting of what was called the Standing Conference of

Regional Arts Associations; it was held in Oxford and on 3 June 1971 I offered those *present some naive thoughts on what arts marketing might be.

I started by putting the arts on a pedestal, giving the arts a special place free from interference; I said that arts organisations *exist to provide and nurture a link between the artist and the public*. I then suggested that the process of bringing the two together had two parts. One was called *Publicity* and the other *Point of Sale*. This very quickly became *Publicity makes them want to buy* and *Sales makes them actually do it*. This simple statement remains for me a crucial concept in marketing. It explains so many failures. It highlights so many deficiencies in organisations. Simple and obvious as it is it is still not widely accepted by arts marketers.

In that same SCRAA paper I said that publicity was made up of *Advertising* and *Public Relations* with the two combining to persuade people to want to buy what was on sale. Later I expanded on this to offer publicity as a function that would motivate people who were already favorably inclined to what was on sale and would also change the attitudes of those who were not at the time favorably inclined. Publicity is thus capable of helping to create audiences now and laying the foundations for attracting future audiences – provided, of course, that it is part of an integrated marketing approach that includes the vital Sales concept.

In January 1993 the Welsh Arts Council published its marketing strategy. I don't wish to disparage a commendable initiative but I will highlight one statement to illustrate my view that there is work to be done *now* in bringing about a consensus on what arts marketing is, what are its components, what parts are played by the components and how they relate one to another.

It is perhaps simplest to say that publicity tells people: What, Where, When, and therefore can only preach to the converted.

*Unfortunately the then Deputy Secretary-General of the Arts Council, Angus Stirling, had to leave the conference just before I delivered the paper and didn't ask for a copy to read on the train. The paper is reproduced in Appendix One

PREACHING TO THE UNCONVERTED AS WELL - ARTS MARKETING THAT LOOKS BEYOND SITTING DUCKS

When I ended my most recent article in the Arts Marketing series I left you with this quotation from the Welsh Arts Council's published marketing strategy (and a very strong hint that I disagreed with it):

It is perhaps simplest to say that publicity tells people: What, Where, When, and therefore can only preach to the converted

In the preceding two articles I also placed considerable emphasis on the need, that I perceive, for a general agreement between practitioners of arts marketing on what is arts marketing, what are its components, what parts are played by the components and how they relate one to another.

This is not mere pedantry. It is my profound belief that if those who practise marketing in the arts do not now come together and agree on the theory, the methodology and the terminology of what they do, they will not make the progress that the recent formation of the *Arts Marketing Association implicitly demands. They will also leave themselves wide open to yet another onslaught from yet another generation of what I once called 'the denizens of Campaignia' with all the time and money wasting and frustration that this would involve. We must plant our standard firmly in the ground and say to our arts manager colleagues, 'This is *our* profession, we know what we are doing, so respect and value us.' And to those who practise marketing in the commercial sector we must say, 'If you want to do business with us you must do it on our terms and respect what we do and why we do it.'

*Formed towards the end of 1993

But we cannot yet make such a confident show. Let's see if we can take the first step forward by examining the statement I quoted above. It says that publicity can only preach to the converted. Now, if this is true one must ask, then who *is* to preach to the unconverted? If you have a marketing theory that works for the arts then you must either provide an answer to that question or base your marketing theory upon the notion that the unconverted are not our responsibility – and if it is not ours, then whose is it? Ruling out those who do not *at this moment* like what we have to sell takes us straight into the commercial marketing camp and very soon we find ourselves thinking that there really is no difference between *our* marketing and *their* marketing. You can see why that statement worried me.

We *do* have to preach to the unconverted. It is one of the reasons why we are justified in taking the taxpayer's money. To what extent you emphasise this goal amongst your many other goals depends on what kind of arts organisation you are and what are your philosophical goals, but you cannot base your marketing theory upon the practice of only shooting sitting ducks; it must embrace the wider target and offer a way of reaching it.

In books and articles and lectures I have suggested that we see publicity as being responsible for making people *want to buy* what we have to sell and that we attach to publicity no greater responsibility than that. Once we have brought people to the boil, once they are ready to buy, we can step in and sell it to them.

The success of our persuasion will always be dependent upon the attitudes *at this moment* of those we are trying to persuade. Those with a favourable attitude to what we are trying to sell may be persuaded. Those who don't like it or, since this is a matter of attitudes, those who think they don't like it as well as those who know they don't like it are going to be harder to persuade because first their attitudes must be changed. (Take heart in the knowledge that attitudes can be changed, they are being changed all the time – if they can't be changed then why have elections? Why have you given up smoking? How does the fashion world survive?).

So publicity has a dual function: first, to persuade those who are already favourably inclined to what we have on offer to want to buy it and secondly, to make more favourable the attitudes of those who are indifferent or hostile to what we have on offer so that they may then be persuaded to want to buy what we have to sell. The first task is the responsibility of what is usually called *Advertising*. The second is the responsibility of a component of *Public Relations*, a complex activity which can be targeted at both converted and unconverted.

Public Relations works in a variety of ways with a variety of different aims and targets and works most visibly when providing the flesh to the bones of persuasive messages conveyed by Advertising; this is *Product PR*. Operating in harness the two are focused on those who are, by virtue of their present attendance performance or by their inclinations (which we may very well have to guess at), within our reach and most likely to respond to what we say about what we have on offer.

Public Relations is also used to give credibility to the combined messages of Product PR and Advertising by establishing the trustworthiness of the body that is presenting and/or housing the event. This is called *Corporate PR* and it is mainly aimed at those who are already favourably inclined towards what is on offer. The underlying thought is that the message about the product may be very appealing but who is delivering the message? Are they telling the truth? If an organisation has a reputation for shoddy work then no matter what it says via Advertising and Product PR its words will be doubted. Corporate PR is slow, painstaking work, requiring the organisation to project itself constantly as it wishes to be seen and then living up to that image. As time goes by, as success follows success, so the corporate image becomes more and more important in this process of persuasion. In an ideal situation the organisation can get to the point where what it is offering becomes attractive simply by virtue of the fact that *this* organisation is doing the offering.

But what of the unconverted? If the processes just referred to can only work on attitudes that are favourable then the next task must be to work on those with unfavourable attitudes. That is, to convert the unconverted – but not by using techniques that only work with those who are already converted. The only hope lies in what may be termed *Educational PR*, the development and implementation of programmes that take people by the hand, as it were, dispelling their prejudices, opening their eyes, helping them to 'get into' what has so far been foreign territory. We have done very little work of this kind and in the present climate are likely to do less but it lies at the heart of what this whole business is about. If we exclude the possibility of ever widening our audiences, if we abandon the ideal, then we fail society and we fail ourselves.

A wider view, then, of Publicity; to be seen as a vital part of arts marketing that is capable of making the most of the potential that exists now and of working to expand that potential. Now, look again at the WAC statement; do you agree with it?

BACK TO FIRST PRINCIPLES -
A FOUNDATION STONE FOR
ARTS MARKETING

It is impossible to overstate the importance of getting the starting point, the fundamental concept, right in the development of any area of human knowledge and activity. If you start with the thought that what we now call 'space' is full of a substance called 'aether' which acts as a medium through which light is transmitted, then any development of this thought will only go so far before the fundamental concept is found to be false. If you observe the pus that forms in an infected wound and postulate that the pus is actually a curative agent necessary to the healing process then it will seem sensible to do things to the wound that will make it produce pus until somebody discovers what the pus actually is and knocks the theory down.

I do not put arts marketing on the same level of importance as physics and medicine but I do believe that just as in the eighteenth century when those disciplines were evolving very rapidly it is most important to determine what is the correct concept upon which to base your further thoughts.

The concept of arts marketing to which I have always adhered, which has influenced everything I have thought, written and spoken is, I believe, the correct one; it is not 'aether' or what was once called 'laudable pus'. It has led no-one up the wrong garden path. Yet I have always wondered why it has failed to persuade people away from what I believe to be other garden paths leading to wrong conclusions.

Perhaps the fault lies in the expression of the idea rather than the idea itself? Perhaps all my work have been influenced by ideas that are, after all, in my head rather than explicitly stated, in print, for all to see. Maybe I have taken too much for granted. For people who have worked in the business for a long time, who subscribe to the underlying philosophy of the job, who have engaged in the inevitable metaphysical discussions on 'why we are all here', I do not think there is a major problem, but for those who are new to it, those who are enjoying some form of vocational training, those who are doing the training without having had any direct practical experience of doing the job and thus engaging in those inevitable discussions and those who are bringing to bear influences (largely commercial and academic) upon how the arts should be marketed, the absence of a clearly stated, unequivocal, starting point – a policy statement, if you like – may account for some of the disagreements and anomalies I have observed and commented on in this column.

Some time ago I included in this column a range of statements from a range of people that attempted to define this starting point. You may remember that I asked several people to contribute and I included five statements that attempted to define arts marketing either by saying what it did and how it was carried out or by saying what it was intended to achieve. I included my own version.

I also included a statement from the Welsh Arts Council's marketing strategy that was sent in by John Matthews. I treated that statement rather harshly at the time, mainly, I think, because its final sentence seemed to pick up on the commercial view that marketing must be wholly customer orientated when all of us who work or have worked in the arts know that we do what we do with artists in mind as well as customers. We are trying to keep going a whole structure of making and selecting art and bringing it into contact with people whilst keeping the whole shebang rolling. We know we cannot say 'the public won't eat margarine so we must stop making and selling margarine.' What I overlooked – and for this I offer my sincere apologies to the author or authors – was the significance of the opening sentence which said: *Marketing is a management discipline which helps an organisation to achieve its financial, social and educational objectives.*

My own objective/definition has a number of virtues but it is not in the complete form that I believe it should be if it is to lay claim to being the *starting point*, the fundamental concept upon which we should all agree and which should inform all subsequent theoretical and practical developments. The thought was right but the expression of it was incomplete.

Let us then combine the two statements into what I would

respectfully suggest should be acceptable to all who work in our business and should be accepted by those who would enter or influence it. I offer it in particular to our newly formed Arts Marketing Association with the suggestion that it forms the basis of its thinking over the years to come. Perhaps it could be embroidered into a sampler or turned into an oath along the lines of the Scouts' and Guides' Promise.

I have asked the good daughters and sons of Caxton to write this statement large – and to italicise the vital addition based on the Welsh Arts Council statement and suggest that this might be the definition of what I shall hereinafter always call (given that italics are at my disposal) *Arts* Marketing so that there can be no confusion with any other kind.

ARTS MARKETING

The aim of *arts* marketing is to bring an appropriate number of people, *drawn from the widest possible range of social background, economic condition and age*, into an appropriate form of contact with the artist and, in so doing, to arrive at the best financial outcome that is compatible with the achievement of that aim.

PART FIVE

A P P E N D I C E S

MARKETING THE ARTS - 1971 paper

WHO IS TO MARKET THE ARTS? - 1988 pamphlet

APPENDIX ONE

This is an historic document as it is the first attempt made in the UK to offer any kind of theoretical basis for work that was hitherto run according to a simple formula based on traditional practices – 'publicity' was all and all publicity was, was leaflets ('throwaways' they were called) and posters produced in quantities governed by the size of the budget. Such a method usually worked well enough if 'stars' were being presented but the advent of a state subsidy system had led to arts presentations involving performers who were not famous. It thus became necessary to think more about how this work should be approached – and that is what I did.

The reader will find ideas here that are ill expressed and, perhaps, slightly at variance with what has been read earlier in the book but, remember please, these words were written nearly twenty five years ago.

MARKETING THE ARTS

Paper produced for the 1971 Summer Conference of the Standing Conference of Regional Arts Associations by Keith Diggle (Director: Merseyside Arts Association)

Introduction

The situation in the Arts is very different from that in Commerce and Industry. It differs in terms of its product and in the way that it is marketed. It is only quite recently that the need to apply marketing techniques to the Arts has been appreciated and, quite naturally, the tendency has been to look to those who practise the craft in other fields to see how their techniques may be applied to our problems. It may be that now those who work in the Arts are ready to produce their own techniques and their own solutions to these problems.

What is Marketing?

Clearly two major factors are involved: the Product and the means by which it is brought before the public. In turn the latter factor may be seen to break down into two basic elements: the means by which the public is informed and persuaded (or motivated) to enter into a psychological commitment with the artistic event and, finally, the translation of that commitment into the appropriate physical action. Thus there are three basic areas which we must consider:

The Product – clearly *what* is to be marketed has a bearing on the *way* it is to be marketed

The Publicity – often thought of as being the entire marketing function but in fact only a part, albeit a major part

The Point of Sale – really the point of commitment and the means whereby the wish is made father to the deed

It may be helpful now to consider each area in turn.

The Product

Here the fundamental difference between the Arts and Industry/Commerce is exposed. In our situation the Product, whatever artistic form it may choose to appear in, is our *raison d'être*; all artistic organisations exist merely to nurture this and to provide a link between the artist and the public. The reaction of the public to the artistic product is, in all normal circumstances, irrelevant to the artist in the short term. It has been proved many times over that public taste lags behind the artist by many years and so the artistic Product must always be the sole responsibility of the artist and must not be influenced by public opinion as manifested at the Box Office. This is not to say that the *means* whereby the Product is introduced to the public should not be influenced by public reaction – indeed it should and a sensitivity to this reaction must be part of the stock-in-trade of the Arts marketer.

In Business the aim is to make a profit and so consideration of the Product cannot take place without consideration of how it is to be sold. There must be maximum feedback throughout the whole marketing chain so that the Product can be modified according to the needs of the market. If the public rejects a Product utterly then profitability demands that the Product be discontinued.

Having established this basic distinction as a matter of underlying principle we must also grant the artistic organisation the right of self-preservation in a commercial world. Thus the long-term needs of the organisation must also be considered and may occasionally over-ride the needs of an individual artistic contributor to that organisation. Although profitability is not the prime concern of the organisation financial stability is vital and no artistic policy can be accepted that will push the organisation beyond the limits of its budget.

Thus, those who market the Arts must accept the Product as it is but those who create the Product must be aware of their rôle in the marketing process.

The Publicity

If the Publicity function is considered in the abstract without any specific relation to any one type of artistic organisation it will be seen that there are two distinct and separate functions within it. These 'sub-functions' are:

Advertising and Public Relations

The distinction between the two is perhaps best expressed by the way in which the media of communication are employed. In Advertising we have absolute control over these media, we buy time and space and we dictate what occupies that time and space. In Public Relations the media have absolute control over us; we give them information, they interpret it as they will and use it as they will.

Another distinction between the two is in their duration. Advertising tends to be finite and aimed at specific objectives, the concert, the play, the exhibition and so on. Public Relations is a continuous process that is from time to time focused on particular objectives.

Thus we speak of an *Advertising Campaign* and a *Public Relations Programme*.

Definitions may be useful here. I would hesitatingly suggest the following in relation to Arts advertising:

'The Advertising Campaign aims to define a potential audience and by means of suitably chosen and exploited media, to create in that potential audience a climate of opinion likely to produce a favourable commitment to the artistic activity that is the subject of the campaign.'

The Institute of Public Relations has agreed upon a definition of the practice of Public Relations as being:

'The deliberate, planned and sustained effort to establish and maintain mutual understanding between an organisation and its public'.

The two functions are not mutually exclusive. Publicity planned for a specific event will require an Advertising Campaign and associated Public Relations activities. A Public Relations programme will certainly have to employ specific Advertising elements.

The Point of Sale

This part of the marketing process deals with the indeterminate period of time between the 'favourable commitment' referred to in the definition of an Advertising Campaign and the translation of that commitment into the appropriate physical action. It is a part of the process that is not widely appreciated.

In the majority of cases it simply means the way in which the public may purchase tickets for an event. Most artistic events involve the payment of money and the sale of tickets is the most usual way of receiving money and reserving places. The system also simplifies accounting and enables checks to be made on the progress of an Advertising Campaign.

The definition of an Advertising Campaign also refers to a 'potential audience' and this implies some form of geographical limit to the campaign. It follows from this that the number and type of ticket sales outlets must bear some relation to this geographical 'target' area.

The underlying principle here must be that the committed person must have every possible inducement offered to encourage him to commit himself finally by the purchase of a ticket. Key factors must therefore be:

The location of ticket outlets

Their hours of opening

Their attractiveness

The quality of their staffing

Special facilities offered: telephone and postal booking services

The period of advance booking (which clearly must coincide with the commencement of the campaign)

The venue for an event is frequently an important ticket sales outlet itself and so these factors must also apply to this as well.

It goes without saying there are important implications here for the Advertising and Public Relations functions so that the advantages of the ticket sales system may be brought to the attention of the public and any disadvantages compensated for.

Responsibilities

It becomes increasingly clear that the Marketing process cannot be the responsibility of one person nor can it be that of one department. It must be the responsibility of the artistic organisation as a whole. The Product is the concern of the person with artistic responsibility, the Publicity that of a department with two main responsibilities – Advertising and Public Relations, the Point of Sale that of Publicity and of everyone concerned with contact with the public. Thus Marketing responsibilities run throughout the arts organisation and cannot be hived off into any one department.

Keith Diggle
3 June 1971

APPENDIX TWO

WHO IS TO MARKET THE ARTS?

This too is an historic document in that it records my serious disquiet in the mid-eighties with the way the Arts Council of Great Britain had taken the initiative over marketing the arts and was busy making a hash of it. The new girls and boys on the block paid scant attention to those, like myself, who had been working hard to develop the ideas and practices from within the industry and the new Marketing and Resources Department was going from strength to strength – in the wrong direction.

It was around this time that I was invited to sit on the advisory panel of what was called the Arts Marketing Scheme *which had been set up by the Office of Arts and Libraries (now Department of National Heritage). The idea of the scheme was to make grants to support marketing projects. It was a development of the idea outlined as an appendix in* Guide To Arts Marketing *where it was called 'Artsbank'. At the time of the Arts Council's takeover bid I was Vice President of the Society of Arts Publicists; at a meeting on 10 January 1986 I put forward a development of the Artsbank idea calling it the 'Arts Marketing Incentive Scheme' (AMIS, for short). By presenting such a scheme to government I believed that much needed support might then be given to the better arts marketers and their employing organisations – and, as the originator of the scheme, the Society of Arts Publicists would benefit in terms of its own standing in the eyes of present and potential members. (The idea of turning SAP into an Institute of Arts Marketing was very much in my mind at that time).*

The SAP committee backed it and on 9 April 1986 the chairman, deputy chairman and myself were at the Office of Arts and Libraries presenting the AMIS document to the civil servant who was responsible for the Arts Council and the OAL's various other responsibilities in the arts. The civil servant (let us call him 'Rodney') listened intently, commented that the idea of having people return grant money once they had succeeded (a fundamental idea of both 'Artsbank' and 'AMIS') would not find favour with his political masters, and said he would think about it.

Two months later, on 2 June 1986, having heard nothing since our meeting with 'Rodney', I was invited to a lunch at the Arts Council in company with PR consultant and member of SAP's committee, Mary Fulton. It was a high level affair attended amongst others by the Secretary General, Luke Rittner, the head of the Marketing and Resources Department, Dylan Hammond, a commercial advertising agency person and 'Rodney'. The purpose of the lunch was to introduce to us an Office of Arts and Libraries initiative, a new scheme to encourage a more positive approach to marketing the arts through special grants. 'Rodney' told us that it would be known as the 'Arts Marketing Scheme' (AMS, for short). Only 'I' was missing.

Not a hint of embarrassment crossed the face of 'Rodney'. It was most definitely the product of his own fertile brain and he told Mary Fulton and I about it with exactly the same degree of enthusiasm and detail as he told the others. 'Hell!' said Mary, sotto voce, *'He's swiped your bloody idea!'. What could we say? What could a couple of innocents like us do up against a veritable Sir Humphrey?*

My invitation to join the advisory panel of AMS only happened after SAP had pointedly asked 'What about us?' when it became apparent that with one exception only commercial folk were to be involved in the advisory/selection process. I was duly appointed. I attended meeting after meeting, collected huge piles of applications, and became profoundly depressed by how the scheme as modified by the civil servants seemed to exclude most applications. Projects had to be 'innovatory; this was the crucial criterion but innovatory in relation to what? Since almost none of the applicants had ever had the chance of working with sufficient money and since virtually no serious development or training had ever taken place, simply promoting a show with half a chance of success would be an innovation. Although we all put on a brave face (it became 'our' scheme and we wanted very badly for it to work) when it ended no-one seriously claimed it as a success. Of course the inevitable conclusion was that arts people weren't very good at marketing and they needed more help from commercial experts and from academics, didn't they?

Some time later I used the moral pressure lever to raise the idea with 'Rodney' of turning the Society of Arts Publicists into the kind of Institute of Arts Marketing I had referred to in Guide To Arts Marketing *with the help of government money. Although he didn't show it, he must have felt some guilt (mustn't he?). I outlined what I had in mind and, at his request, drafted some figures to show what might be involved in setting up a very small office with minimal staffing. He explained that although he found the idea attractive he could not possibly take any action unless the Arts Council were behind the idea as well. He would consult with the head of the Marketing and Resources Department. I went along to petition Mr Hammond on 15 July 1987. He bought me lunch but felt he couldn't back the idea. To 'Rodney' he said 'No'.*

And so, dearly beloved, that is why the Institute of Arts Marketing was not formed in 1986 and the Arts Marketing Association was not able to be created until 1993.

'Rodney' left the OAL soon afterwards to write 'thrillers and chillers' as he put it and did so most successfully; there is no reason to doubt that his plots were wholly original. He was and still is (I have met him socially since that time) a charming and intelligent man but he was then a civil servant and that gave his personality a wholly different dimension.

I wondered what would be the best thing to do next. I was approached by Timothy Mason, then director of Scottish Arts Council, who wanted to focus the attention of his constituency upon arts marketing and asked me what was the next logical step to take, what was going to be the burning issue of the next few years? I suggested that a symposium be organised by SAC together with SAP on the theme of how to address the problem of what I now term the 'Unavailable Audience'. Called Changing Their Minds *and held in Glasgow on 5 February 1988, the symposium attracted around 160 people. Several people from the arts world, including myself, were invited to speak but the star speakers were professors from the University of Strathclyde marketing department who, although more than adequately briefed by organiser John Matthews, proceeded to churn out the standard commercial marketing pap that might have been suitable for first year students in their day of term but was hardly what 'our' people had travelled hundreds of miles to hear; all speakers from the university managed to avoid the topic of the day with complete success. Together with one commercial PR person and a BBC TV executive producer, who actually did address the issue of changing peoples' minds, 'we' saved the day (in that no-one got lynched) but by the skins of our teeth; once again the 'outsiders' seems determined to do us down. (My key note address to this symposium forms the opening of Part Three of this book.)*

With this sad experience still fresh in my memory, the 'swiping' of the AMIS plan, the failure of the OAL Arts Marketing Scheme and the unsuccessful attempt to start an Institute of Arts Marketing behind me I sat down one day to do some pamphleteering. In the booklet, which I produced and published privately from my home address, I made what I hoped would be a constructive argument in favour of arts people being the best ones to develop arts marketing. Ever hopeful of a change in heart I treated the Arts Council of Great Britain and the Office of Arts and Libraries gently and I did not even complain of how 'Rodney' had 'swiped' my 'bloody idea'. I ended the pamphlet by suggesting how best the Arts Council of Great Britain could help us improve the size and range of our audiences.

As far as I am aware, the pamphlet had no effect whatsoever. It did not change what the OAL did nor did it change what the Arts Council's department of Marketing and Resources was doing. It would be satisfying if I could claim for it the demise of the Marketing and Resources Department and, indeed, the Arts Council of Great Britain itself but these things came to pass for different reasons to do with inertia, lack of intellectual weight, bureaucratic bumbledom and the natural organic processes that bring things to life and then kills them off. The pamphlet remains as a little piece of history and nothing more.

WHO IS TO MARKET THE ARTS?

Arts marketing and commercial marketing – the vital difference

In their recently published *Waiting in the Wings*, authors Morison and Dalgleish (pub: American Council for the Arts 1987), say that we must keep searching, *'for the perfect middle ground that will allow the arts to draw upon the rich resources of business acumen without allowing difference in values to distort the primary goals, the definitive purpose of art'*.

They go on to observe, *'When the goal is creating a love affair between people and a certain artist's vision of art, then changing the product does not help to accomplish that end; it betrays it'*.

Commercial marketing, as developed over the past 30 years or so, puts the focus on the customer and his wants. You find out what he wants and you satisfy him profitably. If you discover that he wants something different then you replace or change what you are selling. The objective is profit and everything must be subordinate to that. This was what originally frightened the Arts Council and many others working in the arts in the very early seventies when the idea that the arts could be marketed in a systematic way was first raised. It also provided them with an excuse to ignore the fact that audiences were small and that there might be techniques that could make them bigger. Audiences were created by God and not by man and it was the government's job to cover the inevitable deficit.

When I started to become involved in these matters, the passive acceptance of small audiences shocked me but I found myself very much in sympathy with the arts people's fears about the dangers of allowing the commercial objective to creep in along with commercial techniques; this could so easily lead to 'Sam Goldwynism' and a corruption of the arts ethos. However, it seemed to me that although our objective was certainly different from the commercial world's there was no excuse for failing to use every possible method available for increasing audiences and the financial yield from those audiences.

Can we ignore what the public wants?

This does not mean that I believed the arts should ignore what the customer wants. In Guide to Arts Marketing I said: '*We know that in practice most arts organisations do their best to strike a balance between what is artistically adventurous and worthwhile (and probably more of a box-office risk), and what is likely to receive a more predictably good response. Others follow an even safer course, sticking to known favourites...Each approach is an attempt to respond to some kind of public demand as seen through the eyes of the organisation. It is guesswork, of course...The whole art of programming for an arts organisation is based on a sensitive appreciation of who the market is, what it wants now* **and what it may be persuaded to want in the future** and the relation of those perceptions to what the organisation is capable of delivering' (p33).

Those words in the quotation were not originally emboldened but, in the light of recent developments, it seems necessary to give them greater emphasis.

It has long been a tradition in the performing arts that the most successful activities are those made to happen by impresarios, people – sometimes artists, sometimes managers – with the entrepreneurial talent. Such people often embody an almost natural marketing ability that enables them to gauge what the public taste is at the time and what it may be persuaded to favour shortly. Their marketing is indeed 'market driven' as the phrase goes but it is not a passive activity, dependent upon research findings nor is it based exclusively upon the inclinations that have been created by other forces, it is highly active using most of the techniques of marketing, and in particular public relations, to make people aware of 'attractions' and to be attracted to them.

The traditional impresario works to make a profit for himself and his investors so his emphasis will be on the activities he is fairly sure will be attractive and profitable. Where market research data exists it is used more as a guide to form than as solid evidence. As an entrepreneur he is willing to take risks and to attempt to sell what at first sight would appear to be unsaleable. Successful British organisations like Raymond Gubbay Limited do not appear to be taking risks because their corporate images project such confidence and success that if they choose to promote something there is a good chance of it becoming 'popular' even before the public has been given the chance of responding to it. I am confident, however, that if one were to be a fly on the wall in their offices there are many occasions when success is by no means a foregone conclusion.

It is not given to the majority of arts managers to possess this gambler's golden touch and so an approach based upon an analysis of what is involved in the total process of promoting an event and a methodology which offers a step-by-step system appeared to me to be extremely useful to the arts manager. This is what I set out to do – to provide a sort of junior impresario's kit.

Arts marketing has its own objective, philosophy, analysis and methodology

In 1970 I developed the combination of ideas I termed arts marketing. The essence of arts marketing is to accept the philosophical basis of the work we do (that is, it isn't done for profit and we don't always set out to give the public what it says it wants) whilst using an analysis and methodology – even terminology on occasions – that is derived from arts rather than commercial work. It aims to bring about optimum audience sizes and to yield the best possible finance outcome. I summed it up in a statement made many years ago: *The primary aim of arts marketing is to bring an appropriate number of people into an outcome that is compatible with the achievement of that aim'.*

It was this definition of purpose and function that eventually won for the arts marketing idea the support of the doubters and waiverers in the arts industry; for some years now arts marketing as defined above has not been a controversial topic amongst them. This fact should not be forgotten.

The analysis and methodology

It would not be appropriate to attempt to cover in this publication what has needed almost a complete book to encompass, but a few pointers may be useful at this stage.

In his book, Marketing The Visual Arts, Professor Leslie W Rodger, of Heriot Watt University in Edinburgh, who has 30 years of marketing practice in commercial and industrial organisations, cites the 'four main headings popularised in the marketing literature – the Four Ps of Marketing: Product, Price, Promotion and Place'. Was there ever a lecturer on commercial marketing who did not cite this oversimplified analysis?

The analysis I offer in arts marketing differs in several respects but the most important one is my expansion of the term 'Promotion' to include Publicity (being described as the complementary functions of advertising and public relations something which the commercial world would agree with in theory but in practice, due to the way in which agencies operate, rarely occurs), Sales and Sales Promotion. I also felt that consideration of the market itself was worthy of enshrinement and so it appears in my analysis.

The methodology involves a consideration of the market in terms of its attitudes and behaviour in relation to the art experience that is being marketed. (Along the way it points out that what is being marketed is experience of art rather than art itself). This is a realistic attempt at market segmentation that is far more practical than talk of identifying arts customers by means of their post codes; surely in itself an illustration of belief in divine intervention. This leads the arts marketer into an understanding of the advertising languages that may be used. The emphasis upon Sales reminds the arts marketer that although Publicity may make someone want to buy, it does not follow that he will buy. The Place of the commercial analysis is subsumed by the wider consideration of Sales with the explanation that for a sale to take place there must be a desire to sell, a desire to buy and a place, or communications system, linking the two. Sales Promotion is then used to reduce or eliminate the obstacles that come between the motivated customer and his ultimate purchase – and this in turn connects with considerations of Price.

And so on. It is an approach which, ironically enough, would prove very useful to commercial marketers and is, indeed, the approach used by my own company, Rhinegold Publishing Limited – a totally commercial outfit.

Publications on arts marketing

It is worth noting also that there have been several published guides for practising arts marketers. From the USA there is most notably Danny Newman's *Subscribe Now!*, a seminal work now in its fifth printing, the more recent *Waiting in the Wings*, already referred to, my own *Marketing the Arts* and *Guide to Arts Marketing* and the four volume set of *Marketing Manuals* produced by the TMA with Arts Council assistance. There are many more that deal with specific subjects such as public relations, print buying and so on. All have come from the arts industry, from people prepared to take the time to lay out their experience and thoughts to help their colleagues. None, to my knowledge, have come from outside the arts industry.

The Minister's Arts Marketing Scheme

In very recent times government pressure has made the Arts Council look hard at sources of revenue other than government subsidy. Sponsorship, a horse ridden enthusiastically by the last Minister for the Arts, Lord Gowrie, would help solve the money problem. Marketing was chosen by the present incumbent, Richard Luce; this has been a major theme of his ministry and he has, quite correctly in my view, highlighted the need for improvement in the practice of marketing within the arts industry.

An interesting glimpse of the present state of arts marketing practice came from the many submissions to the Arts Marketing Scheme initiated by Richard Luce in 1987. The scheme was intended to stimulate and reward innovative marketing projects but the selection panel was unable to recommend a sufficient number of candidates to take up the full allocation of £250,000 made available. This selection panel was made up of one civil servant, with considerable experience of the arts world from a governmental point of view, who chaired the meetings, three people whose experience was wholly in the commercial sector and two, of whom I was one and the other Iain Lanyon, whose experience (and kinship) were primarily in the arts. It is significant that this panel's decisions were unanimous.

The Arts Marketing Scheme showed us that arts people – or rather, many of those who applied – were not yet thinking innovatively about marketing so that many applications fell by the 'innovatory' criterion of the scheme. In our deliberations I was constantly aware of how inappropriate it was to demand innovation from people who had probably never in their professional lives enjoyed sufficient funds to do their jobs properly. Many rejected applications were in themselves perfectly sensible ways of spending money on marketing and would probably have succeeded and there was usually no doubt that the money was needed but the projects were not new and so failed.

The historicial context

This inevitably leads me to a brief consideration of the 20 years or so leading up to the Minister's initiative. For the largest part of that period the Arts Council has been at worst hostile and at best lukewarm to the idea that the arts could and should be marketed. People with marketing responsibilities have been very low in management hierarchies, generally untrained (there being few opportunities for training) and badly paid. Arts organisations, addicted to subsidy, could see little point in spending any more money on marketing activities than their generally very small budgets would permit. When an arts organisation, usually led by an inspired individual, did break through and create larger audiences and income there was no official approbation and it was generally held by the religiously minded establishment that the increase 'would have happened anyway' because of any number of factors having nothing to do with the activities. At the most basic level as far as the individual was concerned, a marketing success did not particularly help one's career. Until very recently there was nothing to suggest that the Arts Council was unhappy about this state of affairs nor indeed felt any responsibility for its existence.

Drawing the wrong conclusion from the failure of the Arts Marketing Scheme

Against this background is there any wonder that the Minister's Arts Marketing Scheme, carrying its difficult criterion of innovation, launched hurriedly with no attempt made to help practitioners understand what was expected of them beyond the explanation carried in the application material, largely failed? Yet the unfortunate conclusion that seems to have been drawn is that the people in the arts industry are generally incompetent – incapable of doing their jobs properly. The truth is more likely to be that within the constraints of the arts situation they are doing rather well and with a little help could do much better.

The Arts Council's involvement in 'the mainstream of marketing thought' – the commercial sector

At the behest of the Minister the Arts Council is now taking marketing seriously; it has a Marketing and Resources Department and within it a Marketing Group. It is the duty of this department to bring the arts industry up to scratch in its practice of marketing but, of course, its scope is limited to the scope of the Arts Council, it cannot hope to influence areas such as crafts, museums, film and so on.

At the present time there is every indication that the Arts Council staff favour a close relationship with the commercial sector, with what has been termed by Arts Council's senior management, 'the mainstream of marketing thought'.

This may mean two things in essence: the involvement of very senior commercial marketing people in an advisory and probably voluntary capacity and of suppliers of specific marketing services for which fees will be paid. It also means, by clear implication, that the arts marketers – those that have learned their business within the arts world – are not thought to be in the mainstream of marketing thought.

It is when this inter-face occurs that the distinction between 'marketing' and 'arts marketing' becomes most apparent – a distinction that is important in terms of objectives and the relevance of the experience of the practitioners.

'Marketing' and 'arts marketing' – the crucial difference

I have already referred to the crucial difference in objectives between 'marketing' and 'arts marketing'. This difference is constantly emphasised as people from outside the arts world are invited to offer their opinions on how the arts may increase their audiences. Inevitably they talk of making or selecting product to match the wants of audiences and they say this without apparently any regard to or knowledge of the debate that has gone on in the arts on this topic for the past 20 years – or, indeed, any acknowledgement of the ideas and ideals of arts marketing. Almost without exception the orthodox commercial marketing approach is applied insensitively and ignorantly in the manner of an 18th-century doctor attempting to cure epilepsy by bleeding.

The academic world is similarly guilty

The academic world, where one might expect to find at least flexibility of thought, is similarly guilty. At the symposium, 'Changing their Minds' (Glasgow, 5 February 1988 organised by the Scottish Arts Council and the Society of Arts Publicists) participants from the arts attended eagerly to hear the words of members of the University of Strathclyde Department of Marketing who were asked to open the event. They were perhaps surprised to hear Professor M J Thomas inform them that the marketing concept started with people's needs and wants, required the organisation to decide which needs to meet and then to achieve organisational goals through customer satisfaction. And perhaps equally surprised to hear Professor Gordon R Foxall say that 'genuine customer orientation means being controlled by the customer, it means that ultimately the customer decides what business the organisation is in – not its managers, or those they work for...'. Both these contributors had much to say about marketing but very little to show that they understood the philosophy that guides the arts industry nor that they had attempted to relate what they knew of commercial marketing to the specific situation of the subsidised arts where 'changing their minds' is generally regarded as an important task to be tackled as soon as possible.

Professor Leslie W Rodger, of Heriot Watt University,

Edinburgh, to whom I have already referred, addressed himself to the marketing of the visual arts in the short book written recently for the Scottish Arts Council. Applying the orthodoxy of commercial marketing to the visual arts he completely ignores the one factor that has always made art galleries and museums extremely difficult to market – that they are free and thus have nothing to 'sell' at the moment a potential customer thinks that he might 'buy'. Of course things are not usually given away in the commercial sector but one might imagine that a commercial marketer would spot the importance of this difference and ponder it for a few minutes.

Are commercial marketers better than arts marketers?

Objectives and philosophy aside the next and equally dangerous move is to assume that those who have experience of the commercial world are necessarily expert in the practice, in the nuts and bolts, of marketing as it relates to the arts. Those able to accept invitations to advise free of charge usually enjoy the high status in their companies that permits occasional absences. At this level in a commercial organisation or agency, the marketing sub-activities are handled by a variety of specialist individuals, departments and agencies. In the arts it is more common to have the majority of these activities handled by one person or, at most, one small department. Copy-writing, design briefing, sales promotions, sales, media buying, public and press relations – the arts marketer is usually experienced in the direct practice of all these; the commercial marketer probably not so. Alternatively, the involvement of people with specific skills on a fee basis may occur. Although there may well be, almost certainly are, commercial practitioners with specific skills who cannot be bettered the jack-of-all- trades arts marketer, used to working on low budgets for long hours, is probably the more valuable in the arts situation.

Commercial marketing – higher prices

The price an arts organisation would expect to pay for something as basic as, say, the design and layout of an A3 sales leaflet would be, perhaps, 25% of the price an advertising agency accustomed to commercial prices would charge. Money spent on marketing is a crucial factor. Although it is generally true that arts organisations do not achieve their full earning potential at the box-office because they do not spend enough money on marketing, they can well do without substantial increases in the costs of what they are already buying. There is much evidence to support the view that arts people should be extremely cautious when buying services from agencies accustomed to doing business with wealthier people.

The importance of the small scale commercial supplier

Of course, the arts world does not operate in complete isolation from a commercial sector; it has always worked with relatively small commercial organisations, public relations people, printers and designers in the main and more recently, marketing consultants who have emerged from the subsidised arts sector. These small concerns work in symbiosis with the arts having adjusted their ambitions to match the business potential of their arts clients. Such businesses do not represent a threat to the fragile economies of the arts and, indeed, are arguably vital to them supplying as they do goods and services that cannot be provided from within the arts sector but are yet affordable.

Situations where motivation and reward are not clear

The level at which the commercial sector might become involved with the arts must also be considered. I have said that the involvement may take the form of senior people working voluntarily or it may be on a paid-for basis which will usually involve less senior people. This is, I am sure, an over- simplification. Situations may very easily develop where motivation and reward are not clear. In the business world meetings to discuss possibilities are common, neither party expecting any payment for the discussion but both parties looking for financial gain as the outcome if talks develop into commercial agreements. In the arts meetings are also common but the participants do not always expect financial gain as the outcome. Unless this difference in expectation is understood by both parties there is always the possibility of misunderstandings occurring when commercial people come into contact with arts people. An advertising agency person meeting an arts person may see this as a meeting from which commercial business may develop and will inevitably base his approach on this. The arts person, conditioned to think of the business world as wealthy, successful and if not always philanthropic, likely to be prepared to help out on occasions, may see this meeting as an opportunity to get some free advice from someone who knows much more than he does. In view of their different backgrounds it is likely that the advertising agency person is more likely to achieve his objectives than the arts person.

Risk of upsetting the existing economic balance

Should this occur – and it has, of course, already occurred on countless occasions – the balance between the buying power of the arts organisation and the pricing policy of the small commercial supplier already in the arts business is seriously upset. What business there is goes – probably temporarily – to the newcomer who is at one level offering 'free' advice and on another level supplying services and products the higher cost of which being justified by the 'free' advice. The original supplier, working on small margins and with fewer resources will suffer unnecessarily from this loss of trade.

The arts market is not open ended – an important factor

There is yet another essential difference between the commercial and the arts world. In the normal commercial process the amount of product available to be sold can be in theory limitless and, usually, when the volume of product increases, the unit cost of the product decreases. Thus, provided that there is a direct relationship between marketing expenditure and sales achieved the former may be increased with resultant increase in sales and, because unit cost is falling, profit increases at a disproportionately high rate. In such a situation there is every possible incentive to keep spending money on marketing. In *Marketing the Arts* (1976) I said, '*A serious limiting factor on the marketing of the art experience is the numerical restriction on the number of experiences that can be marketed which is imposed by both the buildings housing the art manifestations and by the intrinsic demands of the art form themselves*'.

Generally, arts organisations are not in an open-ended marketing situation. There is a ceiling on how much they can take in. The buildings in which the arts occur are of finite size and the price that people are willing to pay to enter the buildings to experience the arts has some limit to it. Because of the common circumstances of the arts the buildings may not necessarily be capable of being opened an indefinite number of times. And although the unit cost of the artistic product will fall once the set-up costs have been recovered, from that time on the unit cost will stay more or less the same. It is not as it is with records, tapes, books or bicycles.

Had there been worthwhile trade to be done someone would by now be doing it

This implies that there will be a ceiling on marketing expenditure in most arts situations; where the potential yield is limited there is usually a limit on how much should reasonably be spent in achieving it. It is likely that this ceiling will be too low to sustain a permanent relationship between the arts and the suppliers of services who are accustomed to charging high prices. It could well be that the reason why the commercial sector has not moved in on the arts en masse in the past (other than hit and run consultancy arrangements) is that the occasional forays that there have been have not resulted in sufficiently high rewards. In other words, had there been worthwhile trade to be done someone would by now be doing it on a regular basis.

Relative scale

There is also the matter of relative scale. Arts organisations are generally small with small staffs and many campaigns to run in a year. Commercial companies are usually larger with larger staffs and fewer campaigns to run in a year. Advertising agencies are usually only affordable by larger commercial companies. It must be difficult for someone who has worked in large scale commercial marketing to identify with, much less work with, someone in a small arts organisation.

Many have been seduced

As I have said, the involvement of commercial marketers in the marketing of the arts is not a new thing although the current flurry of activity may make it appear so. People who work in the arts with their lack of formal training, low status, inadequate salaries, working conditions and budgets, tend to have low respect for their own abilities and on the 'greener grass' principle assume that well paid people from the 'real' world (that is truly how it is often expressed) will hold the secret of success. Many have been seduced by the charisma of the denizens of Campaignia. The catalogue of disasters which has followed these flirtations is long and very costly to the arts organisations who do not have the financial resources to absorb losses that might well be shrugged off by a wealthier company. Such happenings are usually concealed to save embarrassment and possible law-suits.

Need for research into earlier experiences

It is one of the unfortunate by-products of having a relatively young staff that the Arts Council has no corporate long term memory (or appears not to have one) and so has no knowledge of the history of these encounters. It may well be that there have been successful operations in which case it would be useful to have these cited and described. In the absence of knowledge a certain amount of research into earlier experiences of arts organisations would have been a valuable precursor to such an important matter as a policy towards the marketing of the arts.

The value of the Arts Marketing Scheme panel meetings

The panel meetings of the Arts Marketing Scheme, involving as they did people from both worlds, were for me extremely educational. I learned much from the people whose experience was outside the arts, they had good analytical ability, thought clearly and positively and expressed themselves directly. But they had virtually no understanding of how the arts industry operates – what it is like to run a small, under funded arts centre, for example, or manage a festival under local government control or with an incompetent lay committee. Iain Lanyon, my arts colleague, and I were able to provide the background to the applications and to explain the likely conditions under which applicants were working. We were able to locate ideas in the context of other similar ideas that had already been tried. The outcome was, as I have already said, a series of unanimous decisions made against the background of criteria which were probably not well considered.

If the panel meetings were a paradigm for future meetings between such different experiences (and I believe they could be) I would say that the 'real' world most definitely has a part to play – but under strict conditions. What then should be the guidelines to make the most of such meetings?

Guidelines for future contact between the two worlds

It is important for such meetings to be at a high level (that is, far away from the nuts and bolts), dealing with strategies, policies and research and for them to take place sufficiently early in the process to bring influence to bear on practice before mistakes are made. This means making full use of senior people who are prepared to give their time voluntarily and know that this is the basis on which they serve. These meetings must also involve people with much experience of arts marketing who will first have their own ideas of what should be done, secondly will have the direct working experience that will ensure that discussion stays on productive lines and finally, will always keep the objective and philosophy of arts marketing firmly to the fore. The 'real' world must not be allowed to dominate the situation – otherwise the vital distinction between commercial marketing and arts marketing, the difference of objective and philosophy and all the other differences listed here will be overlooked.

The need for an Institute of Arts Marketing

Within the arts world there has developed a strong movement towards the improvement of standards of arts marketing practice. Although I may take responsibility for starting it I have not been alone. The considerable size of membership of the Society of Arts Publicists (originally the Scoiety of London Arts Publicists), started over ten years ago, bears testimony to the amount of interest that exists within the industry. There are within this industry – and within the Society – people of considerable knowledge and experience who are passionately committed to helping their younger and less experienced fellows. What has been lacking is the organisational and financial backing to make their skills available nationally through the organisation of training courses and seminars and the provision of consultancy services. there is now the growing opinion that what is needed is an Institute of Arts Marketing that will spearhead and build the movement. Such a body as this would provide the ideal generator for meetings between the two experiences, for initiating research projects, publishing findings, developing training programmes and so on. It would also be a far more appropriate body to handle training in the nuts and bolts sector than the Arts Council. In an admirable initiative the Society of Arts Publicists is now taking steps to investigate the feasibility of setting up an Institute of Arts Marketing.

The rôle of the Arts Council's Marketing and Resources department

What then should be the proper rôle for the Arts Council's new Marketing and Resources department? It has already produced an Action Plan which contains some sensible ideas which it is hoped will be implemented promptly. Of the 23 projects listed one would single out for particular approval those headed, *Business Volunteers for the Arts*, *Development Support Programme*, *Inner City Initiative*, *Tax Reform*, *Funds for the Arts*, *Payroll Giving*, *Involvement of Arts Organisations with DTI Schemes*, *Changing Attitudes to Marketing* (ie within the arts industry), *Market Research* and *Development of New Audiences*, all of which are worthwhile and are logically within the field of interest of a marketing group within that national body. There are within the complete list projects which would probably be better handled by the Association for Business Sponsorship of the Arts and some which would certainly be better in the hands of an Institute of Arts Marketing.

If the Arts Council is wise it will examine most carefully the work done in the field before its Marketing and Resources department came into existence and it will realise that the term 'arts marketing' has its own special meaning for the industry and is not simply a useful conjunction of words. Some clear evidence of respect for the people who have been and are doing the arts marketing job remarkably well under difficult circumstances would not be out of place either.

Without doubt the Arts Council should temper its present enthusiasm for a relationship with the commercial sector with the words of warning I offer here and should bear in mind the safeguards I have suggested.

It is also to be hoped that the Arts Council will regard the proposed Institute of Arts Marketing as a valuable ally, as a means of making the most of the substantial reservoir of accumulated experience, skill and wisdom that is available from within the arts world and as a way of involving and assisting people and organisations whose work falls outside the Arts Council's scope.

A new and important task for the Arts Council

There is more that the Arts Council can do. What I propose is wholly within the purlieu of the Arts Council and it would make the best use of co-operatively inclined members of the commercial sector and it would provide the perfect topic for a working liaison between the exponents of commercial marketing and arts marketing.

The tesk is to find ways of changing public attitudes towards the arts and different art forms. It is generally true that audiences are drawn from those who already have a favourable disposition towards a particular art form. The combination of parental, social and educational influences results in mature individuals with tastes that may be satisfied by our arts organisations, tastes that cannot simply be thought of as 'needs' because they are capable of development (' ...*who the market is, what it wants now* **and what it may be persuaded to want in the future** ...')

Arts organisations generally accept that they must preach to the converted and the willing-to-be-converted most of the time but it goes against the grain with most because in the first instance it is part of the ethos of arts management to be a missionary (albeit a sublimated one) and in the second, it seems wrong to finance the pleasures of the relatively few out of the rates and taxes paid by the many without at least an attempt to make everyone want to join in. There is also the practical view that if more people were favourably inclined towards the arts it would be easier and cheaper to achieve capacity audiences.

It is too easy to dismiss the challenge by saying that it is an educational issue and that we must plan for children to grow up into adults who are aware of the benefits that derive from arts experiences. No-one can deny the importance of this but what of adults now? Changing adult public attitudes *is* possible. It is difficult but it is possible. Attitudes are being changed every day as part of planned, organised programmes in the fields of health, politics, ecology, sociology – almost every area of human interest. The arts suffer because they do not have lobbies and ginger groups working on their behalf. It is a specialised area and one of which we in the arts world have little experience. The commercial sector, however, abounds with knowledge, talent and experience that is highly relevant to this work. This is where the two worlds of the arts and commerce may meet and where the greatest good may be done.

In my keynote address to the Glasgow symposium I said that I could think of no better function for the Arts Council's new Marketing and Resources department than to concentrate almost entirely upon this new task. I went on to say:

'All the indications are that the Arts Council is getting interested in the nuts and bolts of basic marketing. It wants to help you market more effectively. With respect, the people who do the job already can collectively face this challenge. What we cannot do is organise the large scale campaigns to win hearts and minds. Here we need the talent of the big battalions'

Only the Arts Council has the authority and the resources to start this process of public education. It remains to be seen whether it will have the wisdom and courage to do so.

Keith Diggle
July 1988